Green Finance and Investment

Leveraging De-Risking Instruments and International Co-ordination to Catalyse Investment in Clean Hydrogen

Please cite this publication as:
OECD/The World Bank (2024), *Leveraging De-Risking Instruments and International Co-ordination to Catalyse Investment in Clean Hydrogen*, Green Finance and Investment, OECD Publishing, Paris, https://doi.org/10.1787/9a377303-en.

ISBN 978-92-64-42191-2 (print)
ISBN 978-92-64-66832-4 (PDF)
ISBN 978-92-64-91972-3 (HTML)

Green Finance and Investment
ISSN 2409-0336 (print)
ISSN 2409-0344 (online)

Photo credits: Cover © kittirat roekburi/Shutterstock.com.

Corrigenda to OECD publications may be found at: https://www.oecd.org/en/publications/support/corrigenda.html.

Foreword

To put the global economy in a trajectory aligned with the Paris Agreement, more investments in clean energy technologies are urgently needed. In this context, interest for clean hydrogen has grown considerably, as there is a strong case to deploy this technology to decarbonise hard-to-abate sectors. However, very few large-scale clean hydrogen projects already are in construction or operation, as they struggle to reach final investment decision.

In October 2024, the COP29 Presidency published a COP29 Hydrogen Declaration as part of its Action Agenda, aiming to *scale up renewable, clean hydrogen production and deployment and accelerate decarbonisation of existing hydrogen production from unabated fossil fuels to facilitate energy transitions and achieve near-zero GHG emissions from hydrogen production, targeting particularly end-use sectors that are difficult to decarbonise, taking into consideration national circumstances*. This declaration pays particular attention to the need to *support financial and technical assistance to deploy effective, efficient, and scalable instruments, particularly in developing countries, to accelerate investment in renewable, clean hydrogen and its derivatives across the value chain*. Furthermore, 11 national and international development finance institutions (DFI) endorsed a Joint DFI Communique on the 10 GW Lighthouse Initiative and pledged their collective support to *foster collaboration towards bringing renewable hydrogen projects of between 100 MW and 1 GW in size in EMDCs to Final Investment Decision (FID) stage by 2030*, as a contribution to the COP-centred Breakthrough Agenda.

Risk mitigation will be key in attracting and mobilising private capital for clean hydrogen development. Based on novel research of the OECD and the World Bank and inputs from financial sector actors, project developers, and governments, the report stresses that instruments, such as offtake guarantees, political risk and foreign investment insurance, technology guarantees, and partial credit guarantees can help better allocate risks. Importantly, the report argues that these instruments should be integrated within risk mitigation packages, as each project comes with own specific challenges. Moreover, it highlights that supporting policies and a range of enabling conditions are prerequisites to create a conducive investment environment and improve the effectiveness of risk mitigation instruments.

This report provides insights into the landscape of existing international initiatives on hydrogen financing. It underscores key actions to enhance coordination of these initiatives such as the creation of investment platforms to channel capital flows and bilateral cooperation agreements to appraise and finance projects.

At this critical period of increasing the ambition of climate action across all sectors of the economy and recognising the role of clean hydrogen for this purpose, this report informs governments and the financing community in the design and implementation of economic, de-risking and financing instruments for clean hydrogen projects. It has been developed as a collaboration between the OECD's Environment Directorate and the World Bank's Energy Sector Management Assistance Program (ESMAP), building on their joint report Scaling Hydrogen Financing for Development published in the first quarter of 2024. The report lays the groundwork for further joint work under the World Bank-led Hydrogen for Development Partnership (H4D), through its Workstream 3 on "Investment, financing, business models and procurements". Future research could provide new insights on innovative financing mechanisms and scalable business models tailored to the unique challenges of emerging markets and developing economies.

Acknowledgements

This report was developed by the OECD Environment Directorate and the Energy Sector Management Assistance Program (ESMAP) of the World Bank's Energy and Extractives (EEX) Global Practice.

The report is co-authored by Moongyung Lee, Joana Argemí Ribalta, Joseph Cordonnier (OECD), Silvia Carolina Lopez Rocha and Dolf Jean Gielen (the World Bank), with strategic insights from Deger Saygin (OECD) and Michelle Hallack (ESMAP). It was developed by the OECD Clean Energy Finance and Investment Mobilisation (CEFIM) programme, as part of the programme of work of the OECD Working Party on Finance and Investment for Environmental Goals (WPFIEG) under the Environment Policy Committee (EPOC). The team would like to thank Yuval Laster, Head of the Finance, Investment and Global Relations Division at the OECD Environment Directorate and Chandrasekar Govindarajalu at the World Bank for their managerial guidance and support.

The authors are thankful for the feedback received from the following OECD and the World Bank group colleagues: Geraldine Ang, Ariola Mbistrova and Eleonora Moro (OECD); Peter Mockel and Margaret Monyeh (International Finance Corporation); Alan Narayadu (Multilateral Investment Guarantee Agency).

The authors are grateful to external reviewers: Alena Fargère (AKKA Equity); Roberto Gonzalez, Dimitrios Koufos, Gianpiero Nacci and Marise Westbroek (European Bank for Reconstruction and Development); Hyerin Park (ENGIE); Susana Moreira and Julian Reul (H_2Global Foundation); Yoshitaka Hidaka (Japan Bank for International Co-operation); Mphokolo Makara (Standard Bank Group); Pablo Navacerrada Busquets (United Nations Industrial Development Organisation).

The authors extend their gratitude to Alena Fargère for development of case studies presented in this report, enriched by valuable input from the following experts: Jim Brands (Climate Fund Managers); Fabio Grandchamp (Complexo do Pecem); Jacob Englander, Neha Rustagi and Joseph Stanford (Federal Government of the United States); Magued Bahaa, Ahmed Bakly and Heba Youssef (Government of Egypt); Prasad Chaphekar (Government of India); Daisuke Hirota, Wataru Kaneko and Noriya Udagawa (Government of Japan); Ella Carmi, Julien Comiti, Pierre-Germain Marlier and Aleksandra Policha Lebrethon (Hy24 Partners); Janaina Borges de Padua Goulart, Rafael Cavazzoni Lima and Andrea León Cueva (Inter-American Development Bank); Sakshi Jagtap, Naresh Lalwani, Chandrakant Mahalingam and Roshan Mandui (JSW Energy), Prabodha Acharya (JSW Group); Taia Kronborg (Lhyfe); Andrew George, Murray Haynes, Mark Heneghan and Nadine Rodgers-Callan (Marsh); Patrick Hinze and Bernhard Schneider (Munich Re); Joonwoo Cho (Posco Holdings); Marwan Assar (Scatec); Janina Andrea Franco Salazar (the World Bank).

The report benefitted from the insights of a workshop organised on de-risking instruments and international co-ordination for clean hydrogen in emerging markets and developing economies, bringing together over 160 participants. The authors are grateful to Gadi Taj Ndahumba (African Development Bank – African Legal Support Facility); Ana Maria Ruz (Chilean Economic Development Agency); Hyerin Park (Engie); Mphokolo Makara (Standard Bank Group); and Jeroen Weurding (Swiss Re) for their contribution to the event.

The authors are especially grateful to Ria Sandilands for her assistance with co-ordination and communication, and Dominique Haleva and Roberto Lonetti for their editorial support. The authors extend their gratitude to Jehison Hernandez Mujica for his support with the surveys and the infographics.

Table of contents

Tables

Figures

Boxes

Abbreviations and acronyms

CAPEX	Capital Expenditure
CEFIM	Clean Energy Finance and Investment Mobilisation
DFI	Development Finance Institution
ECA	Export Credit Agency
EMDEs	Emerging Markets and Developing Economies
EPC	Engineering, Procurement and Construction
ESMAP	Energy Sector Management Assistance Programme
EU	European Union
FID	Final Investment Decision
IDB	Inter-American Development Bank
IEA	International Energy Agency
IRENA	International Renewable Energy Agency
LCOE	Levelised cost of electricity
LCOH	Levelised cost of hydrogen
LNG	Liquified natural gas
Mt	Million tonnes
OECD	Organisation for Economic Co-operation and Development
OPEX	Operating Expenditure
PPP	Public-Private Partnership
R&D	Research & Development
SPV	Special Purpose Vehicles
UNIDO	United Nations Industrial Development Organisation
WACC	Weighted average cost of capital
WB	World Bank

Executive Summary

Clean hydrogen is instrumental to decarbonise hard-to-abate industry sector but struggling to reach final investment decision

Clean hydrogen offers a major decarbonisation opportunity for both advanced economies and emerging markets and developing economies (EMDEs). It can reduce emissions, boost energy security, and drive economic growth. Based on announced projects, clean hydrogen annual production may increase from under 1 million tonnes (Mt) in 2023 to 40 Mt by 2030, including half in EMDEs. This would require urgent investments, as large-scale projects take years to operationalise. As such, to produce 20 Mt of clean hydrogen by 2030, EMDEs would need to invest on average USD 100 billion annually in the clean hydrogen value chain, including renewable electricity, hydrogen production, storage, transport, and conversion.

The report Scaling Hydrogen Financing for Development, published by the World Bank and the OECD in February 2024, identified that less than 10% of clean hydrogen projects globally have reached final investment decision (FID) due to high perceived risks. De-risking instruments can improve bankability by lowering the cost of capital, reducing production costs, and attracting more private investment. This new OECD and World Bank report examines these instruments and proposes actions to enhance coordination and scale investment.

Combining tailored de-risking instruments in comprehensive risk mitigation strategies is critical to create a pipeline of bankable clean hydrogen projects

An investor survey conducted by the OECD and the World Bank in 2023 shows that the main six categories of perceived risks affecting the development of clean hydrogen projects are uncertainty on the offtake (both volume and price), political and regulatory risks, insufficient enabling infrastructure, technology risks and macroeconomic risks. While lessons from sectors like liquefied natural gas (LNG) and offshore wind are useful, clean hydrogen faces unique challenges, such as a lack of reference price indices, market uncertainty, and the absence of a commercial track record, making it difficult to effectively evaluate the impact of de-risking instruments.

De-risking instruments help projects reach FID by reducing uncertainties and lowering costs, such as optimising debt sizing and cutting capital costs. In 2024, the OECD surveyed over 40 stakeholders, including governments, development finance institutions (DFIs), and private investors. The survey identified key de-risking instruments for clean hydrogen in EMDEs, including contracts for difference, offtake guarantees, foreign currency guarantees, political risk insurance, contractors-all-risk insurance and performance guarantees.

Yet, there is no one-size-fits-all solution: effective de-risking requires a combination of instruments, as each project and country presents unique risks. Careful management of de-risking instruments is crucial to balance risk-return, avoid overlaps and prevent redundant costs. Especially in EMDEs, it is critical to ensure a security package that minimises reliance on public support and boosts private investor confidence in the long term. Moreover, risk mitigation strategies must include enabling conditions like access to infrastructure, demand creation by public and private actors, and sound contractual frameworks to develop a pipeline of investable projects.

International partnerships and co-ordination mechanisms are essential to scale clean hydrogen financing

An increasing number of international initiatives are supporting clean hydrogen projects in EMDEs, led by both global and regional actors. These initiatives focus on research and development, de-risking, financial assistance, capacity-building, policy support and coordination. This report depicts 46 initiatives. More than two-thirds offer direct financial support or de-risking mechanisms, stressing the need for further collaboration to identify projects' risks, increase financing efforts and maximise socio-economic benefits. One half cover EMDEs broadly, while others focus on specific regions. Three-quarters target renewable hydrogen, with a well-balanced coverage of the entire hydrogen value chain.

However, coordination among initiatives for de-risking and financing clean hydrogen remains limited. Investment platforms, bilateral collaborations, and peer-learning sessions among financial institutions can be effective tools to address this gap.

Real clean hydrogen project information reveals critical insights into successful economic, de-risking and financing instruments for reaching final investment decision

Since 2022, the OECD has been collecting data on enabling conditions and financing strategies for clean hydrogen projects. This report analyses 15 new case studies, highlighting the importance of tailored financial and policy frameworks, risk-reducing tools like subsidies and tax credits, and public-private partnerships to attract investment and facilitate scaling. The case studies provide key insights on various areas:

- **De-risking and financing**: effective risk allocation is crucial for securing capital, with instruments like currency hedging and equity stakes in special purpose vehicles playing key roles in large-scale clean hydrogen projects.
- **Government support**: national programmes with targeted subsidies and clear hydrogen-specific policy frameworks are vital for optimising risk allocation and stimulating investment.
- **Partnerships and Implementation**: public-private partnerships and dedicated teams are essential to align financial resources and technical expertise to manage the complexities associated with large-scale hydrogen projects.
- **Replicability and scale-up**: alignment of the projects' objectives with national and international climate policies, tailored business models and sector-specific funding strategies are essential.to address the hydrogen market challenges.

Moving forward: informing international initiatives and countries on de-risking instruments and building partnerships to finance large-scale projects

This new OECD and World Bank report features de-risking instruments for clean hydrogen projects in EMDEs, emphasising their role in attracting private investment. It evaluates asset risk profiles and de-risking tools, based on an investor survey and experience from other sectors. The report highlights the importance of international coordination, public-private partnerships, and knowledge-sharing to overcome investment barriers. It informs the World Bank's 10 GW Lighthouse Initiative and the OECD efforts to help countries accelerate financing for clean hydrogen projects.

Infographic 1. Challenges and solutions for de-risking clean hydrogen

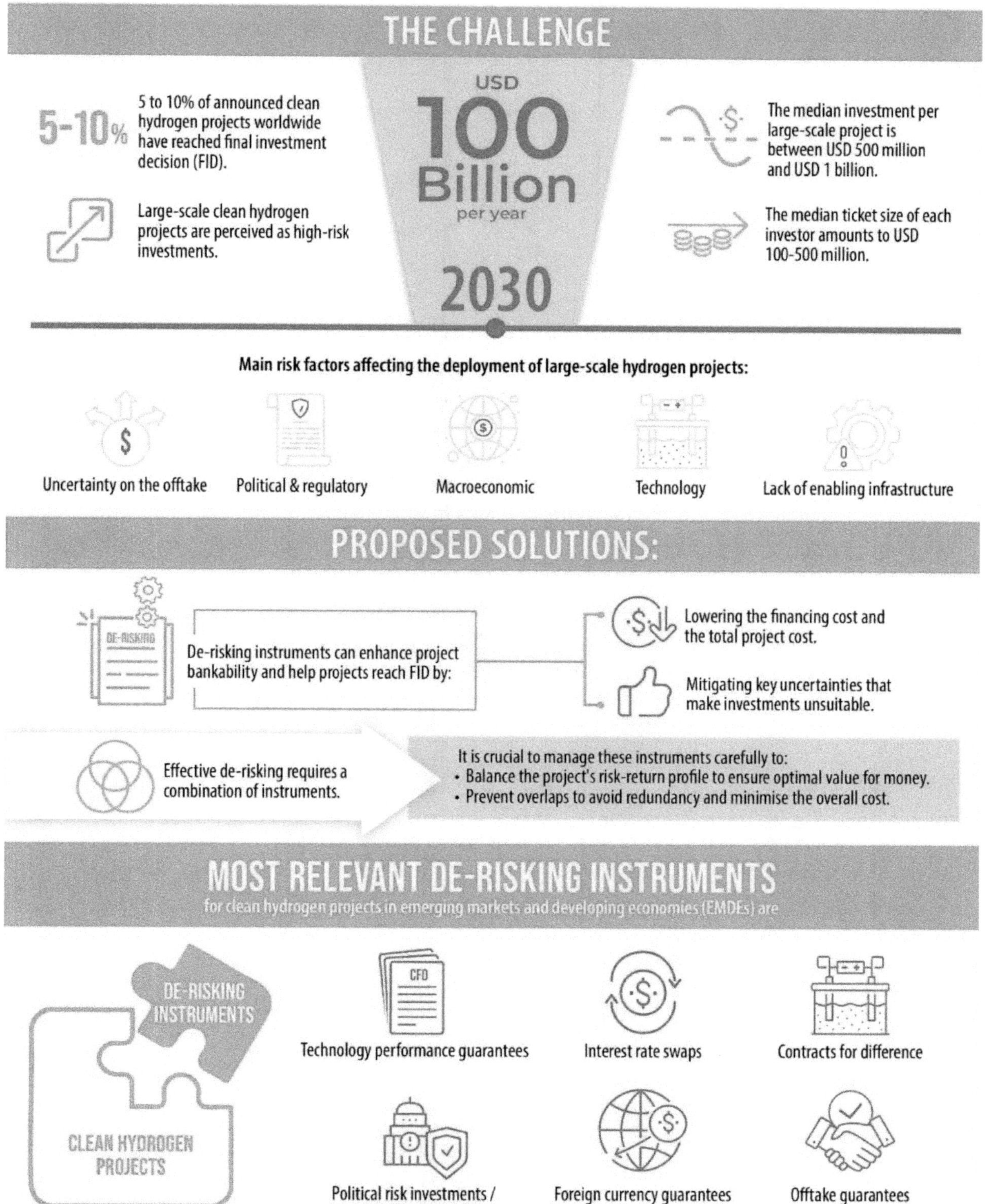

Source: Authors

1 Introduction

This chapter provides a brief overview of the role of clean hydrogen in net-zero emission scenarios. It provides a snapshot of the current status of clean hydrogen financing, highlighting the investment gap against what is needed to achieve climate targets, and underscoring the key risk factors preventing clean hydrogen projects from reaching a final investment decision. Furthermore, the chapter introduces the key stakeholders active in clean hydrogen financing, and their role to unlock investment. Finally, the chapter highlights how this report aims to bridge the knowledge gap and provide a better understanding of the priorities to unlock financing for clean hydrogen projects in EMDEs.

Overview of the role of clean hydrogen in a net-zero emission scenario and current investment challenges

"Clean hydrogen"[1] – and especially "renewable hydrogen" – is emerging as an essential low-carbon technology to realise a net-zero emission energy system by mid-century, aligned with the goals of the Paris Agreement and the UAE Consensus' call to transition away from fossil fuels. The International Energy Agency (IEA) states that in order to achieve a net-zero emission energy system, hydrogen production should grow by a factor 4 to 5 by 2050, from current levels of around 100 million tonnes (Mt) per year (IEA, 2023[1]). In IEA's net-zero emission scenario, nearly all the hydrogen produced in 2050 is clean hydrogen, whereas it represents less than 1% of the hydrogen produced in 2022. According to the latest estimates by the World Bank and the Organisation for Economic Co-operation and Development (OECD), around 20 Mt of clean hydrogen would be produced by 2030 in emerging and developing economies (EMDEs) excluding the People's Republic of China (hereafter "China") - i.e. half of the estimated 40 Mt global clean hydrogen production in the same year (OECD/The World Bank, 2024[2]).

Several EMDEs endowed with large renewable energy potential, and with access to sufficient water resources and land, are well positioned to become renewable hydrogen producers or exporters. Renewable hydrogen can help these countries improve energy security (e.g. through enabling the integration of renewable power to the grid), develop green industrial processes, create green jobs, and improve their trade balances.

Clean hydrogen is also crucial for advanced economies to achieve net-zero emissions. This is already outlined in national and regional decarbonisation and industrial strategies such as REPowerEU of the European Union and the Inflation Reduction Act of the United States (European Commission, 2022[3]) (The White House, 2022[4]). Several advanced economies also benefit from favourable conditions such as abundant renewable energy sources to produce clean hydrogen at low cost. Others may become large demand centres, relying on partially or fully imported clean hydrogen to decarbonise their manufacturing industry, transportation, and power sectors. As 25% to 31% of hydrogen production is expected to be regionally or globally traded by 2050, most countries have an interest in pursuing regional and international collaboration to create hydrogen commercial routes and ensure the success of global decarbonisation efforts (OECD/The World Bank, 2024[2]).

Box 1.1. Hydrogen use and potential in the industry, transport and power sectors

Hydrogen is currently consumed mainly by the manufacturing industry as feedstock in chemical processes. Around 95% of hydrogen production is based on fossil fuels (coal and natural gas) and "consumed where produced" on-site in petroleum refineries, ammonia, and other chemical plants. With new markets and production routes, total clean hydrogen demand in the industry sector could reach around 320 Mt per year by 2050 (IRENA, 2022[5]).

By 2050, clean hydrogen is projected to have a large market share in several sectors and countries, with more than 1 400 large hydrogen projects already announced globally as of December 2023, in particular in the following sectors (Hydrogen Council; McKinsey & Company, 2023[6]):

1. Ammonia and methanol: to substitute the current fossil fuel-based hydrogen in current production processes.
2. Iron and steel: to replace natural gas in direct reduced iron (DRI) production. This process could supersede traditional ironmaking in coal-based blast furnaces.

Figure 1.1. Hydrogen demand in 2020 and projection in 2050 in a 1.5°C Pathway

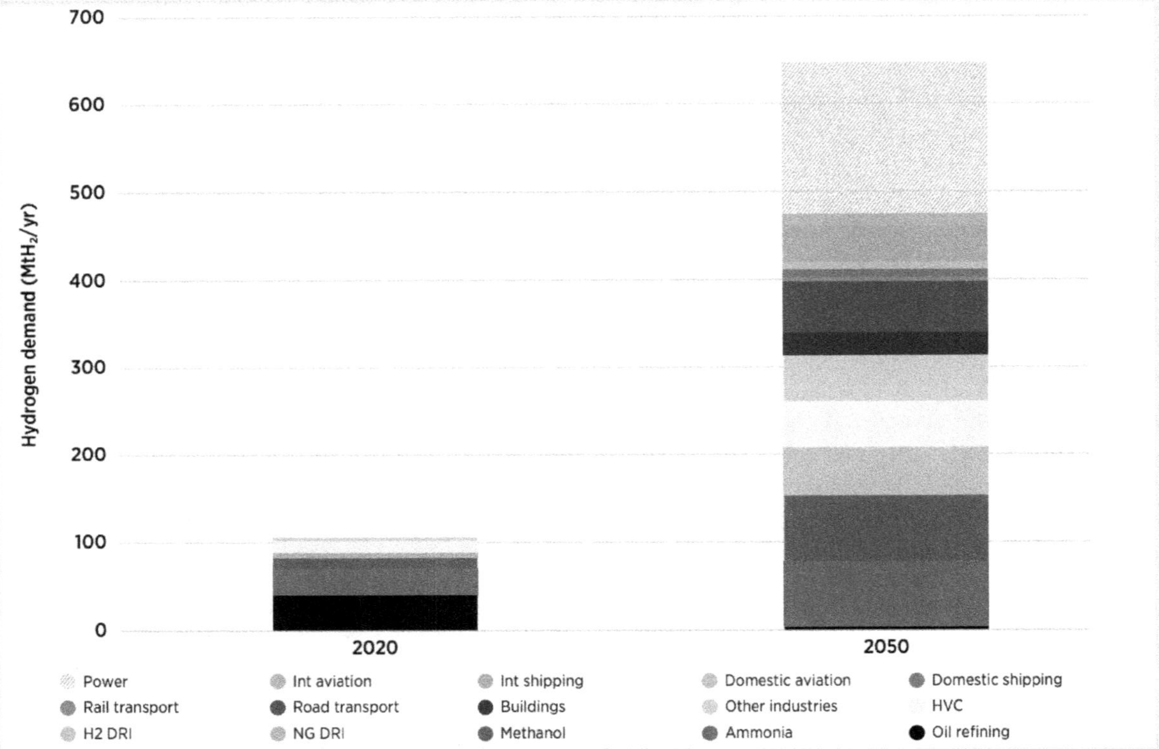

Note: DRI = direct reduced iron; HVC = high-value chemicals; Int = international; NG = natural gas
Source: (IRENA, 2022[5])

The transport and power sectors offer emerging opportunities for renewable hydrogen. In the transport sector, ammonia, methanol and electrofuels[2] produced from renewable hydrogen could provide clean solutions for shipping or aviation. In the power sector, renewable hydrogen can help integrate variable renewable energy sources into the grids, alongside other solutions such as battery storage (IRENA, 2022[5]). For instance, even though this is not done yet at large-scale, hydrogen could be stored seasonally in geological storage and subsequently be used to produce electricity during times of low solar and wind output or high demand.

Despite all these opportunities, clean hydrogen is not a silver bullet, and it is key to prioritise its use where it is the most effective, or when other low-carbon alternatives such as direct electrification are not feasible or less economical. Indeed, producing renewable hydrogen requires water and renewable electricity, and producing it should not divert these resources from other critical applications, such as the decarbonisation of the power grid or agriculture. As an example, the round-trip efficiency of the power to hydrogen to power transformation is typically around 20 to 42% (Escamilla, Sánchez and García-Rodríguez, 2022[7]).

Over the last years, the number of *announced projects* across the clean hydrogen value chain has increased rapidly. In 2023, projections based on projects at the feasibility stage or beyond indicated that global installed electrolyser capacity by 2030 could reach 175 GW, a 30% increase compared to the previous year's projection. This capacity corresponds to around 15 Mt of clean hydrogen that could be produced by 2030, potentially increasing to 40 Mt if early-stage projects are also considered. However, the potential global demand for clean hydrogen by 2030 remains limited to 14 Mt, which is even below the

20 Mt target initially set by the European Union for its domestic demand only. This suggests that stimulating demand creation will be critical to help projects move forward (IEA, 2023[8]). Many private companies are aiming to further develop end-use applications, for instance the 60 renewable ammonia plants (including technology demonstration plans) announced in 2020 and 2021, and the approximately 40 Mt of DRI production capacity expected to be commissioned by 2030[3] which could run on renewable hydrogen (Agora Industry, Wuppertal Institute and Lund University, 2021[9]). Developing a global hydrogen market also relies on infrastructure to store and transport hydrogen and its derivatives. While there are still uncertainties on the best technological options and routes, more than 200 hydrogen infrastructure projects covering pipelines, underground storage and ports are currently under development or in operations (IEA, 2023[8]).

A cumulative investment of USD 1 trillion in production capacity and USD 1 trillion in hydrogen infrastructure and end-use equipment is needed between now and 2030 in order to reach 40 Mt of clean hydrogen global production capacity (OECD/The World Bank, 2024[2]). A quarter to half of these investments are expected to take place in EMDEs. All sources of finance – international, national, public and private – will contribute to close the investment gap. Most of the financing is expected to come from private investors, as for clean energy investment in EMDEs more generally, for which 60% of the finance will need to come from the private sector (IEA, 2023[10]).

The range of current production costs of renewable hydrogen varies from USD 3/kg to USD 10/kg (see Figure 1.2) (OECD/The World Bank, 2024[2]; Lee and Saygin, 2023[11]). The production costs vary notably depending on the capital expenditures (CAPEX) and capacity factors of renewable power generation assets and electrolysers, as well as on the cost of capital. Despite the growing project pipelines for clean hydrogen, it remains uncertain when cost parity with blue hydrogen or unabated fossil-fuels based hydrogen will be achieved. Beyond technology costs, the competitiveness of clean hydrogen will increasingly be determined by the costs of electricity, natural gas, carbon and financing. Future renewable hydrogen production costs are also expected to vary by region, depending on local renewable electricity costs or prices, supply chain specifications (such as grid-connected or off-grid electricity and transport costs), and technological developments.

Figure 1.2. Levelised Cost of Hydrogen Estimates for Renewable Hydrogen Production, 2030–2050

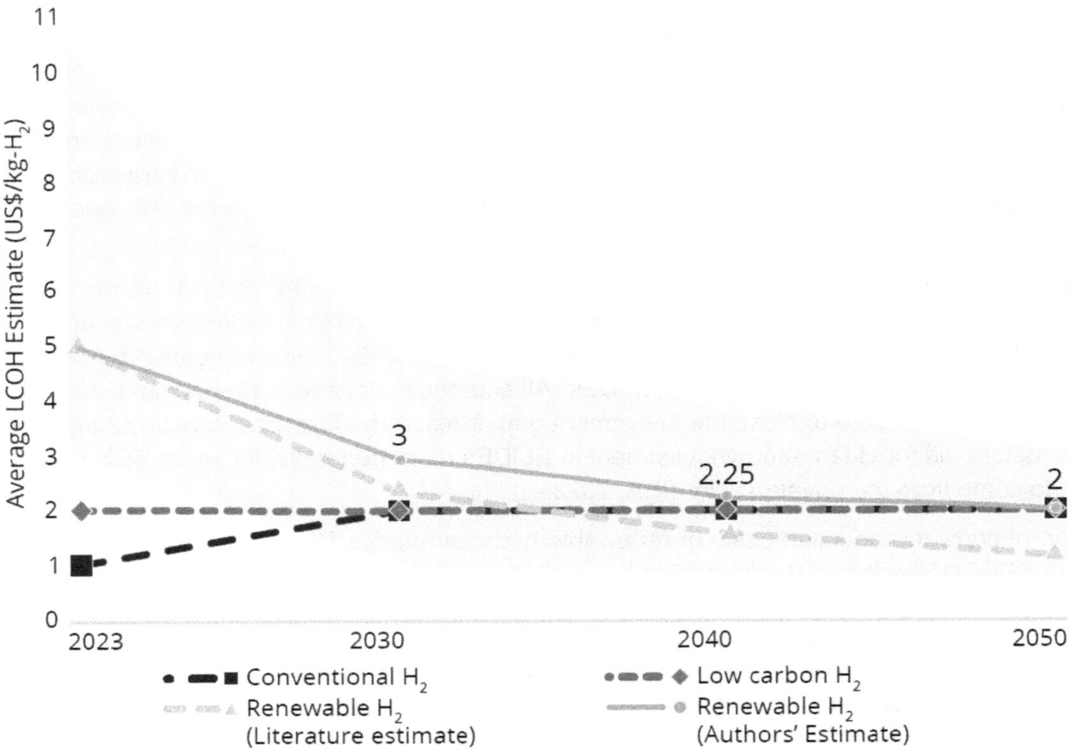

Note: In this chart, "low-carbon hydrogen" corresponds to hydrogen produced from natural gas with carbon capture and storage (CCS)
Source: (OECD/The World Bank, 2024[2])

As a consequence, a limited number of projects have already reached Final Investment Decision (FID).[4] Despite the proliferation of announced projects, the development of hydrogen production is slower than the pace needed to meet net-zero targets. Currently, between 5 and 10% of all announced projects are reaching final investment decision, driven by high risks faced by investors, such as offtake risk, political and regulatory risk, infrastructure risk, technology risk, or construction and completion risk (Lee and Saygin, 2023[11]; IEA, 2023[8]). In the clean hydrogen project pipeline through 2030, only USD 29 billion of investments are at or beyond the FID stage, compared to a total investment pipeline of USD 319 billion. On average, the projects are less advanced in EMDEs than in other country groups, where a 90% share of investment is only announced at the feasibility stage (see Figure 1.3).

Figure 1.3. Breakdown of the global clean hydrogen project pipeline by country group and project phase through 2030 (in USD billion)

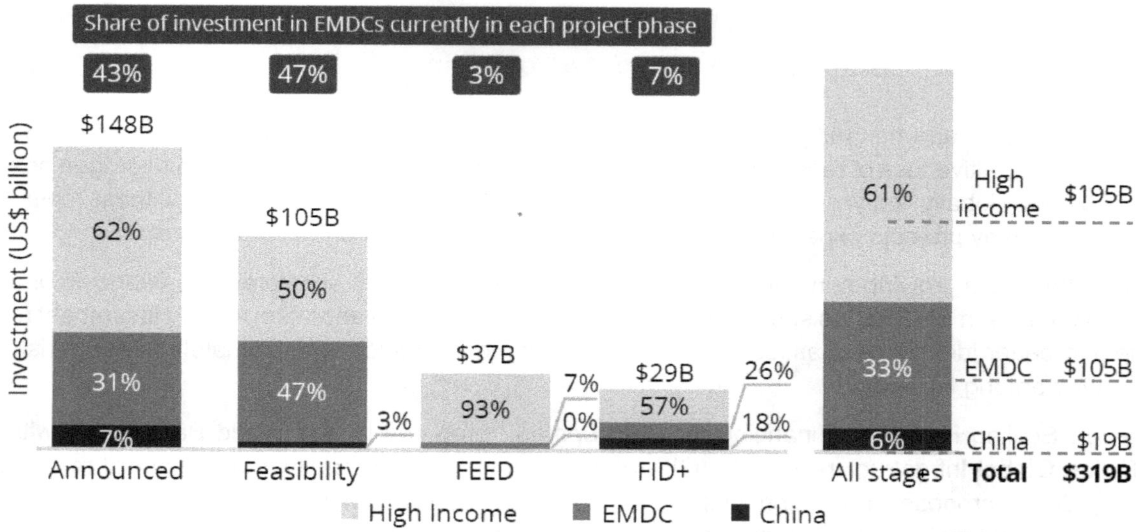

Note: 1) Investment numbers exclude the renewable power component. 2) EMDC: Emerging Markets and Developing Countries; FEED: Front End Engineering Design; FID+ refers to any project at or beyond the FID stage; 3) the numbers in the dark blue labels should be read as follows: 43% of all investment in EMDCs are only announced; 47% of all investment in EMDCs are at feasibility stage; etc.
Source: (OECD/The World Bank, 2024[2])

The role of policy makers and other stakeholders to unlock clean hydrogen financing

Governments, industry actors and financial institutions take action to scale the clean hydrogen market across many countries. As of May 2024, more than 50 national and regional strategies and roadmaps on hydrogen have been drafted or published (IRENA, 2024[12]; Columbia CGEP, 2024[13]). Many stakeholders are developing their activities towards hydrogen across various dimensions: research and development, definitions and certification mechanisms, project development and implementation, policy making, finance and investment, co-ordination and dissemination of projects and initiatives. A key area of interest is how financing, business models, and better cost and pricing data and models could help to create and grow hydrogen markets. This is especially significant because hydrogen is poised to become a globally traded commodity and cost-competitiveness will dictate supply dynamics. Yet, front-loaded project capital structures and country- and sector-specific risks in EMDEs hinder the mobilisation of the urgently needed private capital. Creating and growing markets require improving the enabling investment conditions and the strategic use of limited public finance combined with a suite of risk mitigation measures to leverage private capital.

In some sectors, early movers are likely to reap the benefits of risk-taking by getting higher market share or technological leadership, as the learning curve enables them to achieve quicker cost reduction and secure contracts with customers (Marvin B. Lieberman, 1988[14]). This can lead investors to accept lower returns for first projects (both financed through balance sheets and through special purpose vehicles), when projects are primarily driven by strategic interests and positioning of the companies or sponsors in a new market. However, in many innovative climate change related sectors such as clean energy, innovations and markets have been strongly driven by regulation (Cleff and Rennings, 2012[15]). This is the case when development costs are high compared to the expected market share, market uncertainty is high, and when few actors are ready to bear the risks based on market conditions, which makes the public support indispensable. Therefore, in the clean hydrogen market, in particular in EMDEs, there is an important "early mover risk". In this regard, it is vital to support the first large-scale clean hydrogen projects in these countries.

Priorities to unlock financing for clean hydrogen in EMDEs

Focus on financing and risk mitigation is especially important in EMDEs where the high cost of capital affects the competitiveness of renewable hydrogen projects. While close to 40% of clean hydrogen projects are in EMDEs globally, only six large projects above 100 MW have reached FID in these countries. Furthermore, many projects experience delays driven by financial and non-financial hurdles.

Currently, there is a growing number of international initiatives aiming to accelerate the financing of clean hydrogen projects in EMDEs. As such, enhancing co-ordination and collaboration among incumbent actors can help to better identify risks associated with clean hydrogen projects and ultimately facilitate risk and cost sharing among investors.

The report Scaling Hydrogen Financing for Development, prepared by the World Bank jointly with the OECD, the Global Infrastructure Facility (GIF) and with support from the Hydrogen Council released in February 2024, proposes an action plan to expedite the deployment of clean hydrogen in EMDEs, emphasising four key building blocks: (i) Lighthouse projects; (ii) Policies and institutional framework; (iii) International co-ordination, governance, guidelines and agreements; and (iv) Capacity-building and knowledge sharing (OECD/The World Bank, 2024[2]). Specifically on lighthouse projects, the report presents a 10-gigawatt (GW) initiative to develop lighthouse projects in EMDEs with size ranging from 100 megawatt (MW) to 1 GW, corresponding to around 1 Mt of new renewable hydrogen production capacity before 2030. This initiative could demonstrate viability for all stakeholders and pave the way to scale up clean hydrogen development by unlocking and mobilising private capital (The World Bank, 2023[16]).

Aim, scope and outline of the report

This report's primary aim is to provide a better understanding on the financial risk mitigation strategies and instruments to crowd in private capital for clean hydrogen projects in EMDEs, with a primary focus on renewable hydrogen. The report draws conclusions relevant to projects in OECD and non-OECD member countries. Additionally, the report outlines the landscape of international initiatives around clean hydrogen financing and suggests co-operative mechanisms to strengthen investment in the sector.

The report builds on the expertise developed by the OECD through its Clean Energy Finance and Investment Mobilisation (CEFIM) programme that supports selected EMDEs in the development of policies and instruments to help scale up a pipeline of bankable clean energy projects. It complements three previous publications on clean hydrogen developed under the CEFIM programme: (Cordonnier and Saygin, 2022[17]), (Lee and Saygin, 2023[11]) and (OECD/The World Bank, 2024[2]). Based on desk research, clean hydrogen stakeholder surveys and case studies, **the report focuses on two main areas that can help projects to progress**:

1. Reducing risks and mobilising private capital will be crucial for the establishment and expansion of clean hydrogen markets. Risk mitigation instruments tailored to clean hydrogen project characteristics and specific risks across their value chain have a strong potential to unlock private capital and diversify the capital pool (Chapter 2).
2. Embracing risk mitigation and financing of clean hydrogen requires a well-co-ordinated governance framework. Strong co-ordination and collaboration between international initiatives can notably help to improve mutual knowledge, streamline the identification of promising projects and their

appraisal, and incentivise joint financing. Reaching co-ordination firstly requires creating a detailed mapping to identify the current landscape of international initiatives across the clean hydrogen value chain (Chapter 3).

References

Agora Industry, Wuppertal Institute and Lund University (2021), *Global Steel at a Crossroads. Why the global steel sector needs to invest in climate-neutral technologies in the 2020s.*, http://www.agora-industry.de (accessed on 1 April 2022). [9]

Bigliardi, B. (ed.) (2012), "Are there any first-mover advantages for pioneering firms?", *European Journal of Innovation Management*, Vol. 15/4, pp. 491-513, https://doi.org/10.1108/14601061211272394. [15]

Columbia CGEP (2024), *National Hydrogen Strategies and Roadmap Tracker*, https://www.energypolicy.columbia.edu/publications/national-hydrogen-strategies-and-roadmap-tracker/. [13]

Cordonnier, J. and D. Saygin (2022), "Green hydrogen opportunities for emerging and developing economies: Identifying success factors for market development and building enabling conditions", *OECD Environment Working Papers*, No. 205, OECD Publishing, Paris, https://doi.org/10.1787/53ad9f22-en. [17]

Escamilla, A., D. Sánchez and L. García-Rodríguez (2022), "Assessment of power-to-power renewable energy storage based on the smart integration of hydrogen and micro gas turbine technologies", *International Journal of Hydrogen Energy*, Vol. 47/40, pp. 17505-17525, https://doi.org/10.1016/J.IJHYDENE.2022.03.238. [7]

European Commission (2022), *REPowerEU*, https://commission.europa.eu/strategy-and-policy/priorities-2019-2024/european-green-deal/repowereu-affordable-secure-and-sustainable-energy-europe_en. [3]

Hydrogen Council; McKinsey & Company (2023), *Hydrogen Insights 2023: The state of the global hydrogen economy, with a deep dive into renewable hydrogen cost evolution*, https://hydrogencouncil.com/en/hydrogen-insights-2023-december-update/. [6]

IEA (2023), *Global Hydrogen Review 2023*, IEA, https://www.iea.org/reports/global-hydrogen-review-2023. [8]

IEA (2023), *Net Zero Roadmap: A Global Pathway to Keep the 1.5 °C Goal in Reach*, https://www.iea.org/reports/net-zero-roadmap-a-global-pathway-to-keep-the-15-0c-goal-in-reach. [1]

IEA (2023), "Scaling Up Private Finance for Clean Energy in Emerging and Developing Economies", https://www.iea.org/reports/scaling-up-private-finance-for-clean-energy-in-emerging-and-developing-economies. [10]

IRENA (2024), *Green hydrogen strategy: A guide to design*, https://www.irena.org/Publications/2024/Jul/Green-hydrogen-strategy-A-guide-to-design. [12]

IRENA (2022), *Global hydrogen trade to meet the 1.5°C climate goal: Trade outlook for 2050 and way forward*, https://www.irena.org/publications/2022/Jul/Global-Hydrogen-Trade-Outlook. [5]

Lee, M. and D. Saygin (2023), "Financing cost impacts on cost competitiveness of green hydrogen in emerging and developing economies", *OECD Environment Working Papers*, No. 227, OECD Publishing, Paris, https://doi.org/10.1787/15b16fc3-en. [11]

Marvin B. Lieberman, D. (1988), *First-Mover Advantages*, pp. 41-58, https://www.jstor.org/stable/2486211. [14]

OECD/The World Bank (2024), *Scaling Hydrogen Financing for Development*, OECD Publishing, Paris, https://doi.org/10.1787/0287b22e-en. [2]

The White House (2022), *Inflation Reduction Act Guidebook*, https://www.whitehouse.gov/cleanenergy/inflation-reduction-act-guidebook/. [4]

The World Bank (2023), *World Bank Proposes 10 GW Clean Hydrogen Initiative to Boost Adoption of Low-Carbon Energy*, https://www.worldbank.org/en/news/press-release/2023/11/17/world-bank-proposes-10-gw-clean-hydrogen-initiative-to-boost-adoption-of-low-carbon-energy. [16]

Notes

[1] There is no international consensus on the wording to be used to designate hydrogen based on its emissions or its production pathways. In this report, we call "clean hydrogen" (also known as low-carbon or low-emission hydrogen) hydrogen that is produced with low greenhouse gas emissions, compared to conventional pathways from coal and natural gas. Clean hydrogen can be produced from various sources, including hydrogen production from fossil fuels with carbon capture and storage (CCS) (also known as "blue hydrogen") and from water electrolysis using renewable electricity (known as "renewable hydrogen" or "green hydrogen"). While considering all these pathways, most of the work undertaken in this monograph will mostly relate to renewable hydrogen.

[2] Electrofuels (or e-fuels) are hydrocarbons synthesised from captured carbon dioxide together with hydrogen, such as methanol or jet fuels. They are chemically identical to their fossil counterparts and are therefore a fully inter-changeable substitute.

[3] Corresponding to around 2% of the global steel production.

[4] Final Investment Decision is a crucial milestone in the development of a major project, especially in industries like energy, infrastructure, and large-scale construction. It represents the point at which a company or investor commits significant financial resources to proceed with the project's execution.

2 Risk mitigation strategies to address financing challenges of clean hydrogen projects

This chapter aims to better understand the potential of de-risking instruments and risk mitigation strategies to increase the leverage of public finance for clean hydrogen projects. First, an analysis of the risks faced by these projects describes what can be the role of de-risking instruments, alongside other tools such as economic and financing instruments. Then, the chapter presents a selection of 13 de-risking instruments and their relevance for large-scale clean hydrogen projects. The results from an investor survey focussing on these 13 instruments outlines how these instruments could be prioritised and packaged to build project-level risk mitigation strategy. Finally, key learnings from 15 case studies on clean hydrogen projects as well as economic, de-risking and financing instruments provide evidence on successful strategies implemented to develop and support large-scale clean hydrogen projects in emerging and developing economies.

Key findings

The desk research, investor survey and case studies presented in this chapter point to the following main findings:

- Based on other comparable sectors' experience, **de-risking instruments can have a better leverage than direct financing instruments to mobilise private capital**.
- Because clean hydrogen projects are capital-intensive, **strategic use of de-risking instruments can reduce the total project cost, therefore reducing the need for direct support from public finance to make projects economically viable**. This effect is particularly important in EMDEs, which face higher risks and therefore higher cost of finance than developed economies.
- Based on the investor survey, **offtake guarantees, political risk and foreign investment insurance, technology guarantees, and partial credit guarantees are particularly promising for clean hydrogen projects in EMDEs**.
- However, these **instruments should not be deployed in silos, but should be integrated within risk mitigation packages** to reduce the key risks faced by hydrogen projects.

Definitions

Economic, risk mitigation and financing instruments all have a role to play to mobilise investment for clean hydrogen projects.

- The OECD defines economic instruments as "a means by which decisions or actions of the government affect the behaviour of producers and consumers by causing changes in the prices to be paid for these activities" (OECD, 2008[1]). These can include subsidies, taxes, charges or fiscal transfers.
- De-risking (or risk mitigation) instruments are defined as "instruments that help investors reduce or manage investment and project risks, typically in exchange for a fee, and thus, improve the perceived risk-reward profile of an investment" (WRI, 2012[2]). They include risk-transfer instruments such as insurances, extended equipment warranties, ECA coverage, credit risk guarantee, technology performance guarantees and credit-enhancement instruments such as reserve accounts.
- In this report, they are distinct from financing instruments, which are limited to loan, concessional loans and blended finance approaches, equity and quasi-equity products. The use of financing instruments and the investment approach vary according to the maturity of each step of the clean hydrogen value chain (AIIB and Castalia, 2023[3]).

While all these instruments may be needed to make a clean hydrogen project bankable, the categorisation used in this report is based on the different impact they have on projects. Indeed, economic instruments are primarily developed by governments to influence the behaviour and economic decisions of investors to align them with policy objectives. De-risking instruments aim to transfer some of the risks that investors face to public[1] actors, equipment manufacturers, or insurance companies. The providers of these instruments do not necessarily disburse any funds, as it depends whether the risks that are covered materialise. Financing instruments are provided by investors to pay for the project development, capital operational and maintenance costs.

In this report, instruments relate directly to a measurable re-allocation of financial and investment risks between stakeholders. A wider range of measures can address and seek to remove the underlying barriers that are the root causes of various risks (UNDP, 2013[4]). Several reports provide guidance or stocktake on such measures and suggest ways to create a favourable environment for clean hydrogen development. They cover, for instance, national hydrogen strategies (World Energy Council, 2021[5]) (IRENA, 2024[6]), contracting (Green Hydrogen Organisation, 2022[7]), standards and certifications (IRENA and RMI, 2023[8]), innovation (Cammeraat, Dechezleprêtre and Lalanne, 2022[9]), as well as broader policy toolkits (Hydrogen Council, 2021[10]), (UNIDO, IRENA and IDOS, 2023[11]). The case studies from clean hydrogen projects developed by the OECD between 2022 and 2024 highlight the importance of these non-financial measures, often considered as a prerequisite to developing specific de-risking instruments (see Box 2.1).

Box 2.1. Lessons learnt from OECD case studies: examples of key measures to improve the enabling conditions for clean hydrogen projects

Between 2022 and 2023, the OECD developed 15 case studies of hydrogen projects (see Figure 2.1), targeting primarily large-scale projects that had reached or were close to reaching final investment decision in emerging markets and developing economies (EMDEs). Lessons learnt from these case studies highlight a number of non-monetary measures that are vital to improve the business model for clean hydrogen. These measures highlight a broad set of enabling conditions, not limited to economic, de-risking and financing instruments. Key learnings include the following items:

- **Standards and certification**: common methodologies and interoperability of different hydrogen standards and certification schemes is paramount, notably to facilitate international trade of clean hydrogen and its derivatives for exports-oriented projects.
- **Access to infrastructure**: the availability of power transmission lines, inbound and outbound logistics infrastructures and deep-sea harbours, especially for exports of ammonia, steel or e-fuels, has been decisive for some projects.
- **Green mandates**: visibility on demand creation can be provided by national and regional mandates for specific products and sectors. Thus, business models based on hydrogen derivatives as final products also benefit from green mandates. For instance, synthetic aviation fuel derived from renewable hydrogen must make up 1.2% of all aviation fuel and 42% of the hydrogen used by industry must be renewable by 2030 in the European Union.
- **Partnerships**: a strong network of partners is needed across the value chain as it is challenging for a single actor to cover all aspects. Several project developers rely on vertically integrated partnerships, for instance between a supplier of green electricity, green hydrogen producer and the consumers/offtakers of green hydrogen. For instance, linking power purchase agreements (PPA) and hydrogen sales agreements (HSA) prices can be important to avoid a scissors effect between the project's costs and revenues. Several project developers emphasised the role of public-private partnerships, particularly to develop hydrogen hubs and to ensure common user infrastructures. Others highlighted the role of Joint Ventures (JV) and Special Purpose Vehicles (SPV) with multiple equity partners to better share the risks of the projects.
- **Contractual strategy in construction phase**: choosing highly experienced technologists and reputable engineering, procurement and construction (EPC) firms is essential, but so is the type of contracts, as they govern responsibilities of shareholders. Under an Engineering, Procurement and Construction Management (EPCM), the client has more control of the project, notably on change of scope, planning and associated financial decisions. In some projects, the use of an EPC wrap, where a single contractor is responsible for the entire Engineering, Procurement, and Construction, offers a solution where the EPC firms act as the single entity responsible for mitigating risk and ensuring technical and commercial viability. In this case, investors evaluate not only the EPC firm's capability to deliver the project with the ability to select technology suppliers and contractors and manage interfaces between them, but also that is has a sufficiently strong balance sheet. For instance, Air Products is the primary EPC contractor and system integrator for the NEOM project in Saudi Arabia, and Black & Veatch are taking that role for large-scale projects with production scheduled to commence in 2025 (Merjaneh, 2022[12]).
- **Technical assistance**: there is growing demand for technical assistance for project preparation, pilot projects, and associated financial operations in developing countries. The most commonly offered form of technical assistance to developing countries is awareness and capacity building, followed by the development of assessments and studies related to strategy and policy. At project level, funding for early analytics and diagnostics work can help prepare production cost tools,

market studies, and risk assessments. Developing production cost tools, market studies and risk assessments during the development, construction and operational phases helps to give lenders an increased confidence in the project fundamentals.

Figure 2.1. Overview of case studies of clean hydrogen projects prepared by the OECD in 2022-23

Note: More information about the case studies is available in Annex C: List of OECD hydrogen case studies developed in 2022 and 2023.
Source: (Cordonnier and Saygin, 2022[13]; Lee and Saygin, 2023[14]; OECD/The World Bank, 2024[15])

Methodology

In order to build a better understanding of the use of de-risking instruments for clean hydrogen projects in EMDEs, a three-step approach was followed, including:

- **Desk-based research** to identify and pre-select a subset of risk mitigation instruments;
- An **investor survey** to identify trends and collect insights from stakeholders active in that sector;
- **Case studies** of large-scale hydrogen projects and of economic, de-risking and financing instruments.

The desk-based survey led to an initial screening of more than 50 de-risking instruments that could potentially be used for clean hydrogen projects. Based on the analysis of key risks for this sector, comparison with similar industries and identification of instruments that are available, 13 instruments were pre-selected. The survey, conducted with 41 representatives from industrial corporations, governments, development finance institutions, investment funds, private banks and export credit agencies, collected additional information and expert insights on these 13 instruments. The five case studies on large-scale clean hydrogen projects and 10 case studies on economic, de-risking and financing instruments (see Table 2.1) provide additional insights from actual implementation.

Table 2.1. List of case studies developed for this report

Type	Name	Organisation	Sector and description	Country
Project	Ceará Green Hydrogen Hub	Industrial and Port Complex of Pecém (CIPP)	Clean ammonia	Brazil
Project	Egypt Green Hydrogen	Scatec	Hydrogen production for an existing ammonia plant	Egypt
Project	HyDuqm	Engie, POSCO Holdings	Clean hydrogen and ammonia	Oman
Project	Karnataka project	JSW Group	Captive clean hydrogen project for steel production	India
Project	Lhyfe Grand Canal du Havre	Lhyfe	Clean hydrogen for fertiliser production	France
Instrument (Financing)	Clean H2 Infra Fund	Hy24	Infrastructure fund	Europe, Asia-Pacific, North America and MENA
Instrument (Financing, De-Risking)	Foreign Private Capital Mobilization and Currency Hedging Programme	Inter-American Development Bank, Ministry of Finance of Brazil	Blended Finance and Currency Hedging platform	Brazil
Instrument (De-Risking)	Green Hydrogen Facility to Support Green, Resilient, and Inclusive Economic Development Project for Chile	World Bank, CORFO (implementing)	Sub-loans and risk-mitigation facility, and risk-mitigation reserve accounts (credit enhancement facility)	Chile
Instrument (Economic)	Green Hydrogen Incentives Law	Government of Egypt	Tax credits	Egypt
Instrument (De-Risking)	HySure risk transfer	Munich Re	Product and performance guarantees	Global
Instrument (De-Risking)	Insurance facility	Marsh	Insurance and reinsurance for new and existing green and blue hydrogen energy projects	Global
Instrument (Financing, Economic)	IRA - hydrogen	Government of the United States	Federal tax credits	U.S.
Instrument (Financing, Economic)	Japanese government subsidy scheme	Government of Japan	Contract-for-difference subsidies for domestic and imported hydrogen	Japan
Instrument (Financing, Economic)	National Hydrogen Mission	Government of India	Auction and subsidies	India
Instrument (Financing, De-Risking)	SDG Namibia One Fund	Climate Fund Managers (CFM), The Environmental Investment Fund of Namibia (EIF), Invest International (II)	Investment platform to attract blended finance	Namibia

Note: previous OECD reports include 14 project case studies on clean hydrogen projects (Cordonnier and Saygin, 2022[13]), (Lee and Saygin, 2023[14]), and two case studies on economic, de-risking and financing instruments specific to clean hydrogen, led by H_2Global and the Inter-American Development Bank (Cordonnier and Saygin, 2023[16]).
Source: Authors

Risks faced by clean hydrogen projects

Implication of risks

The risk profile of clean hydrogen remains unknown or high, given the nascent nature of the market and the limited track record of commercially and economically viable projects. EMDEs face higher actual and perceived risks than advanced economies, which contribute to increasing the weighted average cost of capital (WACC)[1] of clean hydrogen projects. This in turn reduces the bankability of clean hydrogen projects and potentially hampers investment (see Figure 2.2).

Figure 2.2. Factors influencing investor's perceived risk

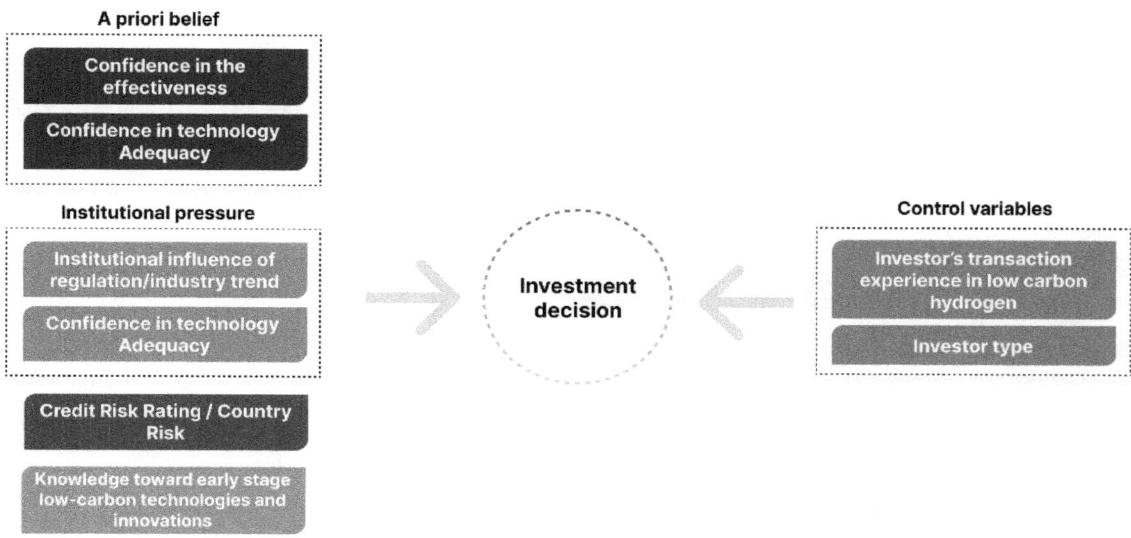

Source: (Lee and Saygin, 2023[14])

Capital-intensive projects like clean hydrogen are sensitive to the cost of finance (Taghizadeh-Hesary et al., 2022[17]) (OECD/The World Bank, 2024[15]). Based on OECD case studies, the CAPEX of large-scale projects with an annual output of at least 20 kt of clean hydrogen ranges between 20-40 k USD per tonne of annual hydrogen production capacity. The breakdown of clean hydrogen projects at low-cost location shows that capital costs (including capital expenditures for electrolyser and renewable electricity generation assets) amount to 70-80% of the total levelised cost of hydrogen (LCOH).[2] Therefore, a higher cost of finance has a significant impact on the LCOH. Holding all other production cost factors constant, an increase in the cost of capital from 9% to 20% can lead to a substantial increase of up to 73% in the LCOH (Lee and Saygin, 2023[14]). Indeed, the cost sensitivity of financing clean hydrogen projects can vary across countries, depending on factors such as infrastructure maturity, regulatory frameworks, political stability, and the availability of reliable EPC contractors (See Figure 2.3). However, the majority of high capital intensity projects such as renewable power generally shows significant sensitivity to the cost of capital in frontloaded structures. The IEA estimates that moving from a WACC of 5% (comparable to the WACC for utility-scale solar PV in AA to AAA credit-rating countries), to a WACC of 9% (comparable to the WACC for utility-scale solar PV in BB to BBB credit-rating countries) would see an increase of the levelised cost of electricity (LCOE)[3] by 34% and 29% for utility-scale solar PV and onshore wind respectively, compared to increases of 10% for coal- and 11% for gas-fired power plants (IEA, 2021[18]).

Figure 2.3. Drivers for the cost of capital for hydrogen projects in developed vs developing countries

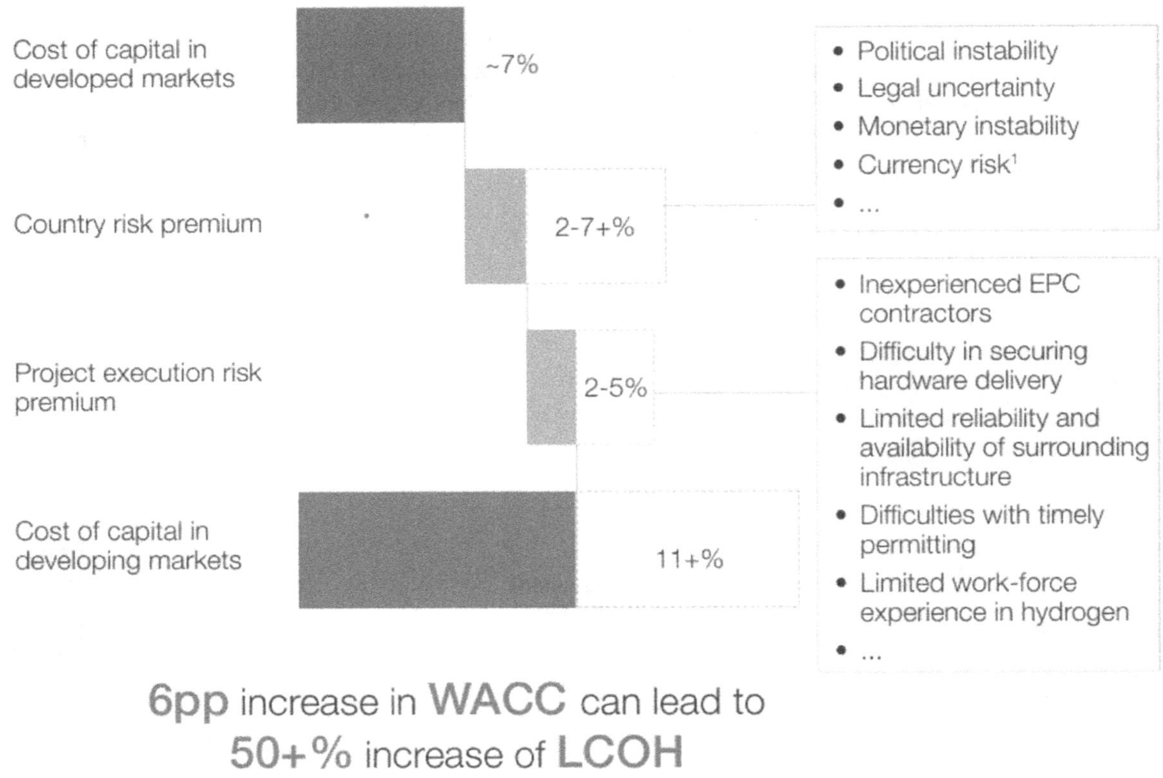

Source: Hydrogen Council and McKinsey (2024)

The capital-intensive nature of clean hydrogen projects makes them more vulnerable to volatile investment climates. For instance, in times of high inflation, as central banks move towards tighter monetary policy, the increased cost of capital will tend to disadvantage high CAPEX projects (e.g. renewables) relative to high OPEX projects (e.g. fossil fuels), as financial costs related to repaying lenders and dividends to investors become one of the largest expenses once the project is built (Montague, Raiser and Lee, 2024[19]). This underscores the need to design and implement tailored de-risking[4] mechanisms or instruments and direct public support measures to address the financing costs barrier (Steckel and Jakob, 2018[20]) (Sweerts, Longa and van der Zwaan, 2019[21]).

The capital structure, informed by the commissioning and operational risks inherent in a clean hydrogen project, is a key consideration to reduce financing costs. It usually comprises debt and equity financing and is determined primarily by debt sizing (i.e. the project finance model mechanics for determining how much debt can be raised for the project) (Firouzi and Meshkani, 2021[22]). Securing substantial debt is crucial to reducing financing costs, as the cost of debt is typically lower than the cost of equity. Debt financing typically involves funding from third parties who have priority in accessing the project's cash flow, beyond equity investors who have limited priority in project cash flow.

Most projects are structured with debt maturities that are shorter than the asset's lifespan or the concession duration. While cash flows during the tail risk aren't included in the collateral, projects with a longer tail are generally considered to have stronger credit profiles. This is because a longer tail can generate value beyond the debt amount, providing the project with greater flexibility to handle unforeseen challenges, negotiate more effectively with lenders, and secure better refinancing terms. Ultimately, this could result in higher recovery rates.

The appropriate amount of debt is limited by a project's ability to cover its capital expenses and operational costs while generating sufficient returns to repay its equity returns, principal, and interest. For projects perceived to be risky, not only are the interest rates higher, but the debt share will be lower, requiring a higher share of costlier equity financing. This balance is crucial for maintaining the project's ability to generate sufficient and predictable cashflow to maintain business operations during market fluctuations (Penev et al., 2024[23]). Therefore, for non or limited recourse projects, the appropriate amount of debt is limited by a project's ability to cover its capital expenses and operational costs while generating sufficient returns to repay its equity returns, principal and interest. For riskier projects, higher interest rates often result in lower debt share ratios, requiring either more expensive equity financing or additional guarantee support, such as insurance or corporate guarantees.

A thorough estimation of risks during the construction and operational phases, and their impacts on the cash generation, is required to provide lenders with confidence in the project's ability to weather potential challenges over the useful life of the project. Therefore, optimal debt sizing also hinges on suitable de-risking instruments and mitigation strategies to improve the financial viability of the project. Because clean hydrogen projects in EMDEs are considered as highly uncertain, they often require a higher level of equity than more mature technology or clean hydrogen projects in advanced economies.

Overview of key risks related to clean hydrogen production

Key risk factors contributing to high financing costs in EMDEs, in particular offtake risk, political and regulatory risk and infrastructure risk (see Figure 2.4), can lead to a cost of capital reaching up to 24% for renewable hydrogen (Lee and Saygin, 2023[14]). Most of the top risk factors identified are influenced by the market's lack of clarity on clean hydrogen demand and traded price, which affects the cash flow forecasts for projects throughout their operation cycle.

Figure 2.4. Key risk factors that are impacting the cost of finance of clean hydrogen projects

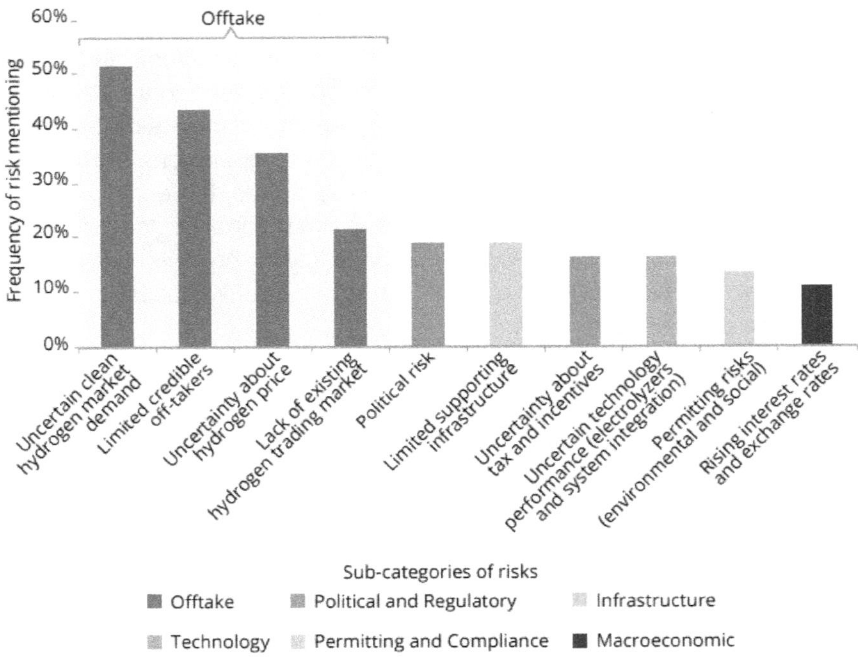

Source: (OECD/The World Bank, 2024[15])

Note: Survey conducted of around 40 investors, financiers, and developers with clean hydrogen project advisory, investment or development experience. The survey focussed on the risks faced for investments in clean hydrogen production projects, but not on investments in other parts of the value chain (electrolyser manufacturing, end-uses, etc.).

Some sub-categories of risks are usually addressed through non-monetary measures. For instance, the lack of water-related infrastructure, power transmission lines, hydrogen storage facility and transmission pipelines, or ports, require the actual physical availability of such assets. In addition, clean hydrogen projects often require collaboration among multiple stakeholders, such as developers, technology providers, investors, and governments. This partnership is essential for addressing challenges related to knowledge-sharing, building project consortiums, and making strategic investments that balance financial and development risks (Hasankhani et al., 2024[24]). Permitting and licensing are usually mitigated by streamlining the permitting process, clarifying institutional responsibilities, reducing the number of process steps, and providing capacity building to programme administrators (Waissbein et al., 2013[25]). In addition, government support such as discount on the land concession fees, tax incentives, exemption of levies until production and offtake ramp-up, could also strengthen the project's viability. On the other hand, financial derisking instruments such as insurance or guarantees, can address other sub-categories of risks throughout a project lifecycle, reduce the overall cost of capital and make the project bankable. These sub-categories of risks are primarily **macroeconomic risks**; **political risks**; **offtake risks**; **design, construction, and completion risks**; and **technology, operational and maintenance risks**.

The **macroeconomic risks** affecting the cost of financing include currency depreciation, high inflation, and interest rate spikes. Clean hydrogen projects are especially exposed to currency depreciation risks if their revenues are denominated in local currency and all or part of their debt is denominated in a foreign currency, usually dollars or euros. For example, the electrolysers that will be used in the first clean hydrogen projects will be imported from high-income countries, mostly from Europe, the UN and East Asia, with repayments to technology providers in foreign hard currencies. These initial projects will thus be exposed to currency risk if the revenues are in local currency. Macroeconomic factors impact the cost of debt financing in a country. As the cost of debt generally reflects the country borrowing rates and additional project risk, the latter being driven by technology maturity, clean hydrogen projects in EMDEs are prone to face high borrowing rates.

Political risks are changes in the legal and political order that may jeopardise the financial viability of clean hydrogen projects. They include modification of laws or regulations, expropriation, limitations in currency convertibility and transferability, and breach of contract, as well as war and civil unrest. Unscheduled changes in the legal framework may affect the financial viability of projects. This is particularly relevant in the nascent clean hydrogen sector, which depends on explicit regulatory supports such as tax incentives, public procurement or subsidies and premium prices, that directly influence the project costs and revenues.

Unscheduled changes in the legal and regulatory framework can significantly impact the financial viability of projects. This risk is especially pertinent in the emerging clean hydrogen sector, where projects rely heavily on regulatory support mechanisms like tax incentives, public procurement, subsidies, and premium pricing to influence costs and revenues. As the market evolves, governments may need to update regulations, a process investors are prepared to navigate, provided that changes are transparent, well-co-ordinated with industry stakeholders, and not applied retroactively.

Political turbulence can cause assets to decline severely in value or to be destroyed, confiscated or partially stranded. Therefore, businesses can be reluctant to operate in developing countries with above-average levels of political instability that threaten their assets and their ability to operate smoothly. Large-scale clean hydrogen projects are especially prone to this type of risks, because of the capital intensity and the life span of these projects.

Offtake risks reflect the high uncertainty on price and volume, notably related to the growth of the clean hydrogen market in coming years. The lack of a merchant market for hydrogen makes that reliable price information is scarce and markets are fragmented. Certain derivatives such as ammonia are already mature markets where price information is readily available, although there usually is no specific index for renewable or clean derivatives to distinguish them from fossil-based ones. Moreover, only few potential offtakers are willing to sign long-term contracts that specify the volume and price of the hydrogen over at least 7-10 years[5], which is often necessary to overcome the offtake risk in this nascent market. This notably stems from the first-mover risk, as clean hydrogen prices are expected to fall rapidly in the coming years, benefitting from a steep learning curve. Even in the case of an offtake contract, lenders require a careful assessment of the balance sheet of the offtaker to verify its creditworthiness.

Design, construction and completion risks can hamper the development of clean hydrogen projects, that bring together multiple stakeholders along an intricate supply chain. Construction and completion risks refer to the possibility of a project not achieving completion within the expected budget and by the expected date.

These risks can result in cost overruns and delays. An accurate estimation of the costs of construction works and equipment[6] to produce clean hydrogen at an early stage of the project is challenging, because of: (i) the limited experience of stakeholders, such as Engineering, Procurement, and Construction (EPC) firms, in large-scale clean hydrogen projects, combined with the lack of established project track records; (ii) consequently, EPC contractors are reluctant to provide comprehensive construction guarantees for these projects, leading to higher costs; (iii) suppliers of critical equipment, like electrolysers, have yet to deliver the required quantities, resulting in underdeveloped supply contract terms, warranties, and guarantees due to the absence of precedent; (iv) the complexity of project design and scope, notably about the renewable power required to operate the electrolysers and the balance of plant or ancillary infrastructure (KPMG, 2022[26]). Furthermore, the lack of infrastructure near the large-scale clean hydrogen project construction site can be challenging. The risk is particularly high in EMDEs, where ports, railways or roads are often not suited to transport heavy equipment, and where the timeline to develop the water and power infrastructure necessary to operate the plant can delay the entire project.

High **technology, operational and maintenance risks** are inherent to nascent sectors such as clean hydrogen, due to a lack of knowledge about the design and technology specifications, for instance for electrolysers. The growth of typical project size for clean hydrogen has been much faster than for batteries, wind or solar. Technical performance risk may become more important if technology or first-of-a-kind projects fail.

In particular, the lack of track record for large-scale projects of at least 100-MW raises questions about the technology performance, durability, and lifetime. This can cause delay in start-ups or business interruptions. On the operational side, partial load has proven to be a challenge for some electrolyser types. The often-harsh EMDE climate conditions can exceed those applied for standards and certification, another source of technology risk. Electrolyser manufacturers face risk of product liability claims if malfunction, defects or improper installation result in injuries (Swiss Re Institute, 2022[27]). Moreover, the electrolyser degradation, maintenance needs and downtime from equipment failure can lower their capacity factor and trigger a loss of revenue.

Environmental and social performance standards are crucial to project viability and operation. For example, clean hydrogen storage and transport involve high-pressure containers and pipelines, which could pose risks to nearby communities in case of leaks or explosions. Failing to assess these risks during the project appraisal phase can lead to significant issues later. The limited number and geographical concentration of suppliers, supply chain vulnerability, as well as the rapid evolution of technology, may also limit the availability and lead time to deliver electrolysers or spare parts. Finally, industrial plants are typically operated continuously and require operating and maintaining the equipment safely. The availability of a skilled workforce can be another limitation for clean hydrogen projects in EMDEs.

The risk of obsolescence also accounts as a technology risk. For instance, hydrogen as long duration energy storage competes with a multitude of other technologies. In such nascent markets and applications, governments' approach may be to let the private sector weed out the least efficient technologies.

The role of risk allocation and de-risking instruments

Investing in nascent technologies and markets such as clean hydrogen implies high risks. Therefore, it is likely that the performance of an investment will be different from expected. Because of this high uncertainty, investors typically demand what is known as a risk premium, which reflects and accounts for risk involved in an investment (Choi, Zhou and Lacton, 2022[28]). This risk premium directly affects the cost of capital. In other words, for a clean hydrogen project, lenders will charge higher interest rates, and equity investors will expect higher returns, compared to an investment in a more mature technology or market.

After having analysed the trends of the clean hydrogen markets and the key risks faced by project developers and investors, and before deep diving into the specificities of risk mitigation instruments, it is important to understand (i) how clean hydrogen projects are structured based on their business models and risk allocation, and (ii) who are the key actors that could provide or develop risk mitigation instruments.

Business models and risk allocation for clean hydrogen projects

The cash flow of clean hydrogen (and derivatives) projects remains likely to be difficult to predict. For instance, projects that are not vertically integrated with renewable electricity generation assets could be exposed to volatile power markets (Craen, 2023[29]). On the other side of the value chain, projects integrated with end-use application may secure the hydrogen offtake but would be exposed to price fluctuation of the markets of oil-derived products from refineries, fertilisers or steel. This can put project developers at risk, especially if most of their competitors do not use clean hydrogen, as the market price may then be decorrelated from the clean hydrogen project's cost structure. Thus, lenders and investors could impose stricter financial terms to increase chances to achieve their expected return on investment.

Blended and climate finance options, with objective key performance criteria set upfront to be met in future or at specific milestones can be incorporated to align incentives which seek to reduce the total cost of financing relative to the technology used and fuel feedstock for hydrogen over the medium to long term.

Several business models have emerged for clean hydrogen, with various project designs and scopes. Because project developers have different financing capabilities and risk appetite, and end-use markets have different dynamics, the project structure needs to be tailored according to several archetypes. This could be a challenge, especially for clean hydrogen projects that involve large-scale, non-recourse or limited recourse structures with multiple stakeholders. Table 2.2 presents four key examples of business models, building on a large number of case studies that provide in-depth information on individual projects: decarbonising existing processes (Model 1); exports (Model 2); utilities going downstream (Model 3); and hydrogen hubs (Model 4) (Cordonnier and Saygin, 2022[13]), (Lee and Saygin, 2023[14]), (OECD/The World Bank, 2024[15]). While these models do not provide a comprehensive overview, they serve to highlight how emerging clean hydrogen projects aim to address sector-specific challenges and provide a sound basis to understand how economic instruments, policy clarity, and risk mitigation strategies can enhance a project's bankability.

A well-designed project can mitigate specific risks and unlock economic opportunities. For instance, as shown in Table 2.2:

- Model 1: Decarbonising existing processes can create a large amount of hydrogen demand and supply with relatively small investments, notably by using existing assets and facilities. It may also limit the risk of stranded assets for companies operating fossil fuel-based plants[7].
- Model 2: Exports can mitigate at least partly the country risk, and benefit from contracts with creditworthy offtakers.
- Model 3: Utilities going downstream enables power producers and original equipment manufacturers (OEMs) to secure an outlet for large-scale renewable electricity generation or for massive volumes of equipment, while diversifying their exposures.
- Model 4: Hydrogen hubs is an option to reduce the exposition of single companies to infrastructure risk, and diversify the end-use for hydrogen production, thereby mitigating the uncertainties of clean hydrogen market uptake in specific markets.

Table 2.2. Examples of business models for clean hydrogen projects

Model 1: Decarbonising existing processes	Model 2: Exports	Model 3: Utilities going downstream	Model 4: Hydrogen hubs
• Oil refineries deploying clean hydrogen *Examples*: Adnoc, Chevron, Ecopetrol, Exxon Mobil, Galp, Reliance, Saudi Aramco, Shell, Sinopec • Gas producing companies deploying clean hydrogen *Examples*: OQ, Qatar Energy, SNAM • Fossil fuel-based power producers deploying hydrogen or ammonia in existing power plant *Examples*: Utilities in Japan and Korea • Ammonia producers deploying clean hydrogen *Examples*: Fertiglobe, OCI, Yara • Steel producers deploying clean hydrogen in existing or new plants *Examples*: Stegra, HYBRIT, JSW Steel	• Existing fossil fuel companies moving into clean hydrogen production *Examples*: BP Australia, Equinor/Scatec Egypt, Sasol South Africa, Shell Oman, Total Eren Mauritania • New players entering the clean hydrogen industry *Examples*: CWP Mauritania, Hyphen Namibia, The Green Solutions Viet Nam	• OEMs and renewable project developers are investing in and/or planning to operate electrolysis plants, as a complementary or diversification activity from their core business *Examples*: Electricity utilities ACWA power, Adani, Engie, Iberdrola; some Chinese photovoltaic manufacturers and Chinese wind turbine manufacturers are entering the clean hydrogen sector.	• Hydrogen hubs are networks of hydrogen producers, consumers, and local connective infrastructure to accelerate the use of hydrogen as a clean energy carrier and feedstock. The hubs are not single facilities but refer to a collection of linked assets that will work together to develop the domestic hydrogen economy. *Example*: The Mission Innovation hydrogen Valleys platform counted 98 hydrogen valleys or hubs worldwide across 33 countries with a total investment volume of USD 173 billion as of 1 August 2024

Note: 1) OEM: Original Equipment Manufacturer; 2) Under Model 1, the reduction of the lifecycle emission reduction can vary greatly in the examples provided; many projects related to clean hydrogen use in fossil-fuel based industrial process only lead to partial emissions reduction. 3) the examples are not comprehensive.
Source: Authors, based on (OECD/The World Bank, 2024[15]), complemented by (UNIDO, 2023[30])

In the absence of a risk management package designed to stabilise the project's cash flow, clean hydrogen projects may struggle to reach final investment decision. Diversifying the risk allocation or utilising risk mitigation solutions to those best able to manage them, whether it be sponsors, insurers, financiers, or governments, is vital to stimulate investment in clean hydrogen. Yet, even when the general risk allocation is adequate and the macroeconomic environment is favourable, a project may still not be financially viable, particularly if the sector or the technology is nascent. There are two main cases for this: first, when a project is unable to generate sufficient revenues to recoup its costs and requires subsidies even without risk or uncertainty; second, when despite an optimal risk allocation, the expected revenues of the project still do not offset the expected risks. Therefore, even when risk mitigation instruments and strategies are being deployed, investment decisions remain fundamentally guided by the market dynamics.

The sector's maturity should also be taken into account when allocating risks. In many mature capital-intensive projects, such as infrastructure or renewables, the private sector bears these risks. However, for clean hydrogen projects, where market transactions are not yet well-established, significant risks typically borne by the private sector should be shared by the public sector (government or DFIs/MDBs) by either co-financing the project or offering financial risk mitigation instruments, notably through Public-Private Partnerships (PPP) (see Box 2.2).

Box 2.2. The example of risk-sharing in Public-Private Partnerships projects

Public-private partnerships (PPPs) combine the deployment of private sector capital and, sometimes, public sector capital to improve public services or the management of public sector assets. By focusing on public service outputs, they offer a more sophisticated and cost-effective approach to the management of risk by the public sector than is generally achieved by traditional input-based public sector procurement (Gerrard, 2021[31]).

Table 2.3. Risk Allocation in typical PPP Project

	Land availability risk	Construction risk	Operating risk	Demand risk	Financial market risk	Disruptive technology risk	Force Majeure risk	Early Termination risk
Water Desalination	Public	Private	Circumstance dependent	Public	Shared	Shared	Shared	Shared
Solar Plant	Circumstance dependent	Private	Private	Public	Shared	Shared	Shared	Shared
Power transmission	Public	Private	Private	Public	Shared	Shared	Shared	Shared
Port	Public	Private	Private	Circumstance dependent	Shared	Shared	Shared	Shared

Notes: 1) The summary matrix identifies a typical risk allocation. However, there are often exceptions or deviations from this typical risk allocation at individual projects level. 2) For water desalination plant, the matrix describes the common risk allocation for a build, own, finance, operate, maintenance and transfer (at the end of the PPP contract) to a contracting authority of a new water desalination project where the potable water is sold to a state-owned single buyer.
Source: Authors adopted from (Global Infrastructure Hub, 2020[32])

In the context of clean hydrogen projects, identifying the right de-risking instruments and determining who is well positioned to bear the associated risks is more complicated. Indeed, the clean hydrogen value chain covers water desalination plants, renewable power generation assets, equipment for the electrolysis, infrastructure to store and transport hydrogen to the end-users, and industrial plants which consume hydrogen. Investment is not limited to greenfield assets, but can also include brownfield ones, such as the retrofit of a natural gas pipeline for hydrogen transportation. While hydrogen project developers are mostly private actors, public actors are often involved in projects as minority shareholders and/or through PPP in part of the value chain, such as infrastructure. In order to de-risk early-stage projects, governments can assume a larger share of upfront development risks by taking a more proactive approach. In a traditional PPP scheme, the public sector typically assumes the offtake risk, while the private sector handles development and operational risks. However, given that hydrogen offtake depends on market conditions, it is necessary to reassess and potentially realign the risk allocation between the public and private sectors.

The complex value chain of clean hydrogen creates a multiplicity of approaches, with a varying level of risks transferred to private actors. As an example: in management and lease contracts in which a private company assumes the management of a public asset for a fixed period but the public authority retains the ownership and investment decisions, limited risks are transferred to the private partner; but when a private company or a public-private joint venture builds and operates a new facility for a period specified in the PPP (long-term) contract, the private partner bears most of the financial and operational risks. In the context of public investment or PPP, an effective risk allocation is essential for delivering great Value for Money (VfM)[8] (Hovy, 2015[33]).

Role of international finance institution, Export Credit Agencies and private actors in providing risk mitigation instruments

In a mapping exercise to better understand the landscape of guarantees for EMDEs, the Climate Policy Initiative identifies four main types of providers: Multilateral Development Banks (MDBs), Development Finance Institutions (DFIs), Export Credit Agencies (ECAs) and Specialised Institutions. The latter are "entities that operate similarly to private sector organizations but are funded by governments and development institutions, generally focusing on guaranteeing specific types of risks in specific situations" (Climate Policy Initiative, 2024[34]).

Existing guarantee facilities with a mandate for climate investments in EMDEs can be scaled with additional capital. Examples include MIGA, GuarantCo, The Currency Exchange Fund (TCX) and the Green Guarantee Company (Systemiq, 2023[35]). In July 2024, the World Bank Group announced pivoting from primarily being a lending institution to also being a mobilising one. The guarantee platform, housed at the MIGA, will be a one-stop shop for all the institution's guarantee business. The platform has three product families: credit guarantees (for loans to the public or private sector); political risk insurance (for private sector projects or public-private partnerships); and trade finance guarantees for public sector risk (Bjerde et al., 2024[36]).

ECAs can be government institutions or private companies that operate on behalf of governments. Such support can take the form either of "official financing support", such as direct credits to foreign buyers, refinancing or interest-rate support, or of "pure cover support", such as export credits insurance or guarantee to cover credits provided by private financial institutions. In 2023, participants to the Arrangement on Officially Supported Export Credits have agreed to allow more generous and flexible financing terms and conditions for a wide range of climate-friendly projects, including clean hydrogen and ammonia. This includes for instance adjusting the minimum premium rates for credit risk for longer repayment terms and obligors with a higher credit risk rating. For Stegra (previously H_2 Green Steel) project in Sweden, Riksgälden (Swedish National Debt Office) provided a green credit guarantee and Euler Hermes an export credit cover for EUR 1.2 bn each. Furthermore, ECAs' tied and untied loans provide competitive interest rates and increase lender confidence in the project. This "anchoring" effect is deemed critical in large-scale projects.

Private investors shall also make use of comprehensive insurance products and guarantees and take some commercial risks on years not covered by government backing to strengthen the de-risking strategy by providing stable cash flows for clean hydrogen projects. New technologies and industrial processes carry risks and uncertainties that can inhibit the affordability of insurance. Thus, businesses need to work with insurers from the earliest stages of development to ensure a match between the available insurance and the risk profile of new initiatives (Howden and BCG, 2024[37]). (Re)insurers can play a key role in the development of the hydrogen economy by providing risk management knowledge and risk transfer options at select points of the value chain. In the short-term, these actors are likely to cover risks that can be mitigated through existing instruments in the construction and supply side, replicating what already exists in other sectors. This includes physical loss during construction, delay in start-up, or operational damages and natural peril causing business interruption risks (Swiss Re Institute, 2022[27]).

The potential of risk mitigation instruments for clean hydrogen remains uncertain

Risk mitigation instruments are currently seldom deployed to support clean hydrogen projects in EMDEs, compared to direct financing and economic instruments such as grants, viability gap funding or tax incentives. Yet, as guarantee instruments and insurance products typically do not require any immediate outlay of capital, and subsequently only in a proportion of cases for the same amount of funding, a larger number of projects can be supported than through other instruments (International Development Finance Club, 2019[38]). The analysis of MDB climate finance mobilisation ratios shows that guarantees show the highest mobilisation ratios, on average mobilising USD 1.5 of private capital for every dollar of MDB capital and outperforming the average mobilisation ratio of loans and equities by six times. However, guarantees represent just 4% of total commitments in the analysed data (Systemiq, 2023[35]). A recent OECD evaluation found that guarantees leveraged 26% of all mobilised private finance between 2018-2020 and were among the preferred risk mitigation tools of private investors (OECD, 2022[39]).

The effectiveness and efficiency of de-risking instruments to mitigate specific risks related to clean hydrogen are yet to be demonstrated. Designing tailored de-risking instruments to address priority risks based on the market context and understanding their leverage can help to increase the cumulated capacity of low-carbon projects deployed for a given amount of public finance spend. Therefore, these instruments (i.e. H_2Global to address offtake risk) could accelerate decision-making of investors and help crowd-in more private finance.

This can be instrumental to meet the Breakthrough Agenda's priority action to "co-ordinate and facilitate access to increased finance and support mechanisms that address obstacles to investment, with the goal of mobilising private investment at scale in emerging and developing economies". Furthermore, a strategic use of tailored risk mitigation instruments can stimulate investment and reduce the cost of capital, thereby reducing the total amount needed to deploy and deliver the 10 GW initiative of the World Bank.

Box 2.3. World Bank's 10 GW Lighthouse Initiative

The 10 GW Lighthouse Initiative seeks to accelerate the deployment of renewable hydrogen in EMDEs by ensuring that a project pipeline representing 10 GW of hydrogen electrolysis capacity reaches final investment decision (FID) by 2030. This goal will be achieved through co-ordinated efforts by multilateral development banks (MDBs) and development finance institutions (DFIs). As of September 2024, ten financing institutions and government entities from Europe, Asia and Latin America have expressed their interest to join this effort.

The 10 GW Lighthouse Initiative will facilitate a joint discussion among relevant actors on how to close the existing financing gap and ensure that limited amounts of concessional and development financing are used to achieve their maximum effect, notably for projects that are moving from early stages of development to FID. Therefore, this activity will facilitate the dialogue between MDBs, DFIs, commercial financial institutions, governments and project developers.

A global project pipeline is currently being mapped to identify projects between 100 MW to 1 GW of electrolysis capacity in EMDCs that can reach FID in the coming years. This activity also encompasses identifying key project barriers and risks hindering the development of clean hydrogen projects. Next step will consist of supporting selected projects on the development of a through package of enabling measures and financing solutions, as well as de-risking mechanisms granted by MDBs and DFIs.

The 10 GW Lighthouse Initiative will document project characteristics and development process to allow future replication and identification of best practices. This activity will also include awareness and outreach actions to disseminate lessons learned.

Source: Authors

Selection of instruments and insights from investor survey and case studies

Selection of relevant risk mitigation instruments

Since clean hydrogen projects are not yet deployed at scale, it is challenging to observe frequently utilised de-risking financial instruments and assess their effectiveness. Furthermore, current clean hydrogen projects cannot progress without substantial economic instruments and policy measures from the public sector. As argued in (Lee and Saygin, 2023[14]), (OECD/The World Bank, 2024[15]), (Craen, 2023[29]) and Fitch, clean hydrogen asset profile present similarities both with energy projects (specifically offshore wind, but to some extent to thermal power plants) and/or LNG projects. Therefore, a comparative analysis of their characteristics can provide valuable insights for clean hydrogen (see Table 2.4).

Clean hydrogen is similar to LNG and offshore wind projects in terms of large project size, long-term capital intensity and technologically complex project structure. Both offshore wind and clean hydrogen projects are in the early stages of development and involve long lead times and complex project structures. This results in high perceived risks during the design, construction, and completion phase. Ownership of offshore wind projects, similar to large-scale clean hydrogen projects, is often concentrated among energy companies (including from oil and gas sector) or large-scale industrial companies (Đukan et al., 2023[40]).

While it is possible to draw analogies between sectors, the asset risk profiles are not fully equivalent:

- The project design for clean hydrogen can be more complex than in these other industries, as it depends on the project's archetype and structure. For example, a co-located module, where renewable electricity is generated and used at the same location as the hydrogen end-users, presents different risks compared to a distantly located module, where renewable electricity is generated in one location, transmitted to power an electrolyser for hydrogen production, and then transported to end-users (OECD, 2024[41]). On the contrary, even though offshore wind farms and LNG plants are complex projects, the projects' design is quite standard in each of these sectors.
- The LNG industry has built a significant transaction track record over the last decades, while the clean hydrogen sector is still nascent. Moreover, cost transparency and competitiveness of clean hydrogen remains challenging, and a clean hydrogen trade market has yet to emerge, whereas the LNG market is valued around USD 100 billion, and it can be traded on multiple natural gas markets worldwide.
- Offshore wind and clean hydrogen projects are both exposed to significant financial risks related to intermittency of production and market price fluctuation (merchant risk). For offshore wind, this is driven by the often highly volatile power markets and curtailment risk, and for clean hydrogen, by the uncertainty and lack of transparency of clean hydrogen price. However, offshore wind projects face a lower demand risk, especially when they are connected to power grids, as their marginal cost of production is limited and some jurisdictions prioritise the offtake of variable renewable electricity over (fossil fuel-based) dispatchable power sources.
- A standalone clean hydrogen project using proven technology could have in principle a similar profile to that of thermal power assets, in particular in terms of technical risk, or in terms of supply risk for natural gas-based power plants. However, health and safety risk for new hydrogen production facilities can be perceived as much higher, notably because of the flammability range, invisibility and explosive characteristics of hydrogen. This would result in overall higher operation risk.

Table 2.4. Asset Risk Profile Comparison of Clean Hydrogen and other relevant sectors

	Clean Hydrogen	LNG	Thermal	Offshore wind	Grey Hydrogen
Capital-intensity	High	High	Moderate	High	Moderate
Project Complexity	High	Moderate	Moderate	High	Moderate
Price risk	Yes (tradable market yet to emerge), expected to be fixed price for first projects	No, commodity price or indexed price (floating)	Moderate, depends on the country and power market structure	Yes	Moderate or No (depends on coal/gas so should be aligned)
Significant capital costs reduction for new projects	Yes (beginning of the learning curve)	No	No	Yes	No
Market Maturity	Low	Advanced	Advanced	Advanced	Advanced (for use in same location as production in large plants)
Profitability	Low or negative	Moderate to High	Moderate to High	Low to moderate	Moderate to high
Operation risk	High	Moderate	High	Low to Moderate	Low
Revenue risk	High	Moderate	High	Moderate, depends on price contract terms/structure	Low to Moderate (for use in same location as production in large plants), depends on price formula
Supply risk	High	High	Moderate	Moderate	Low to Moderate (for use in same location as production in large plants)
Counterparty risk	Yes	No	No	Moderate (pending on contractual arrangement)	Low/No (for use in same location as production in large plants)

Source: Authors, based on (Craen, 2023[29]), (Fitch, 2023[42]), (Natixis, 2021[43]), MIT Energy Initiative
Note: In this table, supply risk refers to potential challenges or uncertainties that may disrupt the availability of essential resources, materials, or components necessary for the project's operations. For example, in LNG projects, supply risks may involve issues such as natural gas availability, disruptions in transportation and shipping, or infrastructure challenges, including problems with liquefaction plants, pipelines, and storage facilities. In renewable energy projects, supply risks might include delays or shortages of key components like solar panels and wind turbines, as well as variability in natural resource availability.

Literature and data on de-risking instruments that have been deployed in renewables, LNG, as well as in green infrastructure projects provide information on the effectiveness of these instruments to enhance the bankability or financial performance of projects. When available, the following criteria were considered to pre-select the most promising de-risking instruments: (i) overall amount of private investment mobilised, and leverage ratio of public finance used; (ii) proven track record of implementation (where data on single instruments was preferred, as it gives a better understanding of their replicability potential, compared to complex packaged risks which may be specific to a given project structure); (iii) proven impact on financing costs if project-level information is available (e.g. in a very few cases, the improvement of the debt-service coverage ratio (DSCR) and its positive on debt sizing has been considered).

Most instruments have a direct cost and a transaction cost when they are applied. These costs must be compared with the potential benefits in order to assess their usefulness in a specific case. The desktop research provided insights on typical assumptions to evaluate the efficiency of de-risking instruments for clean energy projects (see Table 2.5). However, as information about cost and benefits is often case specific and even proprietary, it is difficult to conclude whether the values and assumptions from the literature actually apply to clean hydrogen projects in EMDEs.

Table 2.5. Examples of cost assumptions used in the calculation of the efficiency of de-risking instruments for clean energy projects

De-risking instrument	Description
Public Loan	**Public cost** Assumes public cost is 100% of the loan amount Assumes 3.5x paid-in-capital multiplier
Partial Loan Guarantee	Assumes a partial loan guarantee at 50% of the face value of the commercial loan to avoid moral hazard and recognizing that the electrolyser can be used as collateral. Assumes no matching sovereign guarantee is required by domestic government. **Public cost** Assumes the public cost is a 50% of the guaranteed amount Assumes 3.5x paid-in-capital multiplier **Private cost (fee structure)** Assumes 200 basis points (2%) loan guarantee fee, calculated annually, based on the average outstanding value of the commercial loan covered by the guarantee
Political Risk Insurance	Assumes MIGA coverages for equity holders covering (i) expropriation, (ii) political violence, (iii) currency restrictions, and (iv) breach of contract. Covers 90% of the original face value of equity invested. **Public cost** Assumes the public cost is 10% (loss reserve) of the equity amount covered Assumes 3.5x paid-in-capital multiplier **Private cost (fee structure)** Assumes a 20 basis points (0.2%) front end fee Assumes a 100 basis points (1%) premium payment, calculated annually
Liquidity Reserve Account and Debt Service Reserve Account	**Public cost:** Assumes public cost is 100% of the loan amount Assumes 3.5x paid-in-capital multiplier
Technology insurance (product, performance and availability guarantee)	**Private cost (fee structure):** Assumes a 20 basis points (0.2%) front end fee Assumes a deductible of 37 percent of the repair, rectification and maintenance cost as deductible Assumes a 1000 basis points (10%) co-payment, calculated per event

Note: 1) the cost efficiency of de-risking measure is defined as the difference in the project's net present value (NPV) after implementing the instrument over the cost of the instrument. An efficiency below 1 means that the cost of the instrument is higher than the NPV gains. 2) due to the lack of data on clean hydrogen projects, the values only reflect examples of assumptions for clean energy projects; they would vary depending on the instrument provider and specific projects' conditions, and probably be higher for clean hydrogen, which is less commercially mature than other clean energy technologies. 3) the list is not exhaustive; for instance, in addition to Debt Service Reserve Account, lenders may require a letter of credit to cover short-term payment obligations.
Source: Authors with inputs from (Deloitte, 2024[44]; Munich RE, 2024[45]; Waissbein et al., 2013[25])

Finally, the instruments have also been selected based on their *a priori* suitability to address the main risks faced by clean hydrogen projects (see Figure 2.4). While doing so, the final selection also aims to cover the project lifecycle, including both pre-FID and post-FID salient risks, and present instruments relevant across the clean hydrogen value chain. The final selection of instruments covered in the investor survey is provided in Table 2.6.

Table 2.6. 13 selected instruments description

Risk Category	Instrument	Pre-FID	Post-FID	Value Chain
Macroeconomic Risks	Interest rate swaps	X	X	Cross-cutting
Macroeconomic Risks	Foreign currency guarantee	X	X	Cross-cutting
Political and Regulatory Risks	Political Risk Investment Insurance / Foreign Investment Insurance	X	X	Cross-cutting
Offtake Risks	Partial credit guarantee	X	X	Demand side
Offtake Risks	Contracts for Difference	X	X	Demand side
Offtake Risks	Offtake guarantee	X	X	Demand side
Offtake Risks	Credit default swaps	X	X	Demand side
Offtake Risks	Loan loss reserve (LLR)	X	X	Demand side
Offtake Risks	Syndication of Loans	X	X	Demand side
Technology Risk	Performance guarantees		X	Cross-cutting
Technology Risks	Buyer Credit Guarantees		X	Supply side
Design, Construction, and Completion Risks	Contractors-all-risk insurance		X	Supply side
Design, Construction, and Completion Risks	Liquidated damages		X	Supply side

Source: Authors

Description of selected risk mitigation instruments for clean hydrogen investor survey

Interest rate swaps

Interest rate swaps are forward contracts in which one stream of future interest payments is exchanged for another based on a specified principal amount. Interest rate swaps can exchange fixed or floating rate payments to reduce or increase exposure to fluctuations in interest rates.

Large-scale clean hydrogen projects are likely to be financed through project finance structure, securing a loan amounting to at least 60% of the total project cost (Lopez Rocha, Gielen and Govindarajalu, 2024[46]). Long-term loans in project finance, which depends on the project's success to be repaid, are particularly vulnerable to interest rate fluctuations that may be triggered by inflation and economic cycles. An interest rate swap can provide greater cash-flow predictability and protection from rising rates (Frost Brown Todd, 2023[47]).

For instance, for a clean hydrogen project contracting a EUR 600 million loan structured with a fixed margin plus a floating interest rate linked to the 6 months EURIBOR, a rise in EURIBOR from 2% to 5% could increase annual interest payment from EUR 12 million to EUR 30 million. This would increase the cost of the loan and may put the project in financial distress. However, if the project had contracted an interest rate swap agreement to fix the interest rate at 3%, the annual interest payment would remain stable at EUR 18 million, which would facilitate budget management and increase project's viability.

Foreign currency guarantee

A Foreign Currency Guarantee is designed to protect borrowers from the exchange rate fluctuations, by allowing an obligor to repay funds in the same currency as its revenue stream, or at a pre-determined rate regardless of prevailing market exchange rates over the agreement period (EXIM, 2024[48]) (WRI, 2012[2]).

Clean hydrogen projects in EMDEs can create revenue streams in local currency or in hard currency, depending on the market(s) they are targeting. The expenses in local currency typically include the repayment of the loans contracted to purchase locally manufactured assets, as well as construction costs, and most operational costs. The expenses in hard currency would in principle mainly include the repayment of the loans contracted to cover capital expenditures for imported goods, which can represent the lion's share of the project costs, especially in countries that have a limited industrial base. Therefore, there could be a discrepancy between the share of revenues and expenses in local and hard currency.

For instance, a clean hydrogen project selling 50% of its production to export markets but having 70% of its expenses corresponding to the repayment of a loan in hard currency, a devaluation of the local currency may hinder the loan repayment. While in advanced economies, currency hedging can be done on the financial markets, currency hedges have significant tenor limitations in most EMDEs. Therefore, a foreign currency guarantee could be needed to mitigate the exposure to exchange rate volatility.

Political risk investment insurance and foreign investment insurance

Political Risk Insurance (PRI) protects against borrower failure to repay in case non-commercial risks materialise, such as expropriation, political violence, currency inconvertibility and transfer restrictions, and breach of contract (MIGA, 2011[49]). If such an event occurs and repayments are disrupted, political risk insurance/ guarantees pay out all or a portion of the losses that arise due to the event (WRI, 2012[2]).

In addition to providing compensatory value in the event of claims, PRI can help investors access finance. Investors in EMDEs are often required to get this insurance in order to obtain financing from banks. For lenders, PRI can provide regulatory relief from country risk-provisioning requirements. It can also be used to protect equity investors for termination events that the sovereign may need to compensate for. PRI can be provided by Export Credit Agencies (ECAs), Multilateral Development Banks (sometime through specific branches or agencies), private insurance companies and re-insurers (MIGA, 2011[49]).

Given the large potential of clean hydrogen production in EMDEs, notably in countries suffering from political instability, PRI could be a pre-requisite to help these projects reach Final Investment Decision (FID). Even when it is not necessary, PRI can help project access to better financing conditions. PRI has already been deployed in relatively similar areas as clean hydrogen project, notably for project finance and foreign direct investment, particularly in the oil and gas, mining, and infrastructure sectors (Marsh, 2024[50]).

Given both the large upfront CAPEX and extended tenors of these projects, engaging either a regional or global MDB financing brings a distinct halo effect on the project financing. This may also help alleviate long-term geopolitical stability risk concerns.

Partial credit guarantee

A partial credit guarantee (PCG) is a credit enhancement mechanism for debt instruments such as bonds and loans. It is a promise from the guarantee provider to pay the principal and/or interest up to a pre-determined amount. The guarantee amount is usually expressed as a percentage of principal. Its main objective is to improve the credit profile of borrowers, by decreasing perceived and actual risks of investment losses and that way increases the confidence among investors. Thus, it helps borrowers to diversify their sources of funding, extend maturities, and obtain financing in their currency of choice, hard or local (IFC, 2023[51]). Given the long lifetime of clean hydrogen assets, extending financing tenors using a PCG can be a critical benefit in this sector.

PCG is a well-established mechanism, with over 2 000 such schemes implemented in nearly 100 countries. These schemes typically target specific sectors, regions, or categories of firms or individuals that are considered underserved by the private financial sector (Green, 2003[52]). For instance, according to Marsh & McLennan Companies' Asia Pacific Risk Center database of 10 years of projects in Asia, an estimated 55 to 65 percent of infrastructure projects are not bankable without government or MDB guarantees, because lenders would not be willing to finance the project on a non- or limited-recourse basis (Lu, Chao and Sheppard, 2019[53]).

(Carbon) Contracts for Difference

A Contract-for-Difference (CfD) is a mechanism to incentivise investment in low-carbon technologies by providing stability and predictability to future revenue streams over a long period.[9] It is based on a difference between the market price[10] and an agreed "strike price". The strike price is typically fixed but can also be indexed. CfDs have been widely used in electricity markets, usually based on transparent and liquid indices. However, this approach cannot be directly replicated for clean hydrogen, where no clear price index nor liquid market exist. To address this, an arbitrary reference price can be set, or the natural gas or electricity market prices can be used as a reference. In addition, the market design of hydrogen needs to be strengthened, notably to ensure that there will be sufficient offtake for the clean hydrogen production that benefits from the CfD. More generally for decarbonisation projects, Carbon Contracts for Difference (CCfDs) are being considered, that would use a carbon price level as a reference for emissions reductions below a benchmark baseline (Richstein et al., 2021[54]).

CfDs are usually symmetrical. If the "strike price" is higher than a market price, the CfD provider must pay the clean hydrogen producer difference between the "strike price" and the market price. If the market price is higher than the agreed "strike price", the clean energy provider must pay back the CfD provider the difference between the market price and the "strike price" (IEA, 2019[55]) (Florence School of Regulation, 2023[56]). As such, while it aims to de-risk revenue streams, CfD inherently have a subsidy nature.

CfDs have been proven effective in providing price support for emerging technologies and encouraging desired behaviours by offering stability and predictability of future revenue streams (Ason and Poz, 2024[57]). However, CfDs can come with a high cost for public finance and bias market signal. Thus, the CfD design can be adapted or the scheme can be removed to transfer the risk to the project developers when a technology or industry has become mature enough (Energy Systems Catapult, 2022[58]), (Bouacida, 2023[59]). Currently CfD or similar to CfD models are considered in different jurisdictions including Canada, Germany, Japan, Korea, South Africa (BMWK, 2024[60]; Government of Canada, 2023[61]; S&P Global, 2023[62]; South African Government, 2023[63]).

Offtake guarantee

An offtake agreement is a contract between a buyer and a seller outlining the conditions under which a buyer will purchase a specified quantity of a commodity at a predetermined price. An offtake agreement guarantee is a financial security, such as a letter of credit which is issued by a third party to ensure that obligations under the agreement will be fulfilled, even in case of unforeseen circumstances.

Financial institutions require reliable revenue streams as part of their bankability assessment for a project. Given the low maturity of the clean hydrogen market, long-term (more than 7 to 10 years) hydrogen offtake agreements[11] with creditworthy offtakers, possibly at a fix price, remain the main measure to address the fundamental offtake issue. Including a take-or-pay (or take-and-pay) clause in the agreement further reduces the uncertainty on demand. The role of offtake guarantees, which can be provided by guarantee facilities such as MIGA, is mainly to increase the credibility or backstop these sovereign/SOE agreements. For instance, in clean hydrogen projects involving non-investment grade offtakers, an offtake guarantee can enhance the project's credit profile and improve its bankability assessment. This may be relevant in developing countries which do not have an investment grade rating (for example, where a state-owned utility or company intends to enter into a hydrogen offtake agreement with a producer) (Green Hydrogen Organisation, 2024[64]).

Credit default swaps

Credit Default Swaps (CDS) designed to insure counterparties against the default of a corporate or sovereign debt issuer (Henricot and Piquard, 2022[65]). In a credit default swap contract, the buyer makes a periodic payment similar to the payments on an insurance policy. In exchange, the seller agrees to pay the security's value and interest payments if a default of bankruptcy of the asset owner occurs. The legal terms of credit default swap agreements are highly standardised and have been so for a long time. It has played an important role in the development and increasing liquidity of the CDS market (Bomfim, 2022[66]). While credit default swaps are written on both sovereign and non-sovereign entities, more than 85% of contracts reference non-sovereign entities (Bank for International Settlements, 2024[67]).

For clean hydrogen projects, CDS can be particularly useful in addressing counterparty risk. A CDS allows sponsors, developers, or financiers to transfer the risk of default by a counterparty (e.g., an offtaker) to the CDS seller. Lenders and investors might be more willing to finance the project if they know that default risk is mitigated through a CDS, which could also contribute to securing better financing terms. Additionally, by providing security against default, the project's forecasted cash flow can be stabilised, thereby reducing the overall risk profile of the project. However, given the highly unique nature of clean hydrogen projects and early-stage risk, it may be difficult to obtain a suitable CDS proxy.

Loan loss reserve

Loan loss reserve (LLR) funds are a type of credit enhancement used to improve the credit risk profile of a lender or its investors to obtain better terms of debt repayment. It provides partial risk coverage to lenders, meaning that the reserve will cover a pre-specified amount of loan losses (US DOE, n.d.[68]).

This allows the financial institution to modify its underwriting criteria and accept more risk than it would otherwise. LLR may result in lengthened loan periods, i.e., the timeframe of the loan might be extended from 3 years to 7 or 10 years. The lower risk associated with the LLR coverage may also result in reduced interest rates (US DOE, n.d.[68]). Therefore, LLR can be an effective instrument in the nascent clean hydrogen industry that faces higher risks and uncertainty than other sectors.

A reserve account can notably mitigate O&M risks, as it can temporarily be a source of liquidity to cover downtime, underperformance, or maintenance and repairs in case of technology disruptions. The project operator can borrow from these accounts, and once operations return to normal, the amount that has been borrowed needs to be repaid. In the case of Chile, part of the World Bank loan is used for two such accounts (one for debt service, one for liquidity) that can be used in case of operational problem with electrolysers (see Box 2.4). This tool can even be more effective if it funds are pooled to cover different projects, as it could bundle the effect of occasional recourse of individual projects to the reserve accounts.

Box 2.4. Boosting green hydrogen production in Chile by mitigating operational and technology risk through a liquidity reserve account

Chile is creating a liquidity reserve account (LRA) to cover unexpected short-term technical underperformance in a green hydrogen generation plant. This risk-mitigation instrument is intended to reduce the cost of performance guarantees and strengthen confidence among manufacturing and EPC firms, financiers, and lenders in the performance of the green hydrogen subproject.

Given the short track record of green hydrogen technology, the LRA would be available for the initial five years of a green hydrogen subproject. It would be established based on a percentage (of up to 25 percent of a green hydrogen subproject's revenue). The account would provide additional liquidity and facilitate the subproject's continued operation. The LRA could be triggered solely when subprojects face non-structural technical challenges (especially early on) that could arise because of the early development stage of the green hydrogen industry. Triggers could include the following (among others):

- temporary deviations of operational Key Performance Indicators (KPIs) related to the production, compression, or storage of hydrogen (an operational KPI matrix will be submitted with the subproject application)
- complications arising from the unavailability of component replacements
- excessive costs for repair and replacements as a result of component failure or unexpected performance degradation (beyond the scope of the performance-based maintenance contracting).

Source: World Bank

Syndication of loans

The concept of syndicated financing is closely linked to operations/transactions involving large amounts of capital, such as the acquisition of a company, the opening of a new business unit, the refinancing of a large volume of bilateral debt, relevant investments or the start of a new project. In this case, financing is granted by a group of entities, under the same financial conditions, in order to share the risk among all of them, and it is executed in a single contract, which regulates both the obligations toward the funded party and between the financing entities (BBVA, 2024[69]). The advantage of syndicated lending is that it enables originating banks to share risk across the syndicate. Such risk sharing is valuable if banks are themselves financed in an imperfect capital market and adverse shocks require them to raise costly external capital (Ivashina and Scharfstein, 2010[70]), which is the case for clean hydrogen.

Syndicated loans are often sought for large-scale clean hydrogen projects. For example, Lhyfe secured a USD 28 million green syndicated bank loan indexed to EURIBOR with a 5-year maturity and a bullet payment, structured by Credit Agricole Group with three additional banks (Lhyfe, 2023[71]). The NEOM project, valued at USD 6.5 billion, involved a syndicate of 21 commercial banks, the National Investment Fund, and the Saudi Industrial Development Fund (Lee and Saygin, 2023[14]).

Performance guarantees

Performance guarantees reduce uncertainties regarding construction delays, upfront cost overruns, energy or hydrogen production (capacity factor uncertainty), operation and maintenance cost uncertainty (Deloitte, 2024[44]). They are typically offered by insurance and reinsurance companies.

In the short-term, insurance covers for the hydrogen economy will mainly relate to the production and supply sides. Standard engineering policies could cover the risks inherent in the construction phase of hydrogen production facilities (Swiss Re Institute, 2022[27]), and performance guarantee could apply to the operation phase, in particular for the most critical technology to produce clean hydrogen, i.e. the electrolyser. This can be particularly critical, as electrolyser manufacturers do not necessarily have a strong enough track record to provide sufficient certainty on the performance of their technology in real conditions. Even when they offer contracts that include replacing defective components at their expense, it may be associated with certain risks: indeed, the electrolyser manufacturer may fail to honour its obligation because of insolvency, as most of these actors are not yet profitable (BNEF, 2024[72]).

Under a performance guarantee for a clean hydrogen project, the insurer can bear excessive costs related to the electrolyser's underperformance resulting in a lower hydrogen production. It can include components such as product guarantee (covering against breakdowns and excessive repair or replacement costs) and availability guarantees (covering electrolysers or entire plant's downtime). If the pre-agreed amount for these costs (the deductible) is exceeded, the insurer starts to pay the major portion of the additional warranty costs up to the agreed limit. The manufacturer can bear a certain percentage of the indemnifiable loss as co-payment (Munich RE, 2024[45]).

Buyer credit guarantees

A Buyer Credit Guarantee, provided by a country's export credit agency (ECA), is an instrument that covers most of the risk assumed by a commercial bank towards a foreign borrower or buyer of goods from the home country of the ECA. In other words, a commercial bank provides a loan to a foreign buyer and, instead of that bank assuming credit risk on the foreign buyer, this risk is transferred to an ECA. The Buyer Credit Guarantee covers both the commercial and political/sovereign risks (Cordonnier and Saygin, 2023[16]).

In countries with high-risk profiles, the Buyer Credit Guarantee is key as it unlocks financing and thus enables the foreign buyer to finance the purchased equipment. This is particularly important for clean hydrogen projects, in particular because 90% of the electrolyser production capacity is concentrated in Europe, China and the United States (IEA, 2023[73]). The Netherlands is considering expanding its coverage to guarantees for hydrogen production in EMDE with consumers in Europe (Lopez Rocha, Gielen and Govindarajalu, 2024[46]).

The Buyer Credit Guarantee also benefits the exporter. Indeed, in addition to securing a contract for export, it receives the payment immediately upon deliveries. According to OECD rules (OECD, 2023[74]), the foreign buyer will normally have to make a down payment of minimum 15% of the amount of the order.

Contractors-all-risk insurance

Contractors all risk (CAR) insurance generally covers risks related to physical loss or damage to works during construction. It is often complemented by a delay in start-up (DSU) coverage that provides protection against delays caused by physical damage.

The design, construction and completion of the project, from power generation to hydrogen electrolysis to output production, needs to be carefully co-ordinated to reduce risks. A fixed-price turnkey EPC contract with a reputable company is a solution to mitigate the risks of cost and time overruns. In the absence of such a contract, CAR and DSU provided by insurance companies may offer solutions to mitigate risks related to design, construction, and completion.

Liquidated damages

Liquidated damages are an exact amount of money, or a set formula to calculate the amount of money, a party will owe if it breaches a contract, in order to compensate the injured party for its losses. Liquidated damages must be clearly stated in a section or clause of a contract and agreed upon by the parties prior to entering a contract. Liquidated damages are a variety of actual damages and a remedy for breach of contract (Cornell, 2024[75]).

The risk of delay of construction of the clean hydrogen and derivatives project would ultimately lie with the seller under the sales agreements. The project company/seller would seek to lay off the delay risk on the EPC contractors through delay liquidated damages in the EPC contracts. These should, ideally, be set at a level to match the seller's anticipated liabilities (Craen, 2023[29]). As the clean hydrogen market is nascent, experience of the EPC company will also be critical to inform the adequacy of contractual liquidated damages, which is a provision that seek to match the likely losses that a company will incur or suffer in the event of late completion.

Results from the investor survey

Profile of respondents

Clean hydrogen investors and lenders are a heterogeneous group, including governments, public and private banks, investment funds, (re)insurance companies, technology suppliers, renewable energy companies, utilities, project developers, industrial companies, etc. Each of them needs to adapt its business and/or operating model to align with climate objectives, industrial development targets, regulations and market dynamic, ensuring they remain attractive or competitive while decarbonising to reach net-zero emissions. However, objectives, strategies and viewpoints on acceptable risks may greatly vary across and among actors. Therefore, including in the survey a detailed analysis on the respondents' profile provides great insights on the preference of different investor groups.

A total of 41 respondents took part in OECD 2024 survey on "Risk mitigation instruments for clean hydrogen financing" developed for this report. Seven respondents are from industrial corporations (mostly clean hydrogen producers or project developers), five each from governments and bilateral development banks, four from investment funds, two each from private banks, multilateral development banks and export credit agencies. Other respondents come from diverse organisations, including consulting firms, technical assistance providers, international organisations and research organisations or think tanks.

The respondents have a relatively equal distribution in terms of their business focus on the clean hydrogen value chain. 20 to 26 respondents are investing or aim to invest in the next 18 months in hydrogen production, transport and storage infrastructure or integrated project structure. 16 respondents mentioned investing or planning to invest in the short-term in end-use sector projects.

More than 50% of the respondents declared being involved in 2 to 6 clean hydrogen projects in EMDEs. Only four respondents declared having no role as an investor or advisor for such projects. On the other side, four respondents declared having more than 10 clean hydrogen projects in EMDEs in their portfolio.

The median total investment required for these projects ranges between USD 500 million and USD 1 billion. 16 of these projects have a total investment size below USD 500 million, while 18 of these projects require more than USD 1 billion investment. However, individual ticket size of respondents' organisations is below USD 1 billion in 73% of the cases, confirming that large-scale projects require to build a strong investor pool.

Figure 2.5. Total investment and ticket size of projects under implementation or planned by 2030

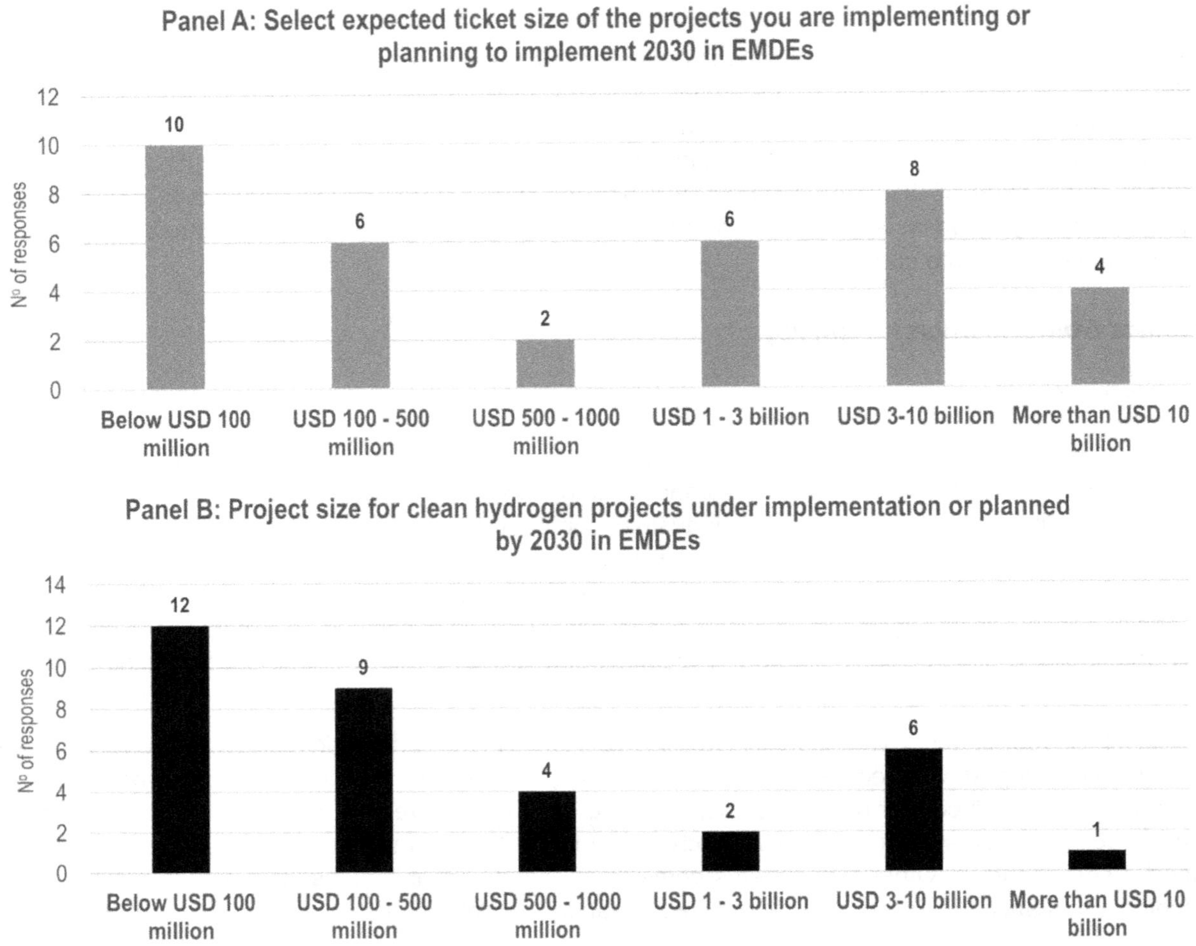

Note: The first graph shows the project size for clean hydrogen projects under implementation or planned by 2030 in emerging markets and developing economies. The second graph shows the respondents' expected ticket size for clean hydrogen projects under implementation or planned by 2030 in emerging markets and developing economies.
Source: Authors

Mapping of de-risking instruments with key risks for clean hydrogen projects

In the investor survey, respondents were asked to assess, for each selected de-risking instrument, its relevance to address six key risks identified in (OECD/The World Bank, 2024[15]): (i) uncertain clean hydrogen market demand, including market uptake, volume commitment and credibility of offtakers; (ii) uncertainty about hydrogen price; (iii) country risk, including political risk, policy reliability and public support predictability; (iv) uncertainty about technology performance; (v) licensing, permitting and completion risks; (vi) interest and exchange rates. Respondents provided a grade to each {instrument, risk} pair, on a scale ranging from 0 (the instrument is not relevant to address this risk) to 3 (the instrument is very relevant to address this risk). Then, all answers for a given {instrument, risk} pair have been averaged to identify the most relevant instruments to address the six risks (see Table 2.6).

Table 2.7. Mapping of risks and instruments

Each instrument has been assessed against 6 key risks, on a scale of 0 (not relevant) to 3 (very relevant)

	Uncertain clean hydrogen market demand	Uncertainty about hydrogen price	Country risk (i.e. political risk, policy reliability, public support predictability)	Uncertainty about technology performance	Licensing, permitting and completion risks	Interest and exchange rates
% of respondents who mentioned this risk in their top 3 risk factors for clean hydrogen projects	51%	35%	19%	16%	14%	11%
Buyer credit guarantees	2	1.8	1.6	1.4	1.3	2
Contractors-all-risk insurance	1.3	1.6	2.2	1.8	1.9	1.6
Contracts for Difference	**2.5**	**2.5**	1.1	1.2	1.3	1.7
Credit default swaps	1.9	1.8	2.1	1.4	1.2	2.2
Foreign currency guarantee	1.4	1.6	2.1	1	1.1	**2.7**
Interest rate swaps	1.4	1.8	1.8	0.9	1.3	**2.8**
Liquidated damages	1.3	1.3	1.4	2	1.5	1.6
Loan loss reserve (LLR)	1.7	2	1.9	1.5	1.6	2.3
Offtake guarantee	**2.6**	**2.6**	1.8	1.5	1.6	1.9
Partial credit guarantee	1.9	1.8	1.9	1.4	1.5	2.2
Performance guarantees	1.7	1.9	1.2	2.2	1.6	1.7
Political risk investment/foreign investment insurance	1.3	1.1	**2.8**	1.3	1.7	2.1
Syndicated loan	1.7	1.6	1.8	1.4	1.7	**2.5**

Note: Highlighted values correspond to cells where an instrument was considered "relevant to very relevant"; "% of respondents who mentioned this risk in their top 3 risk factors for clean hydrogen projects" refers to a survey conducted in 2023 to prepare (OECD/The World Bank, 2024[1]), where a total of 19 risks were listed.
Source: Authors

The survey confirms that stakeholders associate most instruments with the risks that they are specifically designed to address. This is visible when {instrument, risk} pair obtained an average score greater than 2.5 on the 0 to 3 rating scale (in bold in Table 2.7):

- Offtake guarantees and contracts for difference (CfDs) are well-placed to address offtake risk, including both the uncertainty on market demand and clean hydrogen price. Actually, the relevance of all instruments to address demand market risk and price risk is very similar, hinting that these two risks should be addressed jointly.
- Political risk investment insurance/foreign investment insurance are key to address country risk;
- Interest rate swaps and foreign currency guarantee are considered as very efficient way to address interest and exchange rates. Indeed, interest rate hedging tools, such as interest rate swaps, play a crucial role in mitigating the risks associated with floating interest rates in project finance.
- Loan syndication also appear as a potentially very efficient tool to overcome high interest rate. This is explained by the fact that by offering a smaller ticket and investing alongside other lenders, an organisation can gain more comfort in the project and be incentivised to provide better conditions, given that the risks are shared among a larger pool of actors.

The relative grades of {instrument, risk} pairs provide indication on the confidence of respondents about the effectiveness of instruments. For instance, performance guarantee only obtains a grade of 2.2 against technology performance, indicating insufficient coverage of the instrument toward the exposed technology performance risk. This suggests that lenders will continue to face uncertainty about the residual risk associated with technology performance in large-scale clean hydrogen projects. Contractors-all-risks insurance also has a relatively low grade of 1.9 against completion risks, which indicates that respondents may favour instruments not selected here, or other de-risking measures (such as contractual strategies with reputable EPC firms) to mitigate this risk. It also means that insurance companies have a big role to tailor insurance products that are available in the market such as CAR to the specificities of clean hydrogen projects.

The results also provide useful information to make sure that instruments are complementary and do not overlap when building risk mitigation packages:

- Reading the table column by column, one can notice that the key risks identified are unevenly covered by the selected instruments. For instance, only "performance guarantees" are identified as relevant to very relevant to address technology performance, whereas seven instruments are relevant to overcome risks related to interest and exchange rates.
- Reading the table line by line, it is visible that almost all instruments are targeting a specific risk, or a few risks that fall under the same category. For instance, respondents identified instrument credit default swap (CDS) as having a significantly impact the individual risk profiles of investors for macroeconomic risks, which can relate to country risks, interest and exchange rates (Henricot and Piquard, 2022[65]) (see Table 2.7).

Outcome from the investor survey: providing several instruments to help projects reach FID

As there is no single instrument that addresses all risks, instruments must be combined to minimise the overall risk level of a large-scale clean hydrogen project in EMDEs. As some instruments only tackle specific aspects of risks within a broader risk category, their suitability needs to be considered in the project specific context. Typically, the need for a foreign currency guarantee highly depends on the project design, location, cost structure and revenue streams.

Figure 2.6. Prioritisation of de-risking instruments for project financing, depending on a country's credit rating

% of respondents who selected each risk mitigation instrument in the top three instruments that, if available jointly, would provide the highest incentive to secure financing on a non-recourse or limited-recourse project financing.

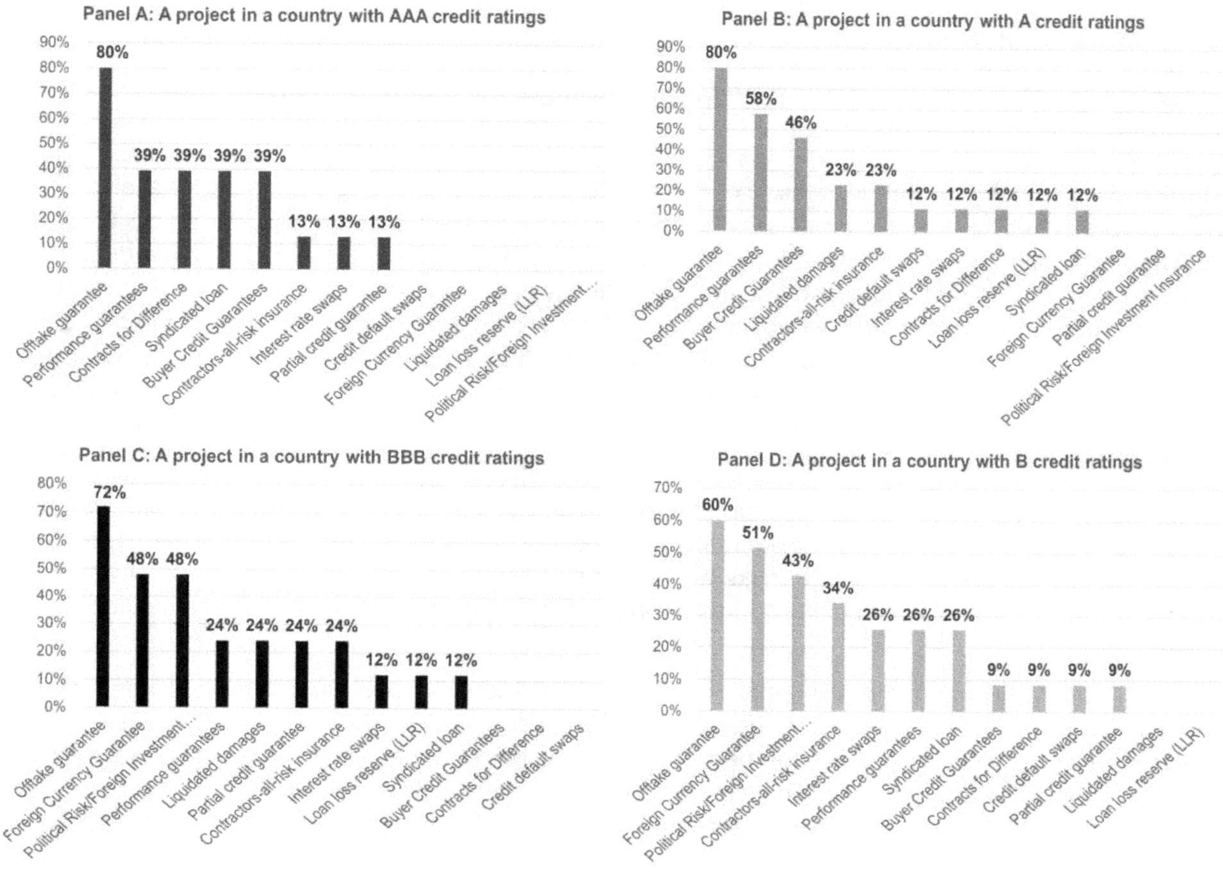

Note: % of respondents who selected each risk mitigation instruments in the top three instruments that, if available jointly, would provide the highest incentive to secure financing on a non-recourse or limited-recourse project financing.
Source: Authors based on OECD/World Bank survey

Typically, projects incorporate various instruments to create a security package that ensures financial viability. For clean hydrogen projects, a survey across different sovereign ratings investigated the optimal mix of instruments to enhance project bankability. The survey revealed that an offtake guarantee is crucial, given the nascent stage of the hydrogen market.

- In AAA credit-rated countries, there is an expectation for tax credits, which are critical for debt and cash flow enhancement, indicating advanced market incentive packages for clean hydrogen, such as the Inflation Reduction Act (IRA).
- In A-rated countries, performance guarantees are prioritized due to the lack of experience in hydrogen technology, such as electrolysers.
- For countries with BBB- to B credit ratings, offtake risk remains a key priority, but there is a growing preference for instruments addressing macroeconomic instability or risks.

In addition, the tail risk of clean hydrogen projects should be appropriately reflected in the design of security package given the long-term asset's lifespan and high capital investment. Tail risk has often been addressed through insurance, contingency planning, and conservative financial structuring to mitigate the potential for severe losses and ensure project stability. Given that insurance products with comprehensive coverage are not yet widely available for clean hydrogen projects, it is anticipated that the development of tailored de-risking insurance products will become increasingly important to address the unique characteristics of these projects.

Learnings from case studies on flagship projects and financing instruments

In addition to the analysis of de-risking instruments in the previous section, the fifteen new case studies (see Table 2.1) provide further insights into effective financing and enabling strategies for scaling clean hydrogen projects. The five project case studies illuminate key approaches to capital mobilisation and structural optimisation for advanced-stage developments, illustrating how carefully crafted financial frameworks combined with development and operational expertise of local project teams can attract investment and drive project progress. The other ten case studies focus on economic, de-risking, and financing instruments, highlighting the value of tailored tools in facilitating a timely final investment decision (FID) by effectively managing risk and securing necessary funding. Together, these case studies offer valuable guidance on establishing the necessary conditions for scaling and replicating clean hydrogen projects globally, addressing financial and operational complexities specific to this emerging technology.

Effective risk mitigation and financing instruments are essential for attracting investment to clean hydrogen, an industry facing high costs, equity constraints, and local currency risks. The examined de-risking tools are designed to reduce or re-allocate risks and increase attractiveness for a broad range of investors. Thereby, these instruments can enable hydrogen projects to progress swiftly from development to FID and implementation.

Public support and economic instruments emerge as critical tools in advancing timely FID and scaling hydrogen projects. Alignment with national and regional policy frameworks, including hydrogen-specific subsidies, creates a conducive environment that both accelerates project timelines and provides the necessary financial backing. Beyond financing, strong partnerships between public and private sectors are essential for risk distribution and ensuring effective coordination of technical and financial resources. The success of studied projects is further strengthened by dedicated sector expertise, ensuring a well-rounded approach to project origination, appraisal, and execution. These collaborations, combined with targeted economic policies, enhance the replicability of clean hydrogen initiatives globally, setting a clear path for decarbonisation at scale.

Public support and economic instruments for timely FID

All studied instruments are tailored to address high-risk tranches of financing, notably development costs, equity financing, and local currency risks. They serve to support clean hydrogen production uptake and decrease the perceived risk for a broader set of more risk-averse investors, thus mobilising significant capital and lowering financing costs. These actions encourage clean hydrogen scale-up both at individual project levels and across global project pipelines.

- Domestic economic instruments, such as tax rebates within IRA's 45V Clean Hydrogen Production Tax Credit in the USA and contract for difference scheme within Japan's low-carbon hydrogen subsidy program, offer OPEX-oriented support to incentivise investments in the clean hydrogen market locally and accelerate project development at scale.
- National clean hydrogen frameworks, such as Egypt's Green Hydrogen Law and India's National Hydrogen Mission, establish regulatory conditions that encourage both local and foreign investment. These policies support projects aimed at domestic and export markets, providing implementation incentives and subsidies.

- Large-scale projects over 1 GW of hydrogen installed capacity, like CIPP Ceara Green Hydrogen Hub in Brazil and HyDuqm project in Oman, benefit from public-private partnerships with available regional and global clean hydrogen policy support, producing clean hydrogen and its derivatives for both domestic and export-oriented markets.

De-risking and financing instruments for capital mobilisation

Several studied instruments address high-risk tranches of financing, including development costs, equity financing, and local market risks. These strategies support clean hydrogen production uptake and reduce perceived risk for a broader set of more risk-averse investors, thus mobilising significant capital and lowering financing costs. These actions encourage clean hydrogen scale-up both at individual project levels and across global project pipelines.

- Private Equity investment funds, such as Hy24 and SDG Namibia One, address specifically clean hydrogen projects, offering targeted expertise and financial resources by employing adaptive equity, quasi-equity investments, and co-investment strategies to facilitate financing of capital-intensive clean hydrogen projects.
- DFI-supported programs, such as Chile Green Hydrogen Facility by the World Bank and CORFO and Eco Invest Brazil by the IDB, use blended finance to reduce costs and risks, enhancing the economic viability of local sustainable projects, including clean hydrogen.
- Hydrogen-specific insurance products, such as Marsh Clean Hydrogen Insurance Facility and Munich Re's HySure product, offer tailored insurance solutions, notably for construction and operational phases, covering project-specific risks and contributing to larger capital mobilisation for clean hydrogen projects.

Impact on project financing structure: insights on development and asset financing

Project Development Financing: instruments supporting project development financing play a crucial role in effective risk allocation for clean hydrogen projects, significantly improving the likelihood of successful implementation. The development costs of large-scale clean hydrogen projects represent a substantial budget, which is challenging to finance on the balance sheet of independent developers or through existing financial solutions due to the perceived risks associated with the emerging industry. Financing instruments that address project development costs, such as reimbursable development loans, equity injections at the corporate level, or project development assistance, significantly increase the probability of timely project development and implementation.

- Hydrogen-specific investment funds, such as Hy24 and SDG Namibia One, enhance project credibility by financing development activities at both corporate and project levels via equity injections. This approach mitigates early-stage development risks, provides a solid foundation for subsequent project phases, and facilitates further private and institutional financing.
- Eco Invest Brazil provides project structuring support through reimbursable financing for project preparation, covering detailed planning and feasibility analysis. This assistance ensures that projects are thoroughly appraised and planned, reducing the risks associated with project origination and enhancing the chances of securing further financing.
- Large-scale projects from 25 MW to 100 MW of hydrogen installed capacity, such as Lhyfe's Green Horizon in France and Scatec Green Hydrogen in Egypt, integrate to a large extend development and operational risks at the project level, allowing prompt project development timelines and extended risk-sharing with private and public financiers.

Project Assets Financing: de-risking and financing instruments facilitate better risk allocation and optimise debt sizing, which are essential for securing the necessary funding for capital-intensive clean hydrogen projects. The instruments range from foreign exchange (FX) hedging solutions to equity stakes in dedicated clean hydrogen projects SPVs (Special Purpose Vehicles).

- Chile Green Hydrogen Facility by the World Bank and CORFO, along with India's National Hydrogen Mission, provide significant CAPEX subsidies (up to 40%), which significantly improve the economic viability of clean hydrogen projects and so facilitate private financing for first-movers in the hydrogen sector.
- Hy24 and SDG Namibia One use adaptive investment, quasi-equity investments, and co-investment strategies to facilitate the financing of project assets. These approaches help allocate risks more effectively between public and private investors, enhancing the overall financing structure of the projects. A dedicated focus on hydrogen projects and strategic long-term commitment ensure that projects have access to substantial and patient capital, thus improving debt sizing and reducing financial uncertainty.
- Flagship projects, such as HyDuqm in Oman and Lhyfe's Green Horizon in France, effectively combine available local public financing, global clean hydrogen incentives with private financing and senior debt to complete necessary funding for clean hydrogen projects at scale.

Improving enabling conditions via partnerships to allocate risk and co-ordinate efforts

Through both public and private partnerships, the studied programmes not only distribute risks more effectively but also coordinate the efforts of diverse stakeholders, thereby creating a robust framework for the successful development, financing and scaling of clean hydrogen projects.

Risk sharing: effective partnerships are essential for distributing risks among various stakeholders, thereby enhancing the viability and attractiveness of clean hydrogen projects. These collaborations account for risk appetite of different actors, ensuring a more balanced risk and capital allocation.

- Chile's Green Hydrogen Facility, Eco Invest Brazil and SDG Namibia One collaborate with international development banks and local government bodies, providing both financial and technical assistance. This multi-stakeholder approach not only distributes risk to facilitate financing but also brings in diverse expertise and resources, enhancing the projects' overall resilience and capacity for success. Successful partnerships are often realised through robust government backing and political will.

Coordination of actors' efforts: coordination between private and public actors is crucial in aligning financial resources and technical expertise, which ensures project implementation and accelerates scaling-up. These partnerships are instrumental in completing necessary financing and creating a cohesive strategy for implementing clean hydrogen projects.

- Hy24 engages financial and technical partnerships with industrial actors. This approach accelerates the hydrogen market's global development by ensuring that projects benefit from the latest technological advancements and industry best practices.

Implementation insights on projects' origination, appraisal and execution

Project Origination and Appraisal: the origination and appraisal stages of project development are critical for ensuring that clean hydrogen initiatives are viable and attractive to investors. Effective strategies and adapted financing instruments at these stages help to identify promising projects and facilitate long-term funding.

- Eco Invest Brazil employs blended finance mechanisms to streamline the origination and appraisal processes. By combining public and private investment, Eco Invest Brazil reduces the risk associated with green projects, making them more appealing to international investors. This approach allows for a thorough evaluation of project feasibility and auction process, ensuring that only the most promising projects proceed to the execution stage.

- Hydrogen-specific private equity investment funds, such as Hy24 and SDG Namibia One, address and finance the development risk of certain projects under their investment portfolio, by leveraging their lower risk aversion due to sector specific approach and dedicated clean hydrogen educated teams.
- Lhyfe's Green Horizon in France leverages public-private coordination and industrial partnerships to optimise resource allocation, aligning technical and financial capacities to reduce project risks and enable successful implementation, while internally addressing an important part of the development effort.

Project Execution: effective execution of clean hydrogen projects is essential for their success. This involves dedicated teams, strong governance, and robust operational frameworks to manage the complexities associated with large-scale, capital-intensive projects.

- Large scale projects' teams of Cearà Green Hydrogen Hub in Brazil, HyDuqm in Oman, and JSW Green Hydrogen in India have established a comprehensive operational framework with dedicated local teams, enabling efficient execution and project scalability.
- Policy frameworks, such as Chile's Green Hydrogen Facility, IRA USA 45V Clean Hydrogen Production Tax Credit framework, and Japan's financing instruments, provide consistent project support for clean hydrogen consumption over long term through contract for different schemes and tax rebates, supervised and implemented by several departments, ministries and government agencies.
- India's National Hydrogen Mission employs a more general structured governance model, ensuring coordination across various stages of execution, from infrastructure development to policy alignment. Chile's Green Hydrogen Facility puts in place a more specific sub-program to finance technical assistance, capacity-building activities, and overall project management to streamline project execution.

Conditions for replicability and scale up

Public support: public involvement provides support frameworks that mitigate risks, ensuring project viability and investor confidence. Alignment with national and international climate policies and objectives (e.g. Nationally Determined Contributions, South Africa's Just Energy Transition Investment Plan, COP28 declaration of intent on certification schemes for hydrogen and derivatives) provides regulatory support and enhances the credibility of projects, making them more attractive to investors.

- Egypt's Green Hydrogen Law and India's National Hydrogen Mission offer regulatory guidance and risk mitigation for investors, making local hydrogen projects, like Scatec Green Hydrogen in Egypt and JSW Green Hydrogen in India, more feasible and aligning them with international climate commitments, driving local and export-oriented production of clean hydrogen and its derivatives.
- SDG Namibia One leverages public finance and policy support from the Environmental Investment Fund of Namibia, providing necessary risk reduction to attract private investment.

Hands-on, hydrogen-specific tailored support: sector-specific expertise and funding are critical for replicating and scaling hydrogen projects. Specialised teams and funding strategies address unique hydrogen market challenges and opportunities.

- Hy24 ensures long-term support for clean hydrogen projects through its substantial funding and dedicated teams. The fund's strategic focus on hydrogen infrastructure and its hands-on governance model enable it to address sector-specific challenges effectively.

- Marsh Clean Hydrogen Insurance Facility and Munich Re's HySure product offer risk management solutions tailored to hydrogen, building confidence for scaling similar projects globally.

Conclusion

In summary, the examined case studies reveal that successful scaling of clean hydrogen projects hinges on well-coordinated public support, risk mitigation through tailored financing instruments and approaches such as blended finance,[12] and robust public-private partnerships. National and regional policies, when aligned with international climate objectives, significantly bolster project credibility and attractiveness, while hydrogen-specific economic tools like subsidies, tax credits, and dedicated insurance solutions foster investment and reduce development risks. Blended finance, strategic equity injections, and adaptive insurance facilities play a crucial role in enabling risk-averse investors to participate, enhancing capital mobilisation. Implementation success is further driven by development capacities of local project teams, clear governance structures, sector-specialised teams, and partnerships that unite technical and financial resources, creating a replicable framework for the global scale-up of clean hydrogen infrastructure.

Public support and economic instruments emerge as critical tools in advancing timely FID and scaling hydrogen projects. Alignment with national and regional policy frameworks, including hydrogen-specific subsidies, creates a conducive environment that both accelerates project timelines and provides the necessary financial backing. Beyond financing, strong partnerships between public and private sectors are essential for risk distribution and ensuring effective coordination of technical and financial resources. The success of studied projects is further strengthened by dedicated sector expertise, ensuring a well-rounded approach to project origination, appraisal, and execution. These collaborations, combined with targeted economic policies, enhance the replicability of clean hydrogen initiatives globally, setting a clear path for decarbonisation at scale.

Public support and economic instruments for timely FID

All studied instruments are tailored to address high-risk tranches of financing, notably development costs, equity financing, and local currency risks. They serve to support clean hydrogen production uptake and decrease the perceived risk for a broader set of more risk-averse investors, thus mobilising significant capital and lowering financing costs. These actions encourage clean hydrogen scale-up both at individual project levels and across global project pipelines.

- Domestic economic instruments, such as tax rebates within IRA's 45V Clean Hydrogen Production Tax Credit in the USA and contract for difference scheme within Japan's low-carbon hydrogen subsidy program, offer OPEX-oriented support to incentivise investments in the clean hydrogen market locally and accelerate project development at scale.
- National clean hydrogen frameworks, such as Egypt's Green Hydrogen Law and India's National Hydrogen Mission, establish regulatory conditions that encourage both local and foreign investment. These policies support projects aimed at domestic and export markets, providing implementation incentives and subsidies.
- Large-scale projects over 1 GW of hydrogen installed capacity, like CIPP Ceara Green Hydrogen Hub in Brazil and HyDuqm project in Oman, benefit from public-private partnerships with available regional and global clean hydrogen policy support, producing clean hydrogen and its derivatives for both domestic and export-oriented markets.

De-risking and financing instruments for capital mobilisation

Several studied instruments address high-risk tranches of financing, including development costs, equity financing, and local market risks. These strategies support clean hydrogen production uptake and reduce perceived risk for a broader set of more risk-averse investors, thus mobilising significant capital and lowering financing costs. These actions encourage clean hydrogen scale-up both at individual project levels and across global project pipelines.

- Private Equity investment funds, such as Hy24 and SDG Namibia One, address specifically clean hydrogen projects, offering targeted expertise and financial resources by employing adaptive equity, quasi-equity investments, and co-investment strategies to facilitate financing of capital-intensive clean hydrogen projects.
- DFI-supported programs, such as Chile Green Hydrogen Facility by the World Bank and CORFO and Eco Invest Brazil by the IDB, use blended finance to reduce costs and risks, enhancing the economic viability of local sustainable projects, including clean hydrogen.
- Hydrogen-specific insurance products, such as Marsh Clean Hydrogen Insurance Facility and Munich Re's HySure product, offer tailored insurance solutions, notably for construction and operational phases, covering project-specific risks and contributing to larger capital mobilisation for clean hydrogen projects.

Impact on project financing structure: insights on development and asset financing

Project Development Financing: instruments supporting project development financing play a crucial role in effective risk allocation for clean hydrogen projects, significantly improving the likelihood of successful implementation. The development costs of large-scale clean hydrogen projects represent a substantial budget, which is challenging to finance on the balance sheet of independent developers or through existing financial solutions due to the perceived risks associated with the emerging industry. Financing instruments that address project development costs, such as reimbursable development loans, equity injections at the corporate level, or project development assistance, significantly increase the probability of timely project development and implementation.

- Hydrogen-specific investment funds, such as Hy24 and SDG Namibia One, enhance project credibility by financing development activities at both corporate and project levels via equity injections. This approach mitigates early-stage development risks, provides a solid foundation for subsequent project phases, and facilitates further private and institutional financing.
- Eco Invest Brazil provides project structuring support through reimbursable financing for project preparation, covering detailed planning and feasibility analysis. This assistance ensures that projects are thoroughly appraised and planned, reducing the risks associated with project origination and enhancing the chances of securing further financing.
- Large-scale projects from 25 MW to 100 MW of hydrogen installed capacity, such as Lhyfe's Green Horizon in France and Scatec Green Hydrogen in Egypt, integrate to a large extend development and operational risks at the project level, allowing prompt project development timelines and extended risk-sharing with private and public financiers.

Project Assets Financing: de-risking and financing instruments facilitate better risk allocation and optimise debt sizing, which are essential for securing the necessary funding for capital-intensive clean hydrogen projects. The instruments range from foreign exchange (FX) hedging solutions to equity stakes in dedicated clean hydrogen projects SPVs (Special Purpose Vehicles).

- Chile Green Hydrogen Facility by the World Bank and CORFO, along with India's National Hydrogen Mission, provide significant CAPEX subsidies (up to 40%), which significantly improve the economic viability of clean hydrogen projects and so facilitate private financing for first-movers in the hydrogen sector.
- Hy24 and SDG Namibia One use adaptive investment, quasi-equity investments, and co-investment strategies to facilitate the financing of project assets. These approaches help allocate risks more effectively between public and private investors, enhancing the overall financing structure of the projects. A dedicated focus on hydrogen projects and strategic long-term

commitment ensure that projects have access to substantial and patient capital, thus improving debt sizing and reducing financial uncertainty.

- Flagship projects, such as HyDuqm in Oman and Lhyfe's Green Horizon in France, effectively combine available local public financing, global clean hydrogen incentives with private financing and senior debt to complete necessary funding for clean hydrogen projects at scale.

Improving enabling conditions via partnerships to allocate risk and co-ordinate efforts

Through both public and private partnerships, the studied programmes not only distribute risks more effectively but also coordinate the efforts of diverse stakeholders, thereby creating a robust framework for the successful development, financing and scaling of clean hydrogen projects.

Risk sharing: effective partnerships are essential for distributing risks among various stakeholders, thereby enhancing the viability and attractiveness of clean hydrogen projects. These collaborations account for risk appetite of different actors, ensuring a more balanced risk and capital allocation.

- Chile's Green Hydrogen Facility, Eco Invest Brazil and SDG Namibia One collaborate with international development banks and local government bodies, providing both financial and technical assistance. This multi-stakeholder approach not only distributes risk to facilitate financing but also brings in diverse expertise and resources, enhancing the projects' overall resilience and capacity for success. Successful partnerships are often realised through robust government backing and political will.

Coordination of actors' efforts: coordination between private and public actors is crucial in aligning financial resources and technical expertise, which ensures project implementation and accelerates scaling-up. These partnerships are instrumental in completing necessary financing and creating a cohesive strategy for implementing clean hydrogen projects.

- Hy24 engages financial and technical partnerships with industrial actors. This approach accelerates the hydrogen market's global development by ensuring that projects benefit from the latest technological advancements and industry best practices.

Implementation insights on projects' origination, appraisal and execution

Project Origination and Appraisal: the origination and appraisal stages of project development are critical for ensuring that clean hydrogen initiatives are viable and attractive to investors. Effective strategies and adapted financing instruments at these stages help to identify promising projects and facilitate long-term funding.

- Eco Invest Brazil employs blended finance mechanisms to streamline the origination and appraisal processes. By combining public and private investment, Eco Invest Brazil reduces the risk associated with green projects, making them more appealing to international investors. This approach allows for a thorough evaluation of project feasibility and auction process, ensuring that only the most promising projects proceed to the execution stage.
- Hydrogen-specific private equity investment funds, such as Hy24 and SDG Namibia One, address and finance the development risk of certain projects under their investment portfolio, by leveraging their lower risk aversion due to sector specific approach and dedicated clean hydrogen educated teams.
- Lhyfe's Green Horizon in France leverages public-private coordination and industrial partnerships to optimise resource allocation, aligning technical and financial capacities to reduce project risks and enable successful implementation, while internally addressing an important part of the development effort.

Project Execution: effective execution of clean hydrogen projects is essential for their success. This involves dedicated teams, strong governance, and robust operational frameworks to manage the complexities associated with large-scale, capital-intensive projects.

- Large scale projects' teams of Cearà Green Hydrogen Hub in Brazil, HyDuqm in Oman, and JSW Green Hydrogen in India have established a comprehensive operational framework with dedicated local teams, enabling efficient execution and project scalability.
- Policy frameworks, such as Chile's Green Hydrogen Facility, IRA USA 45V Clean Hydrogen Production Tax Credit framework, and Japan's financing instruments, provide consistent project support for clean hydrogen consumption over long term through contract for different schemes and tax rebates, supervised and implemented by various departments, ministries and government agencies.
- India's National Hydrogen Mission employs a more general structured governance model, ensuring coordination across various stages of execution, from infrastructure development to policy alignment. Chile's Green Hydrogen Facility puts in place a more specific sub-program to finance technical assistance, capacity-building activities, and overall project management to streamline project execution.

Conditions for replicability and scale up

Public support: public involvement provides support frameworks that mitigate risks, ensuring project viability and investor confidence. Alignment with national and international climate policies and objectives (e.g. Nationally Determined Contributions, South Africa's Just Energy Transition Investment Plan, COP28 declaration of intent on certification schemes for hydrogen and derivatives) provides regulatory support and enhances the credibility of projects, making them more attractive to investors.

- Egypt's Green Hydrogen Law and India's National Hydrogen Mission offer regulatory guidance and risk mitigation for investors, making local hydrogen projects, like Scatec Green Hydrogen in Egypt and JSW Green Hydrogen in India, more feasible and aligning them with international climate commitments, driving local and export-oriented production of clean hydrogen and its derivatives.
- SDG Namibia One leverages public finance and policy support from the Environmental Investment Fund of Namibia, providing necessary risk reduction to attract private investment.

Hands-on, hydrogen-specific tailored support: sector-specific expertise and funding are critical for replicating and scaling hydrogen projects. Specialised teams and funding strategies address unique hydrogen market challenges and opportunities.

- Hy24 ensures long-term support for clean hydrogen projects through its substantial funding and dedicated teams. The fund's strategic focus on hydrogen infrastructure and its hands-on governance model enable it to address sector-specific challenges effectively.
- Marsh Clean Hydrogen Insurance Facility and Munich Re's HySure product offer risk management solutions tailored to hydrogen, building confidence for scaling similar projects globally.

Conclusion

In summary, the examined case studies reveal that successful scaling of clean hydrogen projects hinges on well-coordinated public support, risk mitigation through tailored financing instruments and approaches such as blended finance,[13] and robust public-private partnerships. National and regional policies, when aligned with international climate objectives, significantly bolster project credibility and attractiveness, while hydrogen-specific economic tools like subsidies, tax credits, and dedicated insurance solutions foster investment and reduce development risks. Blended finance, strategic equity injections, and adaptive insurance facilities play a crucial role in enabling risk-averse investors to participate, enhancing capital mobilisation. Implementation success is further driven by development capacities of local project teams, clear governance structures, sector-specialised teams, and partnerships that unite technical and financial resources, creating a replicable framework for the global scale-up of clean hydrogen infrastructure.

References

AIIB and Castalia (2023), *Financing clean hydrogen in Asia and beyond: Catalyzing the development of this emerging industry*, https://www.aiib.org/en/about-aiib/who-we-are/infrastructure-for-tomorrow/green-infrastructure/pdf/AIIB-Castalia_Financing-Clean-Hydrogen-in-Asia-and-Beyond_Sep-2023.pdf. [3]

Ason, A. and J. Poz (2024), *Contracts for Difference: the Instrument of Choice for the Energy Transition*, https://www.oxfordenergy.org/wpcms/wp-content/uploads/2024/04/ET34-Contracts-for-Difference.pdf. [57]

Bank for International Settlements (2024), *BIS Data Portal*, https://data.bis.org/. [67]

BBVA (2024), *What is a syndicated financing?*, https://www.bbvacib.com/insights/news/what-is-a-syndicated-financing/. [69]

Bjerde, A. et al. (2024), *New platform leverages power of guarantees to boost private financing*, https://blogs.worldbank.org/en/voices/new-platform-leverages-power-of-guarantees-to-boost-private-financing?cid=ECR_LI_worldbank_EN_EXT_profilesubscribe. [36]

BMWK (2024), *Press release: Important step for global hydrogen ramp-up – Germany will work with H2Global to import green hydrogen products on a large scale from 2027*, https://www.bmwk.de/Redaktion/EN/Pressemitteilungen/2024/07/20240711-h2global.html. [60]

BNEF (2024), *Electrolyser Manufacturing 2024: Too Many Fish in a Tiny Pond*, https://www.bnef.com/login?r=%2Finsights%2F33679. [72]

Bomfim, A. (2022), "Credit Default Swaps", *Finance and Economics Discussion Series*, Vol. 2022/023, pp. 1-27, https://doi.org/10.17016/feds.2022.023. [66]

Bouacida, I. (2023), *Developing hydrogen for decarbonisation in Europe: how relevant are contracts for difference?*, https://www.iddri.org/en/publications-and-events/policy-brief/developing-hydrogen-decarbonisation-europe-how-relevant-are. [59]

Bruner, R. et al. (1998), "Best Practices in Estimating the Cost of Capital: Survey and Synthesis", *Financial Practice and Education*, Vol. 8/no. 1 (Spring-Summer), pp. 13-28, https://www.hbs.edu/ris/Publication%20Files/Best%20Practices%20in%20Estimating%20the%20Cost%20of%20Capital%20Survey%20and%20Synethesis_e59fb55c-eeac-4abe-9ae9-04c4c623e8c3.pdf. [76]

Cammeraat, E., A. Dechezleprêtre and G. Lalanne (2022), "Innovation and industrial policies for green hydrogen", *OECD Science, Technology and Industry Policy Papers*, No. 125, OECD Publishing, Paris, https://doi.org/10.1787/f0bb5d8c-en. [9]

Choi, E., L. Zhou and V. Lacton (2022), *How to De-risk Low-carbon Investments*. [28]

Climate Policy Initiative (2024), *Landscape of Guarantees for Climate Finance in EMDEs*, https://www.climatepolicyinitiative.org/wp-content/uploads/2024/02/Guarantee-Report-Final-2024_FINAL.pdf. [34]

Cordonnier, J. and D. Saygin (2023), "Financing solutions to foster industrial decarbonisation in emerging and developing economies", *OECD Environment Working Papers*, No. 226, OECD Publishing, Paris, https://doi.org/10.1787/24a155ab-en. [16]

Cordonnier, J. and D. Saygin (2022), "Green hydrogen opportunities for emerging and developing economies: Identifying success factors for market development and building enabling conditions", *OECD Environment Working Papers*, No. 205, OECD Publishing, Paris, https://doi.org/10.1787/53ad9f22-en. [13]

Cornell (2024), *Wex: Liquidated damages*, https://www.law.cornell.edu/wex/liquidated_damages. [75]

Craen, S. (2023), *Financing a world scale hydrogen export project*, https://www.oxfordenergy.org/wpcms/wp-content/uploads/2023/01/Financing-a-world-scale-hydrogen-export-project-ET-21.pdf. [29]

Deloitte (2024), *Financing the Green Energy Transition: Innovative financing for a just transition*. [44]

Đukan, M. et al. (2023), "The role of policies in reducing the cost of capital for offshore wind", *iScience*, Vol. 26/6, p. 106945, https://doi.org/10.1016/j.isci.2023.106945. [40]

Energy Systems Catapult (2022), *Input to BEIS Select Committee Call for Evidence: Decarbonisation of the power sector*, https://committees.parliament.uk/writtenevidence/109645/pdf/. [58]

EXIM (2024), *Foreign currency guarantee*, https://www.exim.gov/solutions/loan-guarantee/foreign-currency-guarantee (accessed on 31 July 2024). [48]

Firouzi, A. and A. Meshkani (2021), "Risk-based optimization of the debt service schedule in renewable energy project finance", *Utilities Policy*, Vol. 70, p. 101197, https://doi.org/10.1016/j.jup.2021.101197. [22]

Fitch (2023), *Spotlight: Project-Financed Green Hydrogen*, https://www.fitchratings.com/research/infrastructure-project-finance/spotlight-project-financed-green-hydrogen-02-05-2023. [42]

Florence School of Regulation (2023), *Contracts-for-Difference*, https://fsr.eui.eu/contracts-for-difference/. [56]

Frost Brown Todd (2023), *Considerations for Commercial Borrowers: Mitigating Uncertainty and Risk with Interest Rate Swaps*, https://frostbrowntodd.com/considerations-for-commercial-borrowers-mitigating-uncertainty-and-risk-with-interest-rate-swaps/. [47]

Gerrard, M. (2021), *What are public-private partnerships, and how do they differ from privatizations?*, International Monetary Fund, https://www.imf.org/external/pubs/ft/fandd/2001/09/gerrard.htm. [31]

Global Infrastructure Hub (2020), *PPP Risk Allocation Tool*, https://ppp-risk.gihub.org/ (accessed on 26 July 2024). [32]

Government of Canada (2023), *2023 Fall Economic Statement*, https://www.budget.canada.ca/fes-eea/2023/home-accueil-en.html. [61]

Green Hydrogen Organisation (2024), *Key considerations for green hydrogen offtake agreements*, https://gh2.org/sites/default/files/2024-05/GH2_Considerations%20for%20Hydrogen%20Offtake%20Agreements_2024.pdf. [64]

Green Hydrogen Organisation (2022), *Green Hydrogen Contracting for People and Planet: Guidance and good practice for decision makers*, https://gh2.org/sites/default/files/2023-01/GH2_Contracting%20booklet_A5_2023_0.pdf. [7]

Green, A. (2003), *Credit Guarantee Schemes for Small Enterprises: An Effective Instrument to Promote Private Sector-Led Growth?*, http://www.unido.org/file-storage/download/?file_id=18223. [52]

Hasankhani, M. et al. (2024), "Unveiling complexity of hydrogen integration: A multi-faceted exploration of challenges in the Dutch context", *Journal of Cleaner Production*, Vol. 434, https://doi.org/10.1016/j.jclepro.2023.139927. [24]

Henricot, D. and T. Piquard (2022), *Credit Default Swaps and Credit Risk Reallocation*, https://abc-economie.banque-france.fr/sites/default/files/medias/documents/wp860.pdf. [65]

Hovy, P. (2015), *Risk Allocation in Public-Private Partnerships: Maximizing value for money*, https://www.iisd.org/system/files/publications/risk-allocation-ppp-maximizing-value-for-money-discussion-paper.pdf. [33]

Howden and BCG (2024), *The bigger picture: The $10 trillion role of insurance in mobilising the climate transition*, https://www.howdengroup.com/sites/g/files/mwfley561/files/2024-06/the-bigger-picture-whitepaper.pdf. [37]

Hydrogen Council (2021), *Policy Toolbox for Low Carbon and Renewable Hydrogen: Enabling low carbon and renewable hydrogen globally*, https://hydrogencouncil.com/wp-content/uploads/2021/11/Hydrogen-Council_Policy-Toolbox.pdf. [10]

IEA (2023), *Global Hydrogen Review 2023*, IEA, https://www.iea.org/reports/global-hydrogen-review-2023. [73]

IEA (2021), *The Cost of Capital in Clean Energy Transitions*, https://www.iea.org/articles/the-cost-of-capital-in-clean-energy-transitions#. [18]

IEA (2019), *Policy and Measures Database: Contract for Difference (CfD)*, https://www.iea.org/policies/5731-contract-for-difference-cfd (accessed on 31 July 2024). [55]

IFC (2023), *Structured and Securitized Products: Partial Credit Guarantees - Product Description*, https://www.ifc.org/content/dam/ifc/doc/2023/ifc-product-description-partial-credit-gurantees.pdf. [51]

International Development Finance Club (2019), *A brief overview of Blended Finance*. [38]

IRENA (2024), *Green hydrogen strategy: A guide to design*, https://www.irena.org/Publications/2024/Jul/Green-hydrogen-strategy-A-guide-to-design. [6]

IRENA and RMI (2023), *Creating a global hydrogen market: Certification to enable trade,*, https://www.irena.org/-/media/Files/IRENA/Agency/Publication/2023/Jan/IRENA_Creating_a_global_hydrogen_market_2023.pdf?rev=cad6962f55454a46af87dec5f2e6c6e8. [8]

Ivashina, V. and D. Scharfstein (2010), "Loan Syndication and Credit Cycles", *American Economic Review: Papers & Proceedings*, Vol. 100, pp. 57-61, http://www.aeaweb.org/articles.php?doi=10.1257/aer.100.2.57. [70]

KPMG (2022), *How to evaluate the cost of the green hydrogen business case? Assessing green hydrogen production costs*, https://assets.kpmg.com/content/dam/kpmg/be/pdf/2022/hydrogen-industry-1.pdf. [26]

Lee, M. and D. Saygin (2023), "Financing cost impacts on cost competitiveness of green hydrogen in emerging and developing economies", *OECD Environment Working Papers*, No. 227, OECD Publishing, Paris, https://doi.org/10.1787/15b16fc3-en. [14]

Lhyfe (2023), *Lhyfe successfully closes its first corporate syndicated loan for an amount of €28m*, https://www.lhyfe.com/press/lhyfe-successfully-closes-its-first-corporate-syndicated-loan-for-an-amount-of-e28m/. [71]

Lopez Rocha, S., D. Gielen and C. Govindarajalu (2024), *Financing Hydrogen projects in Emerging Markets and Developing Countries*, https://energypost.eu/financing-hydrogen-projects-in-emerging-markets-and-developing-countries/. [46]

Lu, J., J. Chao and J. Sheppard (2019), *Government Guarantees for Mobilizing Private Investment in Infrastructure*. [53]

Marsh (2024), *Political Risk*, https://www.marsh.com/en/services/political-risk.html. [50]

Merjaneh, Y. (2022), *Realising green hydrogen's potential*, https://meconstructionnews.com/53710/realising-green-hydrogens-potential. [12]

MIGA (2011), *World investment and political risk*, https://doi.org/10.1596/978-0-8213-8478-7. [49]

Montague, C., K. Raiser and M. Lee (2024), "Bridging the clean energy investment gap: Cost of capital in the transition to net-zero emissions", *OECD Environment Working Papers*, No. 245, OECD Publishing, Paris, https://doi.org/10.1787/1ae47659-en. [19]

Munich RE (2024), *Innovative Risk Transfer Solutions – A Contribution to the Success of the Green Hydrogen Industry*, https://www.munichre.com/content/dam/munichre/contentlounge/website-pieces/documents/MunichRe-Hydrogen-Whitepaper_en.pdf/_jcr_content/renditions/original./MunichRe-Hydrogen-Whitepaper_en.pdf. [45]

Natixis (2021), *Green & Sustainable Financing green hydrogen's development: clearing the hurdles*, https://gsh.cib.natixis.com/site/T_rRFifyaz6SK8y7TKR4rw/api-website-feature/files/download/12141/h2_financing_-_uk_def_2.pdf?file_type=media_files. [43]

OECD (2024), *Stakeholder meeting for Egypt's low-carbon hydrogen development*, https://www.oecd.org/en/events/2024/01/stakeholder-meeting-for-egypts-low-carbon-hydrogen-development.html. [41]

OECD (2023), *Arrangement on Officially Supported Export Credits*, https://one.oecd.org/document/TAD/PG(2023)7/en/pdf. [74]

OECD (2022), *Climate Finance Provided and Mobilised by Developed Countries in 2016-2020: Insights from Disaggregated Analysis*, Climate Finance and the USD 100 Billion Goal, OECD Publishing, Paris, https://doi.org/10.1787/286dae5d-en. [39]

OECD (2022), "OECD blended finance guidance for clean energy", *OECD Environment Policy Papers*, No. 31, OECD Publishing, Paris, https://doi.org/10.1787/596e2436-en. [77]

OECD (2008), *OECD Glossary of Statistical Terms*, OECD Publishing, Paris, https://doi.org/10.1787/9789264055087-en. [1]

OECD/The World Bank (2024), *Scaling Hydrogen Financing for Development*, OECD Publishing, Paris, https://doi.org/10.1787/0287b22e-en. [15]

Penev, M. et al. (2024), *Capital Structure for Techno-Economic Analysis of Hydrogen Projects*, https://www.nrel.gov/docs/fy24osti/90103.pdf. [23]

Richstein, J. et al. (2021), *Carbon Contracts for Difference: An assessment of selected socioeconomic impacts for Germany*, https://www.diw.de/en/diw_01.c.815986.en/nachrichten/new_report_from_climate_friendly_materials_plattform_has_bee__an_assessment_of_selected_socio-economic_impacts_for_germany.html. [54]

S&P Global (2023), *Clear guidelines, formation of CfD schemes likely to unlock Asian hydrogen market in 2024*, https://www.spglobal.com/commodityinsights/en/market-insights/latest-news/energy-transition/122923-clear-guidelines-formation-of-cfd-schemes-likely-to-unlock-asian-hydrogen-market-in-2024. [62]

South African Government (2023), *Green hydrogen commercialisation strategy*, https://www.idc.co.za/wp-content/uploads/2023/11/GHCS-Full-Report-17Oct23-Public-Submission.pdf. [63]

Steckel, J. and M. Jakob (2018), "The role of financing cost and de-risking strategies for clean energy investment", *International Economics*, Vol. 155, pp. 19-28, https://doi.org/10.1016/j.inteco.2018.02.003. [20]

Sweerts, B., F. Longa and B. van der Zwaan (2019), "Financial de-risking to unlock Africa's renewable energy potential", *Renewable and Sustainable Energy Reviews*, Vol. 102, pp. 75-82, https://doi.org/10.1016/j.rser.2018.11.039. [21]

Swiss Re Institute (2022), *De-risking the hydrogen economy – Bridging the protection gap*, https://www.swissre.com/dam/jcr:300e7069-1bef-418d-85fb-aa3ba2863fba/ep-de-risking-the-hydrogen-economy.pdf. [27]

Systemiq (2023), *Better Guarantees, Better Finance*, https://www.systemiq.earth/wp-content/uploads/2023/06/Blended-Finance-Taskforce-2023-Better-Guarantees-Better-Finance-1.pdf. [35]

Taghizadeh-Hesary, F. et al. (2022), "Green finance and the economic feasibility of hydrogen projects", *International Journal of Hydrogen Energy*, Vol. 47/58, pp. 24511-24522, https://doi.org/10.1016/j.ijhydene.2022.01.111. [17]

UNDP (2013), *Derisking Renewable Energy Investment: Key Concepts Note*, https://www.undp.org/publications/original-drei-report. [4]

UNIDO (2023), *Assessment of low carbon hydrogen production, demand, business models and value chain in Egypt: Main findings*, https://www.unido.org/sites/default/files/files/2023-06/Low-Carbon-Hydrogen-Assessments-in-Egypt-Highlights-UNIDO.pdf. [30]

UNIDO, IRENA and IDOS (2023), *Green hydrogen for sustainable industrial development: A policy toolkit for developing countries*, https://www.unido.org/sites/default/files/files/2024-02/Green%20hydrogen%20for%20Sustainable%20Industrial%20Development%20A%20Policy%20Toolkit%20for%20Developing%20Countries.pdf. [11]

US DOE (n.d.), *Loan Loss Reserve Funds*, https://www.energy.gov/scep/slsc/loan-loss-reserve-funds#:~:text=Loan%20loss%20reserve%20(LLR)%20funds,better%20terms%20of%20debt%20repayment. [68]

Waissbein, O. et al. (2013), *Derisking Renewable Energy Investment. A Framework to Support Policymakers in Selecting Public Instruments to Promote Renewable Energy Investment in Developing Countries.* [25]

World Energy Council (2021), *Hydrogen on the horizon: National hydrogen strategies*, https://www.worldenergy.org/assets/downloads/Working_Paper_-_National_Hydrogen_Strategies_-_September_2021.pdf. [5]

WRI (2012), *Moving the Fulcrum: A Primer on Public Climate Financing Instruments Used to Leverage Private Capital*, https://www.wri.org/research/moving-fulcrum. [2]

Notes

[1] The cost of capital (or cost of finance) is a critical component in modern finance theory for making investment or divestment decisions, economic profit forecasts, and enhancing performance efficiency (Bruner et al., 1998[76]). The cost of capital includes both the cost of debt and the cost of equity and is usually called weighted average cost of capital (WACC) in project finance transactions. It represents the rate of return that investors expect to earn on their investments. In this paper, cost of capital, cost of finance, WACC and financing costs are used interchangeably.

[2] The levelised cost of hydrogen (LCOH) is a measure of the average net present cost of hydrogen production over a project's lifetime. It factors in all costs related to hydrogen production, including capital, operating, maintenance, fuel, and other expenses. These costs are divided by the total hydrogen output. The LCOH is typically measured in USD/kg.

[3] The levelised cost of electricity (LCOE) is a measure of the average net present cost of electricity generation for a power plant over its lifetime. The LCOE is typically measured in USD/MWh.

[4] De-risking means reallocating, sharing, or reducing the existing or potential risks associated with an investment. Allocating risks in an effective manner decreases the risk premium for equity and debt providers, thus reducing the expectations of equity returns and improving lending terms. (OECD/The World Bank, 2024[15]).

[5] The risks faced by offtakers depends on various parameters such as the sector, market, geographical location, etc. Examples of business models are provided in Table 2.2.

[6] For electrolysis, basic capital expenditures (CAPEX) cover the electrolyser system (stack); all necessary balance of plant (drier, cooling, de-oxo, and water de-ionization equipment); civil, structural, and architectural works (building and foundations); and power supply (electricity grid connection or renewable generation).

[7] The impact would depend on each process and industry. For instance, as Scope 3 emissions account for 80-95% of total carbon emissions of oil and gas companies, the avoided emissions by using clean hydrogen are very small compared to the remaining emissions from burning the fuels. Thus, the risk of stranded asset remains high.

[8] European Investment Bank states that a "PPP project yields value for money if it results in a net positive gain to society which is greater than that which could be achieved through any alternative procurement route".

[9] This definition applies notably for renewable electricity or hydrogen, and is the one used in this paper when referring to CfDs. More generally (but not considered in this paper), CfD is a financial derivative contract that can be concluded on a number of different products, such as interest rate swaps.

[10] In principle, the choice of reference price can be agreed upon freely and is not necessarily the current market price.

[11] BNEF launched a **Hydrogen Offtake Agreement Database** that tracks 149 offtake agreements for clean hydrogen and derivatives. The total volume is 7.9 Mt per year (nearly half in the form of ammonia). According the BNEF database by September 2023, only 13% of the contracted volume (or 1 million metric tons/year) is binding. Another 7% are pre-contractual agreements with a solid chance of becoming binding contracts. The remaining 80% are either memorandums of understanding or unspecified (BNEF, 2024).

[12] For more information on blended finance use for clean energy, see (OECD, 2022[77]).

[13] For more information on blended finance use for clean energy, see (OECD, 2022[77]).

3 Landscape and co-ordination of international initiatives for clean hydrogen financing

While risk mitigation and financing instruments for clean hydrogen in EMDEs contribute to the viability and bankability of first-mover projects, the clean hydrogen industry nevertheless needs a robust and well-co-ordinated framework to sustain its growth. Achieving effective co-ordination first requires a clearer understanding of the international initiatives and actors involved in financing clean hydrogen. This awareness will help identify key funding gaps and highlight areas where additional investment is needed to scale up and enhance the effectiveness of climate finance in EMDEs. Co-ordination is crucial for harmonizing project identification and appraisal processes, as well as facilitating joint financing efforts for clean hydrogen projects. This chapter provides an overview of existing international initiatives and offers suggestions on how better co-operation among them can improve assistance and financing for clean hydrogen projects in EMDEs.

Key findings

The scoping analysis maps out 46 international initiatives involved in the financing of clean hydrogen projects in EMDEs. Three quarters of the mapped initiatives are led by multilateral development banks, development financing institutions and international organisations.

The mapping exercise found that the main financing mechanisms offered by these actors are concessional finance and de-risking guarantees for clean hydrogen projects, with high presence of multilateral development banks and development finance institutions. Specifically, loans are found as the predominant financing products, and guarantees, auctions and credit facilities are the most deployed instruments to take risks.

Co-ordination between stakeholders can further accelerate clean hydrogen financing by harmonising project identification and appraisal processes and offering joint financing activities for clean hydrogen projects. Based on desk research and supported by a stakeholder poll, international investment platforms to channel investments, bilateral contracts between stakeholders to strengthen collaboration, and knowledge-exchange activities are the most relevant tools to increase co-ordination among stakeholders. Yet, further research on the current progress of these co-ordination tools in emerging markets as well as their implementation is needed to determine the relevance of finance co-ordination for the clean hydrogen economy.

Introduction

Currently, there are many actors operating at the international level, which have become crucial in the financing of clean hydrogen. These range from purely financing actors (i.e., multilateral development banks, development financial institutions and export credit agencies) to bilateral co-operation agencies, international organisations delivering capacity-building and technical knowledge, and other specialised initiatives (Asian Infrastructure Investment Bank, 2023[1]).

Whether purely financing stakeholders, development agencies or multilateral organisations, these actors are in prime position to support clean hydrogen development and bridge the investment gap, especially in EMDEs. Indeed, international actors can support clean hydrogen by providing financing and de-risking mechanisms, as well as funding R&D studies and offering technical assistance for capacity-building (Lee and Saygin, 2023[2]; NewClimate Institute, 2024[3]). As the landscape of international financing actors for clean hydrogen expands, co-ordination among their activities is critical for sustained market growth.

This chapter presents a mapping exercise of the international initiatives that are involved in clean hydrogen development in EMDEs across the value chain. Furthermore, the study provides a broad perspective on the role of international co-ordination to build a sustainable financial ecosystem, facilitating the long-term scaling of clean hydrogen projects.

Methodology

This chapter is based on a scoping analysis to gain a baseline understanding of the global landscape of initiatives conducted by international actors in the field of clean hydrogen financing in Emerging Markets and Developing Economies (EMDEs). The international initiatives considered are those:

- Being carried out by an international actor involved in clean hydrogen financing, or a domestic actor with an international scope;
- targeting emerging markets and developing economies;
- aiming to contribute to clean hydrogen financing and development;

- covering at least one of the six areas of work identified in this study (i.e., R&D, de-risking, financial assistance, capacity-building, policy and regulatory support, and co-ordination).

This exercise provides a breakdown of six areas of work (Figure 3.1) and eight steps of the value chain (Figure 3.2) (IEA, 2022[4]; UNIDO, 2024[5]). The results of the mapping exercise were complemented with evidence from an expert survey and further discussed comprehensively through consultations and bilateral discussions with hydrogen experts from financial, industry and policymaking sectors.

The analysis expands on the role of co-ordination in clean hydrogen development, including the most relevant tools to co-operate as well as its positive impacts. Desktop research and literature review of international co-ordination initiatives in climate finance constituted the core of the analysis. This was further complemented by the results of an online poll conducted during the OECD and the World Bank Stakeholder Workshop on "De-risking Instruments and International Co-ordination for Clean Hydrogen in Emerging Markets and Developing Economies", organised on 18 July 2024.

Figure 3.1. Areas of work of international initiatives on clean hydrogen

Note: This figure only contains the areas of work considered in this study.
Source: Authors

Figure 3.2. Steps of the clean hydrogen value chain

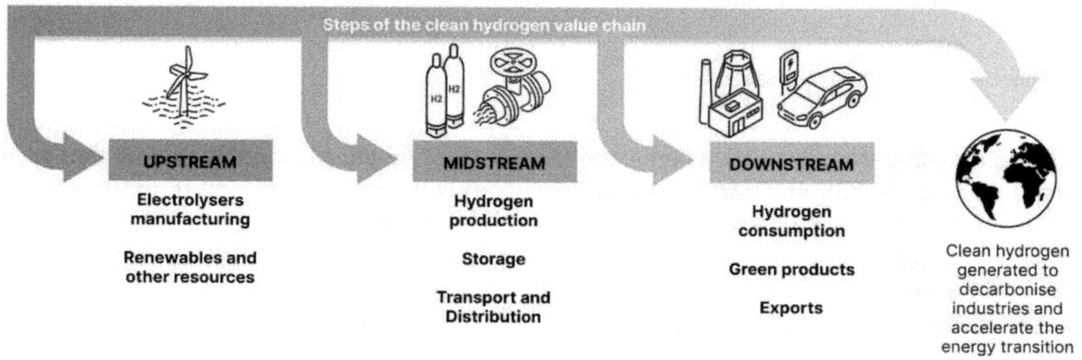

Note: The figure shows the distribution of steps of the hydrogen value chain considered in this study.
Source: Authors

While this analysis delves into a new topic such as the co-ordination of financing initiatives for clean hydrogen, the available data to feed the study presents inherent limitations. These limitations primarily stem from the absence of available information on the co-ordination initiatives carried out between financing institutions. Moreover, the set of co-ordination tools considered in this study has been gathered from different energy sectors. Consequently, relying solely on the list of tools of this study may not provide a precise representation of the options available.

Results of the mapping

Figure 3.3. International actors and initiatives on clean hydrogen development in emerging markets and developing economies

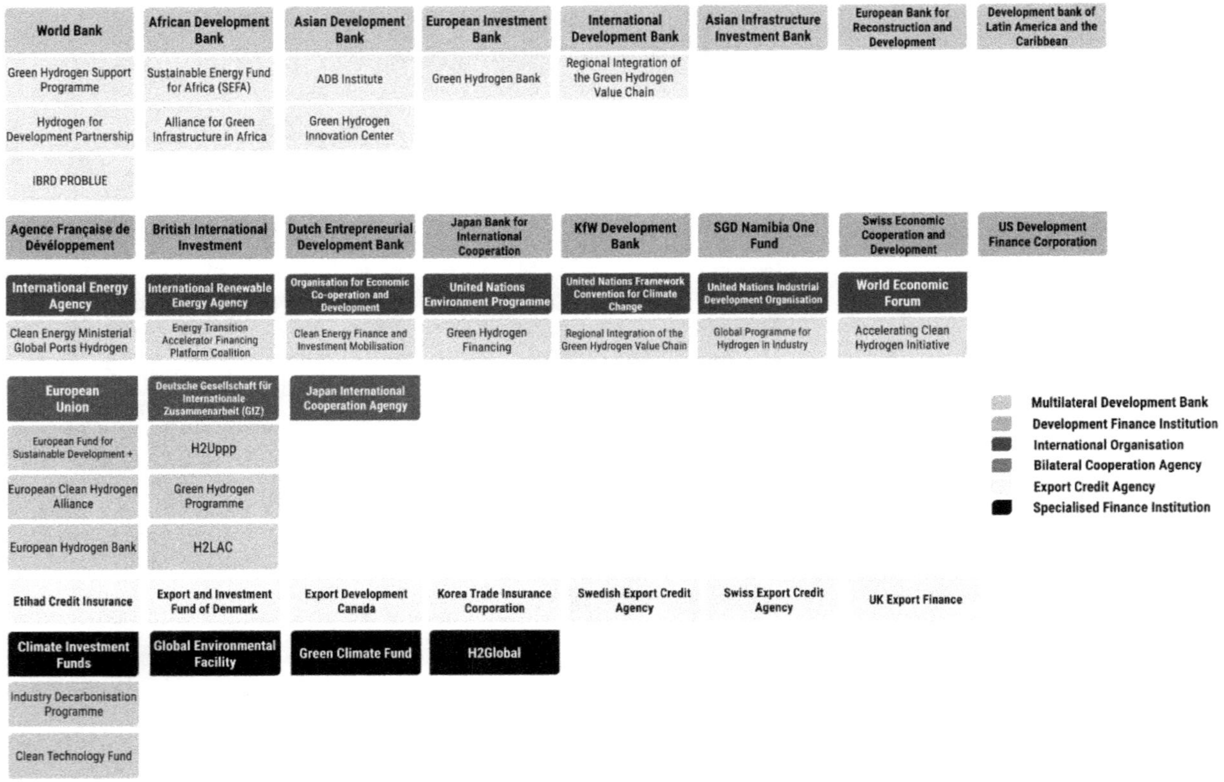

Source: Authors, based on the mapping exercise.

The mapping resulting from this study has identified a total of 46 international initiatives that are devoted to accelerating clean hydrogen financing in EMDEs. Across these initiatives, more than half are directly led by Multilateral Development Banks (38%), Development Finance Institutions (17%) and International Organisations (15%). The rest of initiatives are undertaken by government-led agencies and other institutions, such as Export Credit Agencies (13%), Bilateral co-operation agencies (13%) and other specialised financing initiatives (4%). This analysis shows an overview of the different international actors comprised in the mapping.

Figure 3.4. Landscape of the international actors on clean hydrogen in emerging economies and developing countries

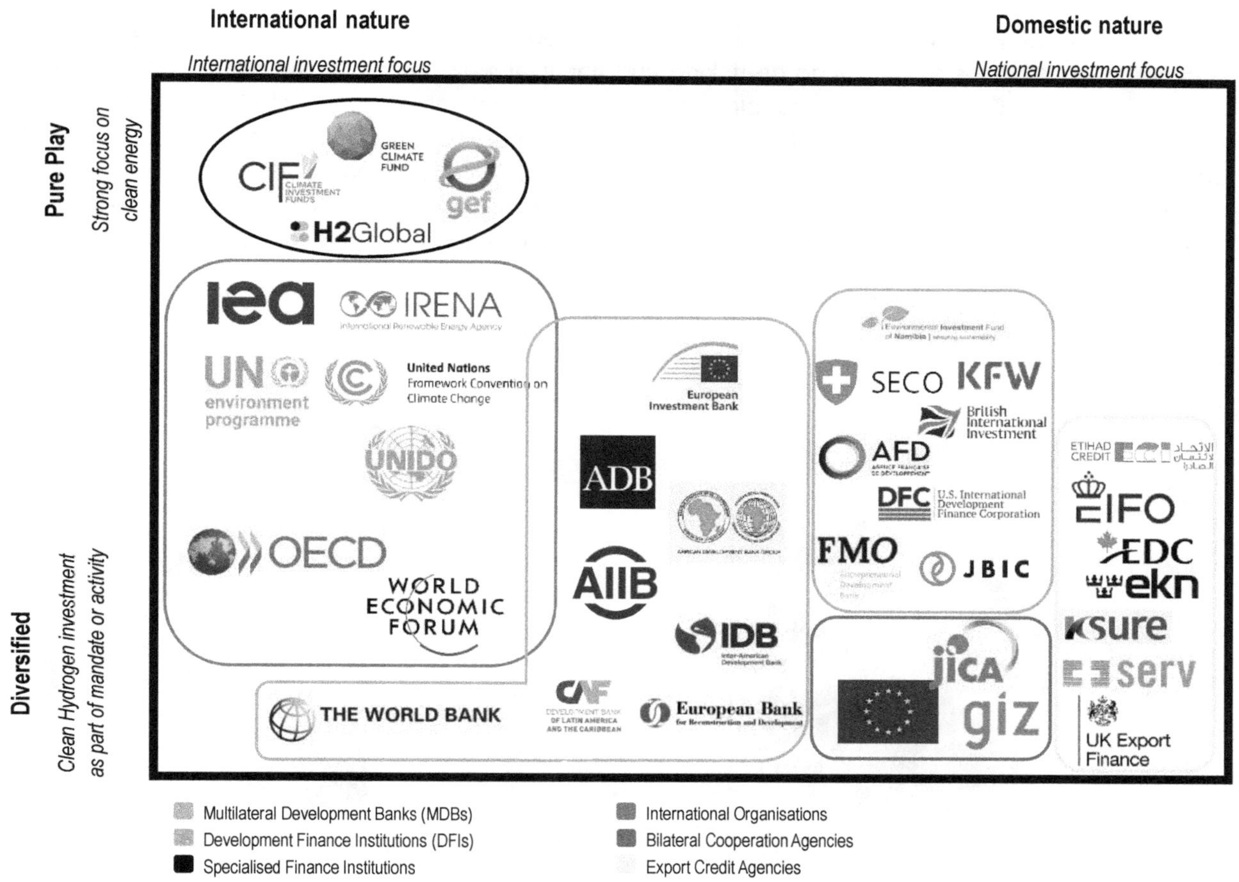

Note: This figure contains only the international actors considered in this study.
Source: Authors

The initiatives identified fall under the following categories:

- Activities embedded into the mandate of actors such as the Japan Bank for International Co-operation[1];
- Specific programmes such as the World Bank's Hydrogen for Development Partnership[2] or International Renewable Energy Agency (IRENA)'s Energy Transition Accelerator Financing Platform[3];
- Collaborations between different international actors, as it is the case the Climate Investment Funds[4], a climate finance partnership between the World Bank Group, the African Development Bank, the Asian Development Bank, the European Development Bank, and the Inter-American Development Bank.

Furthermore, the mapping shows that **most of the initiatives cover EMDEs without specific country target** (25 initiatives). The rest of initiatives are geographically concentrated in Africa and Asia, accounting for 9 and 7 initiatives, while Latin America and the Caribbean, and the Middle East host 3 and 2 initiatives accordingly.

The mapping shows that **72% of all the identified initiatives target renewable hydrogen**, while the remaining 28% cover broader forms of clean hydrogen, including hydrogen produced from natural gas and carbon capture and storage (i.e., low-emissions hydrogen). It is yet worth noting that international financing actors have no consensual definition of "renewable" hydrogen, and that the lack of a clear difference with other forms of hydrogen production can mislead the mapping exercise.

Concessional finance and guarantees are the most common instruments identified in the mapping exercise when it comes to delivering de-risking and financial assistance. These instruments are mostly used by MDBs and DFIs, accounting for almost a third of all initiatives each. The study shows that most of the initiatives offer concessional products, being loans the most common financing product (40% of the total of instruments declared). Additionally, almost half of total initiatives offer risk mitigation instruments for clean hydrogen projects. The most offered de-risking instruments are guarantees (50%), followed by auctions, credit facilities, hedge funds, green bonds, insurances and Contracts for Difference.

Figure 3.5. Number of financing and de-risking instruments offered by international initiatives on clean hydrogen

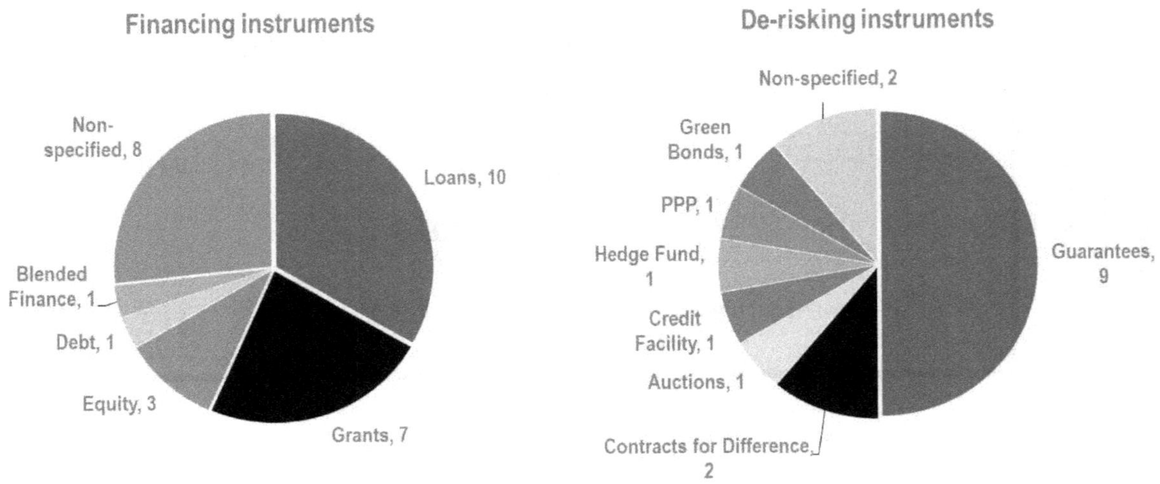

Source: Authors, based on the mapping exercise.

It is worth mentioning the role of export credit agencies (ECAs) in deploying de-risking instruments. While clean hydrogen is still entering into the scope of ECAs, 40% of de-risking initiatives in the mapping are covered by these agencies (see Figure 3.6).

Figure 3.6. Number of international initiatives providing financing and de-risking instruments for clean hydrogen

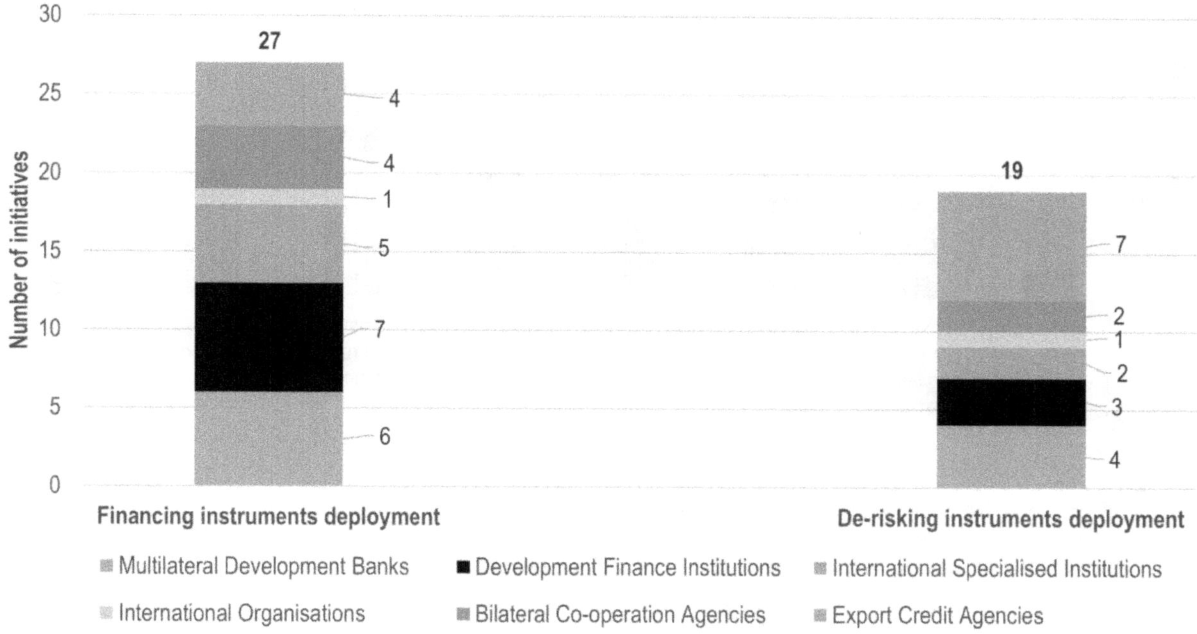

Source: Authors, based on the mapping exercise.

International actors also devote resources to **hydrogen research, capacity building, and policy and regulatory support**. The study shows that a third of all financing initiatives are involved in R&D programmes, 18% deliver capacity building activities, and 8% provide policy support.

In addition, 16% of the total amount of international initiatives cover the whole hydrogen value chain. The rest (84%) target a specific step (or steps) of the value chain. According to the expert survey conducted for the purpose of this study, the initiatives appear very balanced across the steps of the hydrogen value chain. Yet, it is worth mentioning that electrolyser manufacturing stands out for being disregarded (with only 3 initiatives).

Moreover, Figure 3.7 shows that research and analysis and policy and regulatory support are the most common areas of work of international actors.

Figure 3.7. Number of international initiatives by area of work and step of the value chain

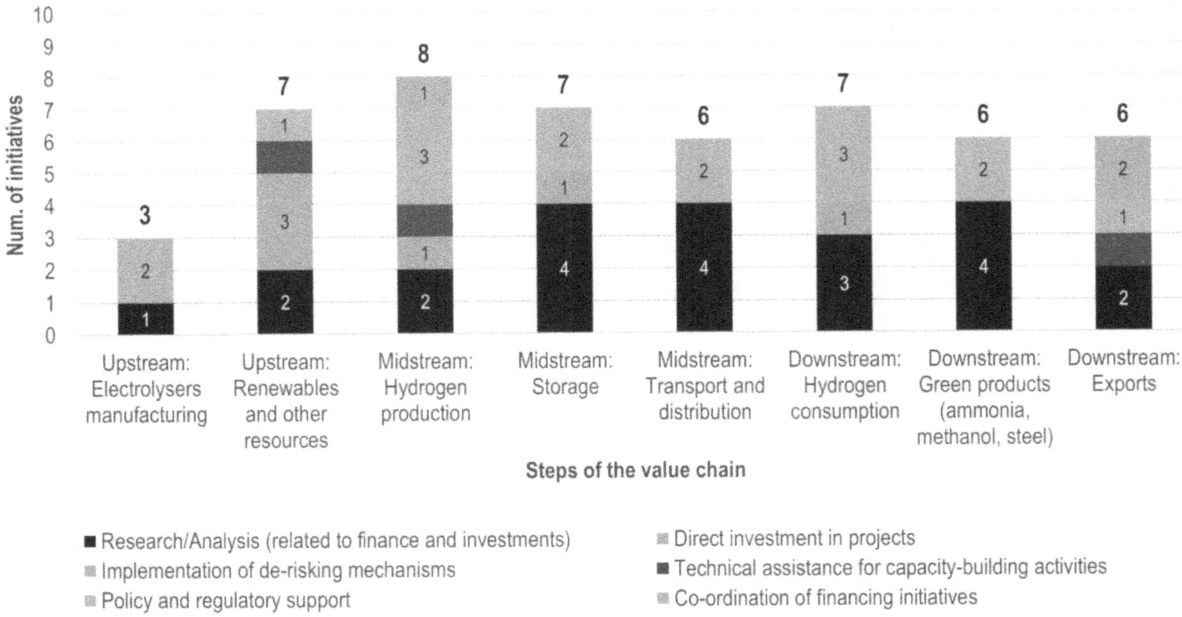

Note: The data in this graph only reflects the information provided by survey's respondents, which is a subset of the total number of initiatives identified in the mapping.
Source: Authors

Key takeaways

There is a proliferation of international initiatives involved in the financing of clean hydrogen in EMDEs. The number of announced initiatives for clean hydrogen financing is expanding rapidly across the value chain, leading to a very populated sector. In this context, clear boundaries and a certain level of co-ordination between initiatives is key to avoid duplication of activities and ensure a clear understanding of their area of work.

R&D, capacity building and policy support are crucial components in the support of clean hydrogen financing in EMDEs. International actors, more particularly MDBs, have been identified to be key players in the development of policy and regulations, as well as capacity building and research on renewable hydrogen (NewClimate Institute, 2024[3]). MDBs can play the following roles to support hydrogen development: (i) knowledge creation, by providing technical assistance for the collection of data estimates on potential demand and exports for hydrogen; (ii) capacity-building, including supporting governments in contract negotiations and offering training programmes for workforce; and (iii) policy and regulatory support, such as supporting the integration of certification schemes or regulatory reforms across the hydrogen value chain. Indeed, international actors use research, capacity-building and policy support to build knowledge around the financing needs of clean hydrogen and create the enabling regulatory conditions for its development. This is particularly important in EMDEs, given the limited supply of public finance to support R&D and capacity-building programmes (Climate Policy Initiative, 2024[6]).

International initiatives support clean hydrogen projects across the whole value chain, by taking a cross-cutting approach which can help to integrate all parts of the value chain and optimise their socio-economic benefits. Some financing institutions have already integrated such an approach, by targeting projects that cover multiple segments of the hydrogen value chain. An example of these is Namibia's

Hyphen green hydrogen project carried out by Hyphen Hydrogen Energy company and financed by the Government of the Republic of Namibia (GRN). The project targets green hydrogen and ammonia production for domestic and international markets (OECD Clean Energy Finance and Investment Mobilisation, n.d.[7]). Additionally, the project is part of the Socio-Economic Development (SED) Framework, an initiative launched in 2023 by the Namibian company and the GRN, with the aim to use the project for employment generation, local procurement, skills development and enterprise and supplier development (Hyphen Africa, 2023[8]).

Disclosing information on clean hydrogen activities is key to ensure a well-co-ordinated hydrogen sector. International actors need to provide details of their activities around clean hydrogen, including what their programme is and how it operates, which instruments they offer, and which project profile they prioritise (i.e., programme's structure, phase of the value chain, geographic location). This information can become crucial to facilitate exchanges of best practices and return on experience based on real projects. Eventually, this can help better understand the conditions to make projects investable, promote partnerships between public and private actors at domestic and international level, and ensure a more balanced risk and capital allocation.

The co-ordination tools used for international financing initiatives on clean hydrogen

Why co-ordination is important for clean hydrogen development in EMDEs?

International co-ordination, understood as the deliberate alignment of actions to achieve common goals, can play a key role in the development of clean hydrogen, particularly when financial support is challenged by operational, regulatory and risk-related constraints. This is particularly relevant in EMDEs, where the limited access to public finance and high financing cost prevents them from reaping the opportunities of clean hydrogen.

Co-ordination of initiatives in such a populated sector is key to avoid overlapping or duplication, align strategies, and mutualise tools and resources. Accountability and leadership are crucial for steering the complex hydrogen sector, which can be reinforced by strong co-ordination between investors, project developer and policymakers.

International co-ordination can help develop the clean hydrogen market and boost economic growth, which represents a major opportunity for EMDEs. First, it can connect public agencies with international investors and promote a better understanding about the financing needs to promote market growth. Second, it can help to position countries as an attractive location to develop green projects and solutions. Third, it presents an opportunity to use foreign investment to catalyse economic development, job generation and institutional capacity-building (Green Hydrogen Organisation, n.d.[9]).

The benefits of international co-ordination to accelerate clean hydrogen financing

Enhancing co-ordination could help to accelerate the financing of clean hydrogen, by (i) scaling-up investments in clean hydrogen projects, (ii) promoting the adoption of de-risking mechanisms by leveraging donors' guarantees and other financing instruments, and (iii) offering a collaborative platform for tackling clean hydrogen financing issues and share best financing practices.

Scaling-up investment in clean hydrogen projects. The co-ordination of financing initiatives, in particular, could help streamline investments, connect these with suitable investment opportunities and financing operations, and improve the financial services offered to project developers (OECD, 2023[10]; ETTG, 2022[11]). In parallel, co-ordinated policies are critical for ensuring a reliable and orderly clean hydrogen development, thus creating a liquid market for investors.

International co-operation leads to successful financial interventions. For instance, in 2023, the Chilean Economic Development Agency (CORFO) announced a USD 1 billion fund, which aims to provide loans and grant credits with low interest rates and long-term tenures to cover potential financial and technology risks associated to renewable hydrogen projects. In this context, a strong co-ordination between CORFO and other IFIs involved, including the European Investment Bank, KfW Development Bank, the World Bank and the International Development Bank, was critical to secure risk-sharing between stakeholders, address gaps in risk coverage occurring in individual instruments and offer a comprehensive risk sharing framework (CORFO, n.d.[12]; Martin, 2023[13]).

Offering a platform for tackling clean hydrogen financing issues and sharing best financing practices. Enhancing co-ordination between international initiatives can foster exchange of best practices and help to identify and address investment opportunities and bottlenecks. An example is the Asia Pacific Green Hydrogen Alliance (APAC), an initiative led by the Green Hydrogen Organisation and Breakthrough Energy, that aims to accelerate renewable hydrogen production in the Asia and the Pacific region by offering a platform to catalyse financing, strengthen policy and financing incentives, and accelerate sustainable production, use and exports of renewable hydrogen (Green Hydrogen Organisation, n.d.[9]). APAC aims to crowd in investments for hydrogen projects by:

- Promoting partnerships among financing institutions and governments;
- Proposing innovative financing solutions to de-risk investments;
- Identifying policy instruments and actions needed for financial close;
- Supporting the adoption of fiscal terms, incentives, and standards and certifications to promote sustainable investments in the sector.

An overview of the current co-ordination initiatives and tools for clean hydrogen financing

International co-ordination of initiatives is key for the development and financing of the clean hydrogen sector. The mapping conducted in this study shows a proliferation of initiatives by different stakeholders and in different areas. It has been previously argued that where multiple initiatives exist, a certain level of co-ordination can build on their complementary characteristics, such as their specific area of work, their geographical focus, or their project targets (IEA, 2021[14]). Indeed, co-ordinating initiatives have emerged in the areas of R&D, capacity-building and policy support. Two examples are the IRENA Collaborative Framework on Green Hydrogen and the WEF Accelerating Clean Hydrogen Initiative, being multilateral initiatives focused on knowledge dissemination and capacity-building. The Hydrogen Council is another example of co-ordinating initiative focusing on promoting clean hydrogen solutions for industrial decarbonisation goals (IEA, 2021[14]).

Box 3.1. The Breakthrough Agenda

The Breakthrough Agenda, launched by 45 World Leaders at COP26, and now backed by 47 governments, sets out and tracks the progress of priority international actions under the Hydrogen Breakthrough. These actions are organised along five main dimensions: (IEA, 2023[15])

Standards & Certification: Accelerate and fully resource the implementation of a co-ordinated programme of work to develop a comprehensive portfolio of international renewable and low carbon hydrogen standards and to facilitate associated certification schemes.

Demand Creation & Management: Strengthen demand for renewable and low carbon hydrogen by coordinating the agreement and announcement of packages of firm and sustained public and private commitments for the large-scale use renewable and low carbon hydrogen that displaces fossil fuel use in a wide range of applications and takes into account the need for just transitions.

Research & Innovation: Drive a significant increase in the number and geographical distribution of new, innovative hydrogen research and demonstration projects across a diversity of hydrogen's high-value end use sectors, backed by mechanisms to broaden and more rapidly share learnings from projects.

Finance & Investment: Enhance the overall public offer of international assistance for clean hydrogen projects, by coordinating and facilitating access to increased finance and support mechanisms that address obstacles to investment, with the goal of mobilising private investment at scale in emerging and developing economies.

Landscape Co-ordination: Enhance the co-ordination and transparency of international collaboration on clean hydrogen.

Landscape map of key international hydrogen initiatives

In 2022, the Breakthrough Agenda released a mapping of public and private initiatives carried out by actors with a global scope to showcase the landscape of international collaboration on low-carbon and renewable hydrogen.

Figure 3.8. Landscape map of key international hydrogen initiatives

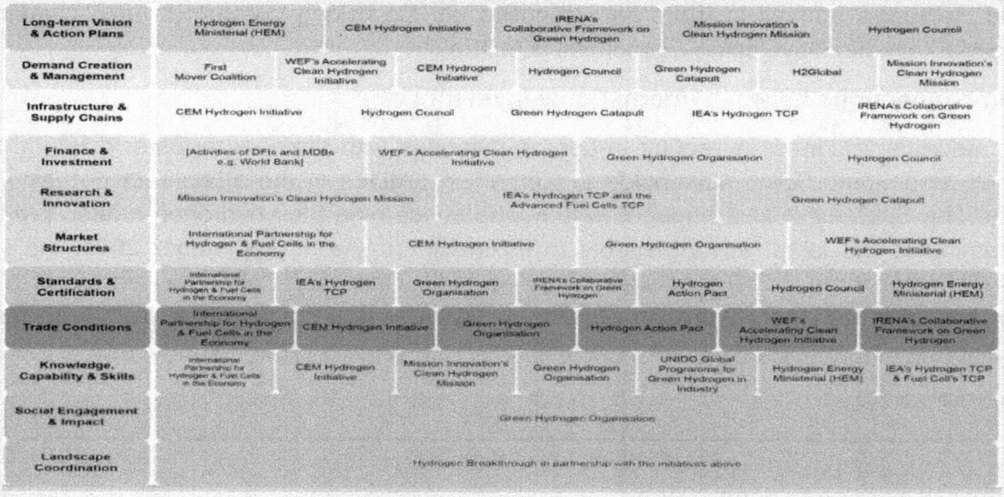

Source: (IEA, 2022[4])

There are only a few cases of co-ordination between initiatives for de-risking and financing, compared to other areas such as R&D or capacity-building. The mapping exercise identified three initiatives that aim to co-ordinate investments across the hydrogen sector. One of them is the World Bank's Hydrogen for Development Partnership, which aims to build evidence and eventually lead to co-ordination of investments around different hydrogen workstreams (see Box 3.2).

Box 3.2. The World Bank Hydrogen for Development (H4D) Partnership

The Hydrogen for Development (H4D) Partnership is a global initiative launched by the World Bank Energy Sector Management Assistance Programme (ESMAP) in 2022 with the aim to foster international co-operation for clean hydrogen deployment in EMDEs. Composed of 42 stakeholders, including business associations, hydrogen clusters, academia, public agencies and development institutions, it serves as a platform for knowledge sharing, capacity building, and boosting international co-operation to promote clean hydrogen financing.

The actions undertaken by the H4D Partnership are:

Research and knowledge production

The H4D Partnership releases reports, handbooks and technical papers on five different work streams across the hydrogen value chain: (i) clean hydrogen technologies, infrastructure and systems integration; (ii) enabling policy and regulatory frameworks; (iii) investment, financing, business models and procurement; (iv) socioeconomics and sustainability; and (v) hydrogen uses in industry.

Recent publications include the WB-Hydrogen Council report "Sufficiency, sustainability, and circularity of critical materials for clean hydrogen" (2022), and the OECD-WB report "Scaling Hydrogen Financing for Development" (The World Bank and Hydrogen Council, 2022[76]; OECD/The World Bank, 2024[1]).

Capacity-building and peer-learning

The H4D Partnership organises monthly capacity building workshops on various topics across the hydrogen value chain. For instance, in 2024, the World Bank, in collaboration with the Government of Brazil, hosted a webinar titled "Hydrogen Production, the Role of Storage, and Transportation-Related Infrastructure." Furthermore, in 2024, the World Bank and the OECD co-organized a side event during the World Hydrogen Summit in Rotterdam, focused on "De-risking Clean Hydrogen Investments in Emerging Markets and Developing Economies (EMDEs)."

Fostering connections between international investors

The H4D Secretariat convenes regular in-person meetings with partners to foster dialogue between North-South and South-South stakeholders, supporting EMDEs in the attainment of their hydrogen objectives. The Secretariat also engages with MDBs concerning their hydrogen-related programmes and disseminates the latest advancements to its members. As of September 2024, the H4D has successfully hosted three H4D Partners Meetings—in India, Chile, and Colombia—designed to catalyse long-term financing for clean hydrogen projects in EMDEs, with contributions from both public and private sectors.

Source: (World Bank, n.d.[16])

Co-ordination tools are key to ensure a certain level of co-operation and harmonisation between international financing initiatives. To identify the current co-ordination initiatives within the hydrogen sector, and gain insights into the most effective tools to promote financing co-ordination, an expert survey was conducted.

According to the expert survey, co-ordination of financing initiatives is lacking in the hydrogen sector. Regardless, almost 60% of responding stakeholders believe that financing co-ordination is needed across the whole value chain.

There are several tools that are relevant to co-ordinate finance for clean hydrogen. Yet, this study has only considered seven of them, based on the desk research and other sectors' best practices (European Investment Bank, 2022[17]; Ahman, Arens and Vogl, 2020[18]; The World Bank, 2021[19]):

- Global rule-making organisation acting as managing entity;
- Bilateral contracts of collaboration or co-ordination between financial institutions;
- Memorandums of Understanding between governments, financial actors or specialised institutions;
- Multilateral informational meetings between international financial institutions;
- International investment platforms to channel capital flows;
- Non-legally binding international rules;
- Voluntary international mechanisms to track investments.

Based on the survey respondents, the most relevant co-ordination tools are international investment platforms to channel capital flows, bilateral contracts of collaboration or co-ordination between financial institutions, and multilateral informational meetings between international financial institutions.

Figure 3.9. Survey Results - The most suitable co-ordination tools to strengthen co-ordination of financing activities for clean hydrogen

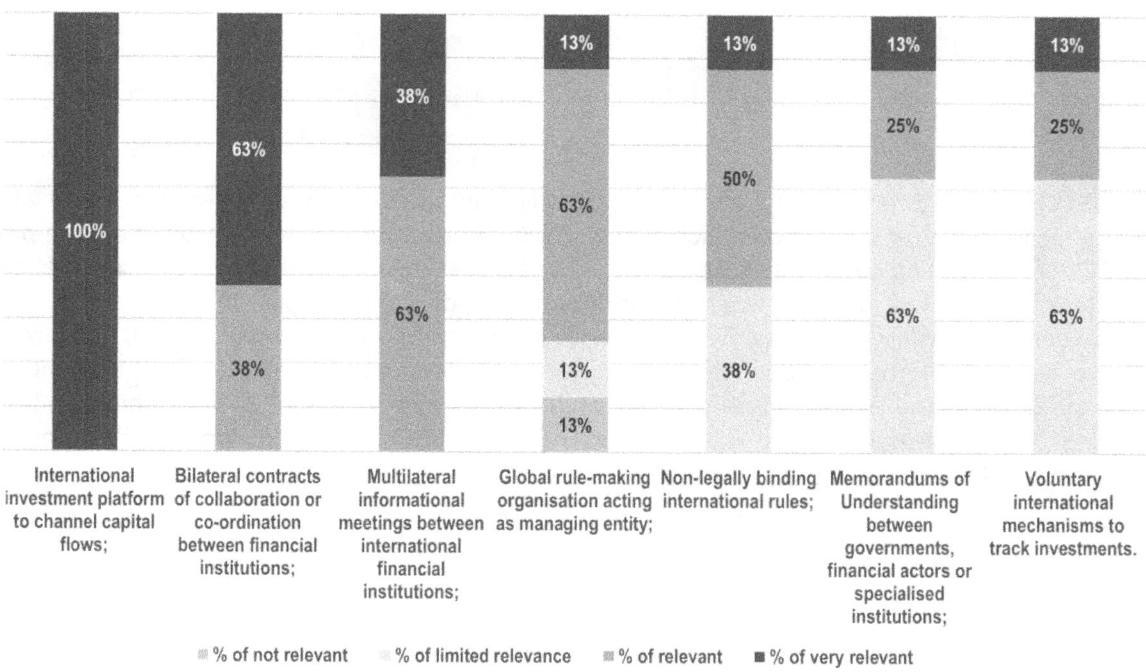

Note: Participants were asked to rate the importance of the seven tools in a ranking scale from least to most relevant, according to their relevance to strengthen co-ordination of financing initiatives for clean hydrogen. The blue stacked bars show the percentage of participants who gave the grade to the given tool.
Source: Authors

These co-ordination tools have many benefits for clean hydrogen development. In a poll conducted during the OECD and World Bank stakeholder workshop on "De-risking Instruments and International Co-ordination for Clean Hydrogen in Emerging Markets and Developing Economies" in July 2024, participants stated that co-ordination can effectively help to accelerate clean hydrogen financing and development by leading to joint financing partnerships, multi-stakeholder platforms to re-direct capital flows, and transparent interactions between stakeholders to harmonise processes and share best practices.

Figure 3.10. Poll Results – How can co-ordination accelerate clean hydrogen development?

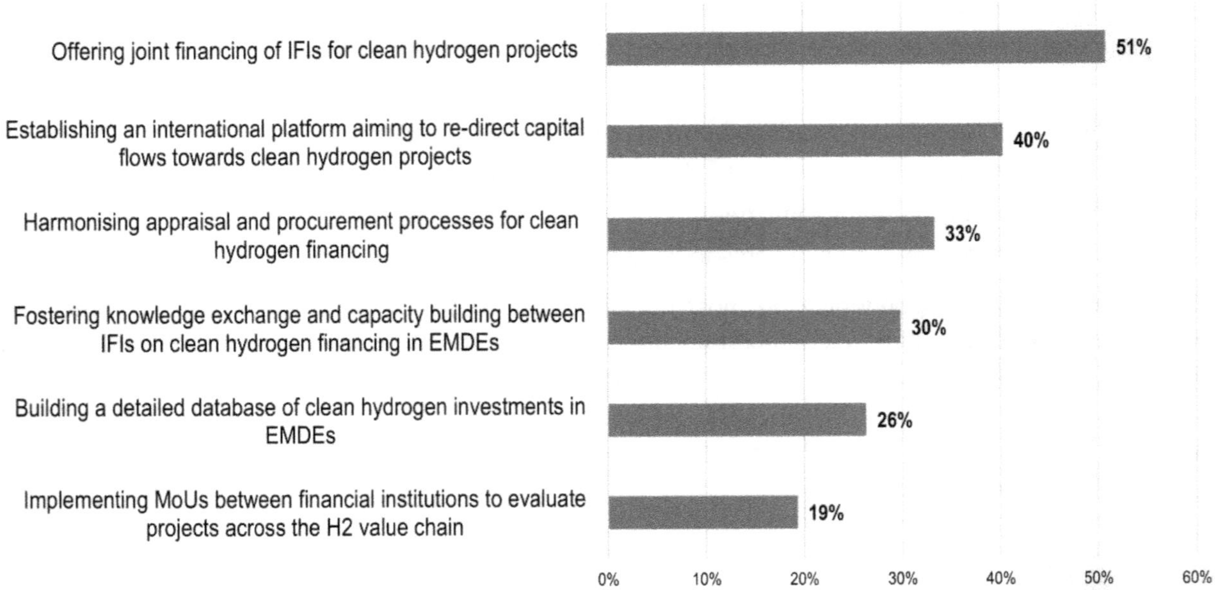

Note: Participants were asked to rate the importance of the six different co-ordinating tools to accelerate clean hydrogen development in EMDEs.
Source: Authors

The OECD intends to leverage its analytical capabilities to strengthen the evidence base on effective policies, economic, de-risking and financing instruments to support large-scale clean hydrogen projects. The OECD's convening power could be instrumental to disseminate such findings, but also to foster and facilitate dialogue and collaboration among investors, governments and project developers. The development of this joint report has paved the way for the Joint DFI Communique on the 10 GW Lighthouse Initiative, signed by 12 national and international development finance institutions on 14 November 2024 during the COP29. The World Bank Group will serve as the convener of the 10 GW Lighthouse Initiative, providing organisational support and facilitating coordination among participating institutions (Breakthrough Agenda, 2024[20]).

References

Ahman, M., M. Arens and V. Vogl (2020), *International Cooperation for decarbonizing energy intensive industries - Towards a Green Materials Club*, https://lup.lub.lu.se/search/files/88197690/Working_paper_Green_Materials_Club_IMESEEES_report_117.pdf. [18]

Asian Infrastructure Investment Bank (2023), *Financing Clean Hydrogen in Asia and beyond*, https://www.aiib.org/en/about-aiib/who-we-are/infrastructure-for-tomorrow/green-infrastructure/pdf/AIIB-Castalia_Financing-Clean-Hydrogen-in-Asia-and-Beyond_Sep-2023.pdf. [1]

Breakthrough Agenda (2024), *Joint DFI Communiqué: Supporting the 10 GW Renewable Hydrogen Lighthouse Initiative*, https://breakthroughagenda.org/wp-content/uploads/2024/11/10-GW-Joint-Communique_13November202477.pdf (accessed on 28 November 2024). [20]

Climate Policy Initiative (2024), *Discussion Paper: Financing Industrial Decarbonization: Challenges and Solutions for India's Iron and Steel Sector*, https://www.climatepolicyinitiative.org/wp-content/uploads/2024/04/Financing-Industrial-Decarbonization.pdf. [6]

CORFO (n.d.), *Corfo website*, https://www.corfo.cl/sites/cpp/movil/webingles. [12]

ETTG (2022), *Enhancing coordination between European donors, development agencies and DFIs/PDBs*, https://www.dev-practitioners.eu/media/documents/ETTG-Enhancing_coordination-brief-september-2022.pdf. [11]

European Investment Bank (2022), *Unlocking the hydrogen economy - stimulating investments across the hydrogen value chain: Investor perspectives on risks, challenges and the role of the public sector*, https://www.eib.org/attachments/publications/unlocking_the_hydrogen_economy_en.pdf. [17]

Green Hydrogen Organisation (n.d.), *APAC Green Hydrogen Alliance*, https://gh2.org/apac-alliance. [9]

Hyphen Africa (2023), *Hyphen Hydrogen Energy and The Government of the Republic of Namibia Launch Socio-Economic Development Framework for country's first Gigawatt-scale Green Hydrogen Project*, https://hyphenafrica.com/press/hyphen-hydrogen-energy-and-the-government-of-the-republic-of-namibia-launch-socio-economic-development-framework-for-countrys-first-gigawatt-scale-green-hydrogen-project/. [8]

IEA (2023), *Breakthrough Agenda Report 2023*, https://www.iea.org/reports/breakthrough-agenda-report-2023. [15]

IEA (2022), *Breakthrough Agenda*, https://iea.blob.core.windows.net/assets/49ae4839-90a9-4d88-92bc-371e2b24546a/THEBREAKTHROUGHAGENDAREPORT2022.pdf. [4]

IEA (2021), *Enhancing Collaboration Between Multilateral Initiatives*, https://iea.blob.core.windows.net/assets/55bc172a-901e-4718-8f57-8455565c9da2/Enhancingcollaborationbetweenmultilateralinitiatives.pdf. [14]

Lee, M. and D. Saygin (2023), "Financing cost impacts on cost competitiveness of green hydrogen in emerging and developing economies", *OECD Environment Working Papers*, No. 227, OECD Publishing, Paris, https://doi.org/10.1787/15b16fc3-en. [2]

Martin, P. (2023), *Chile tops up green hydrogen fund to $1bn and pledges to protect producers against certain 'financial risks'*, https://www.hydrogeninsight.com/production/chile-tops-up-green-hydrogen-fund-to-1bn-and-pledges-to-protect-producers-against-certain-financial-risks/2-1-1470847. [13]

NewClimate Institute (2024), *Green Hydrogen for Sustainable Development: The Role of Multilateral Development Banks*, https://newclimate.org/sites/default/files/2024-05/NewClimate_Green%20Hydrogen%20for%20Sustainable%20Development_may2024.pdf. [3]

OECD (2023), *Public Investment in Bulgaria: Planning and Delivering Infrastructure*, OECD Public Governance Reviews, OECD Publishing, Paris, https://doi.org/10.1787/b73ef3b4-en. [10]

OECD Clean Energy Finance and Investment Mobilisation (n.d.), *Green Hydrogen*, https://www.oecd.org/en/about/programmes/clean-energy-finance-and-investment-mobilisation/scaling-up-finance-for-clean-hydrogen.html. [7]

The World Bank (2021), *National - Subnational Coordination for Investment Attraction: The Case of Spain*, https://documents1.worldbank.org/curated/en/503651614752434734/pdf/National-Subnational-Coordination-for-Investment-Attraction-The-Case-of-Spain.pdf. [19]

UNIDO (2024), *Mapping of financial and technical assistance of clean hydrogen for developing countries*, https://hydrogen.unido.org/sites/default/files/2024-05/MAPPING-digital-final.pdf. [5]

World Bank (n.d.), *Hydrogen for Partnership*, https://www.esmap.org/Hydrogen_for_Development_Partnership_H4D. [16]

Notes

[1] For more information on Japan Bank for International Co-operation's activities: https://www.jbic.go.jp/en/information/today/today_202310/jtd_202310_pj1.html.

[2] For more information on World Bank's Hydrogen for Development Partnership: https://www.esmap.org/Hydrogen_for_Development_Partnership_H4D.

[3] For more information on IRENA's Energy Transition Accelerator Financing Platform: https://etafplatform.org/.

[4] For more information on Climate Investment Funds: https://www.cif.org/cif-funding.

Annex A. Methodology for the review of de-risking instruments, investor survey and case studies

To support the analysis of Chapter 2, a three-step approach was followed, including:

- Desk-based research to identify and pre-select a subset of risk mitigation instruments;
- An investor survey to identify trends and collect insights from stakeholders active in that sector;
- Case studies of large-scale hydrogen projects and of economic, de-risking and financing instruments.

Desk-based research

The desk-based research consisted in collecting examples of instruments from academic papers and grey literature. The review focussed primarily on clean hydrogen-related reports, but due to the lack of evidence, it was extended to comparable sectors, such as offshore wind and Liquefied Natural Gas (LNG). To select these comparable sectors, the methodologies of credit rating agencies were reviewed to verify the similarities and differences of the risk and credit profile of assets in these sectors. Then, a broader set of publications and databases was explored, as clean energy and LNG are more mature sectors than clean hydrogen (see Table A A.1). Through this screening, more than 50 instruments were identified. To shorten this "long list", evidence on the use and effectiveness of identified instruments was collected, and the list of instruments was further screened against expert interviews, notably those carried out in 2022 and 2023 to prepare previous OECD reports on hydrogen financing and case studies (see Annex C).

Table A A.1. (Non-exhaustive) list of reviewed work

Organisation	Publications/Database
African Development Bank	Initiative for Risk mitigation in Africa (IRMA)
Asian Infrastructure Investment Bank	Financing Clean Hydrogen in Asia and beyond
Cities Climate Finance Leadership Alliance (CCFLA)	Financial Instruments Toolkit
Clean Energy Ministerial	Database
Climate Policy Initiative	A Map of Risk Mitigation Instruments for Clean Investment
Deloitte	Financing the Green energy Investment
European Investment Bank	Unlocking the hydrogen economy stimulating investment across the hydrogen value chain
Green Hydrogen Organization (GH2)	Hydrogen financing brief Getting the right blend
Inter-American Development Bank (IDB)	MDBs Risk Mitigation Instruments for Infrastructure Investment
International Energy Agency (IEA)	Reducing the Cost of Capital
International Transport Forum (ITF)	Mobilizing Private Investment in Infrastructure: Investment De-risking and Uncertainty
IPP Journal	Database

Organisation for Economic Co-operation and Development (OECD)	De-Risking Institutional Investment in Green infrastructure
S&P Global	Capital IQ
Swiss RE institution	De-risking the hydrogen economy Bridging the protection gap
United Nations Development Programme (UNDP)	Derisking Renewable Energy Investment
United Nations Industrial Development Organization (UNIDO)	Mapping of financial and technical assistance of clean hydrogen for developing countries
World Resources Institute (WRI)	Moving the Fulcrum A Primer on Public Climate Financing Instruments Used to Leverage Private Capital

Note: The list is not exhaustive. For instance, the reviewed work include additional research papers such as (Steckel and Jakob, 2018[1]), (Craen, 2023[2]), or (Taghizadeh-Hesary et al., 2022[3])

Investor survey

The investor survey on "Risk mitigation instruments for clean hydrogen financing" developed for this report was carried out by the OECD between June and July 2024. A total of 41 respondents took part in the survey, primarily from organisations providing risk mitigation instruments. Among them, seven are from industrial corporations, five each from governments and bilateral development banks, four from investment funds, two each from private banks, multilateral development banks and export credit agencies. Other respondents come from diverse organisations, including consulting firms, technical assistance providers, international organisations and research organisations or think tanks.

The investor survey: (i) identifies which finance providers are implementing or could implement (some of) these instruments; (ii) helps to understand and prioritise the risk mitigation instruments that can trigger investment decision from private capital providers, depending on their investor profile and risk appetite. The survey is divided into 3 parts:

- Part 1 focuses on the profile of respondents. It is key to analyse the relevance and understand the rationale behind responses, especially when survey data are distributed unevenly depending on respondents' profile.
- Part 2 examines the current landscape of risks and perceived cost of capital for clean hydrogen projects, building on the previous work from (Lee and Saygin, 2023[4]) and (OECD/The World Bank, 2024[5]). It also asks respondents to evaluate the effectiveness of the 13 selected instruments from the desk-based research against key risk factors that drive the high cost of financing of clean hydrogen projects in EMDEs. In addition, it explores the potential use of credit default swaps for financing clean hydrogen projects, particularly in emerging and developing economies.
- Part 3 aims to explore on the most appropriate combination of de-risking instruments that could be provided jointly for large-scale clean hydrogen projects, depending on the country credit ratings, ranging from AAA to B.

Case studies

The case studies gathered and presented in this report cover (i) selected large-scale clean hydrogen projects that have reached or are likely to reach Final Investment Decision; (ii) economic, de-risking and financing instruments being deployed to support the development of the clean hydrogen market. They complement previous ones collected on hydrogen projects and on the financing of industrial decarbonisation (see Annex C). The case studies have been selected from EMDEs wherever possible, or from developed economies, when the learnings could also benefit EMDEs. Consolidated insights and lessons learnt are incorporated in the main text of this paper. The case studies are available in Annex D.

The case studies have been identified through preliminary desk research, followed by interviews with experts from the organisations implementing the instruments and developing the projects. Each case study has been reviewed and vetted by the relevant organisations. The case studies aim to show the diversity of clean hydrogen projects under feasibility or development, and the availability of a wide range of instruments. The selection of the final set of case studies is based on the quality of documentation and information provided, the maturity of the instruments and projects, and the possibility to draw lessons from them. It also illustrates the diversity of conditions, depending on the country or region where the case studies apply. Therefore, the case studies provide concrete examples of how the risks to finance clean hydrogen can be overcome in various contexts.

The project case studies follow the following outline:

- **Basic description**: project status, positioning in the hydrogen value chain, key numbers (e.g. hydrogen production volume, investment amount);
- **Project rationale**: targeted markets, job creation, trade opportunities;
- **Governance**: industrial consortium, public-private partnership;
- **Business Model**: LCOH, economic viability vs. existing processes, viability barriers;
- **Enabling market conditions**: if measures such as feed-in tariffs, contract for difference, tax relief, offtake agreements, have been put in place to enable the project;
- **Financing**: public or private financing; participation of development finance institutions; equity/debt ratio; risk-taking and seniority of debt;
- **Other lessons learnt (optional)**: additional caveat or opportunity that could provide value to countries or companies engaging in similar projects.

The instrument case studies follow the following outline:

- **Instrument – theoretical concept**: actors involved, financial and contractual flows, key advantages and challenges to implement the instrument;
- **Supported project(s) description**: overall envelope and number of projects supported, country, industry subsector, size of investment, governance and implementation of the solution;
- **Impact of the solution on the project(s)**: advantages vs conventional financing; impact on business model or access to finance; explanation of how improving the enabling conditions can complement the economic, financial or de-risking solution;
- **Lessons learnt and replicability**: effectiveness of implementation, mobilisation of private capital, disbursement of funds in case of de-risking instrument, conditions for replicability.

The lessons learnt from the case studies are grouped and summarised below. The key learnings are structured around the following categories:

- De-risking and financing instruments for capital mobilisation
- Public support and economic instruments for timely FID
- Impact on project financing structure
- Improving enabling conditions via partnerships
- Implementation insights
- Conditions for replicability and scale-up

References

Craen, S. (2023), *Financing a world scale hydrogen export project*, https://www.oxfordenergy.org/wpcms/wp-content/uploads/2023/01/Financing-a-world-scale-hydrogen-export-project-ET-21.pdf. [2]

Lee, M. and D. Saygin (2023), "Financing cost impacts on cost competitiveness of green hydrogen in emerging and developing economies", *OECD Environment Working Papers*, No. 227, OECD Publishing, Paris, https://doi.org/10.1787/15b16fc3-en. [4]

OECD/The World Bank (2024), *Scaling Hydrogen Financing for Development*, OECD Publishing, Paris, https://doi.org/10.1787/0287b22e-en. [5]

Steckel, J. and M. Jakob (2018), "The role of financing cost and de-risking strategies for clean energy investment", *International Economics*, Vol. 155, pp. 19-28, https://doi.org/10.1016/j.inteco.2018.02.003. [1]

Taghizadeh-Hesary, F. et al. (2022), "Green finance and the economic feasibility of hydrogen projects", *International Journal of Hydrogen Energy*, Vol. 47/58, pp. 24511-24522, https://doi.org/10.1016/j.ijhydene.2022.01.111. [3]

Annex B. Methodology and results of the mapping of international financial initiatives and co-ordination mechanisms for clean hydrogen

This section describes the methodology used for the chapter "International financial initiatives and co-ordination mechanisms for clean hydrogen", composed of two different parts. Part 1 focuses on a mapping exercise of the financial initiatives conducted by international financial actors for clean hydrogen development in Emerging Markets and Developing Economies (EMDEs). Part 2 addresses the co-ordination mechanisms that are available for international financial actors across the whole hydrogen value chain, and studies how these can be harnessed to create better alignment and collaboration between them.

Part 1

The mapping exercise of the key international initiatives identified in the existing hydrogen landscape is based on a consultation with experts from international financial institutions (IFIs), who are actively engaged in the development of clean hydrogen. The consultation was based on an expert survey with the aim to identify the financial initiatives carried out by the abovementioned stakeholders, and the co-ordination mechanisms used between them. The questionnaire was distributed to approximately and answers were collected over a period of one month. A total of 12 stakeholders provided insightful responses to the questionnaire, coming from different types of IFIs, including Multilateral Development Banks, Development Finance Institutions, Export Credit Agencies (ECAs) and investment funds.

The consultation was complemented with bilateral discussions with specific financial institutions which provided detailed information and understanding regarding their activities driving clean hydrogen financing in EMDEs.

The survey was composed of two sections. The first one aimed at providing an overview of the international financial initiatives and actors across the hydrogen value chain. Respondents were requested to indicate the areas of work, financial activities and steps of the clean hydrogen value chain they were most active in through a matrix table.

- The following areas of work were considered:
- Research/Analysis (related to finance and investments)
- Direct investment in projects
- Implementation of de-risking mechanisms
- Capacity-building activities
- Policy and regulatory support
- Co-ordination of financing initiatives

The steps of the value chain contemplated were:

- Upstream: Electrolysers manufacturing

- Upstream: Renewables and other resources
- Midstream: Hydrogen production
- Midstream: Storage
- Midstream: Transport and distribution
- Downstream: Hydrogen consumption
- Downstream: Green products
- Downstream: Exports

The second section of the survey addressed the main mechanisms used to facilitate co-ordination among IFIs. The aim was to gain insights into which collaboration mechanisms are available for international financial actors, and how much co-ordinated the landscape of clean hydrogen is, ultimately influencing financing, market growth and development. Respondents were asked to indicate the initiatives and mechanisms best suited to strengthen co-ordination and avoid duplication of activities, especially in developing countries.

- Respondents were presented with seven co-ordination mechanisms (ranked from most to least binding):
- Global rule-making organisation acting as managing entity;
- Bilateral contracts of collaboration or co-ordination between financial institutions;
- Memorandums of Understanding between governments, financial actors or specialised institutions;
- Multilateral informational meetings between international financing institutions;
- International investment platform to channel capital flows;
- Non-legally binding international rules;
- Voluntary international mechanisms to track investments.

Part 2

- Segment two delves into the available mechanisms to facilitate co-ordination between international financial initiatives for clean hydrogen. Accordingly, the results from Section 2 of the survey served as a basis to support this analysis.
- The co-ordination mechanisms were further identified through desktop research and deep dives into international financial actors that have either implemented or are developing mechanisms to foster co-ordination and alignment of initiatives associated with clean hydrogen.
- In light of the potential of co-ordination mechanisms to promote synergies and collaborations between IFIs and to catalyse investments, this chapter provides recommendations for international financial actors as well as policymakers involved in clean hydrogen to support the adoption and implementation of these mechanisms.

Figure A B.1. Mapping exercise of international initiatives for clean hydrogen in EMDEs [Panel 1]

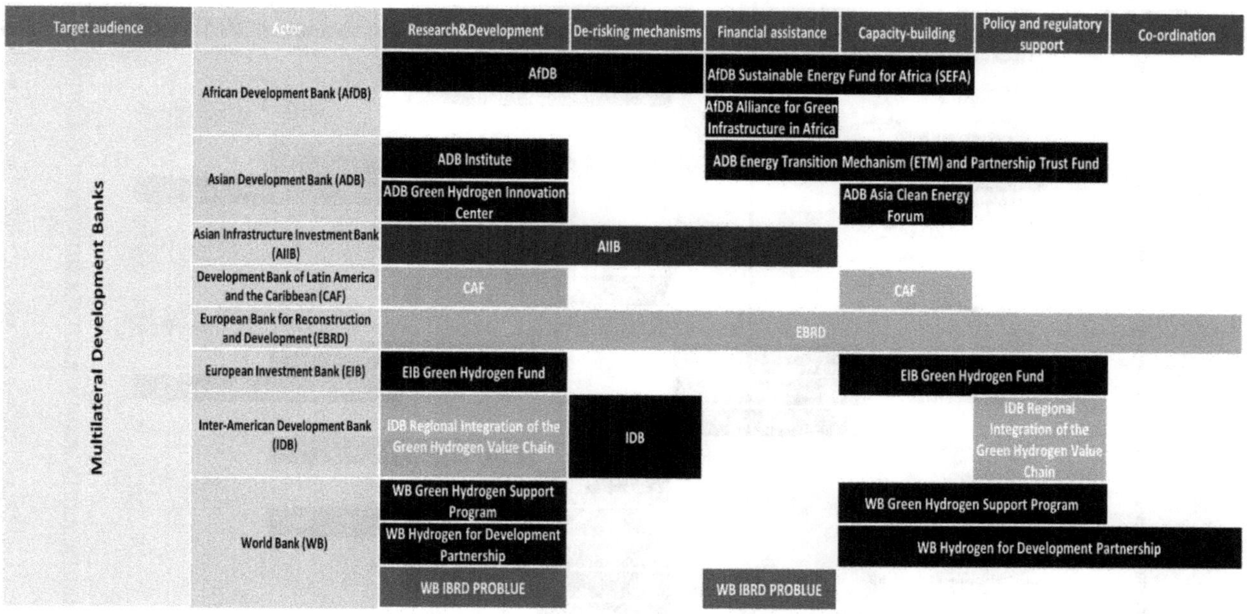

Note: The initiatives are coloured based on the step of the value chain they cover. Grey: Cross-cutting, dark blue: upstream phase, blue: midstream phase, light blue: downstream phase, black: non-specified.
Source: Authors

Figure A B.2. Mapping exercise of international initiatives for clean hydrogen in EMDEs [Panel 2]

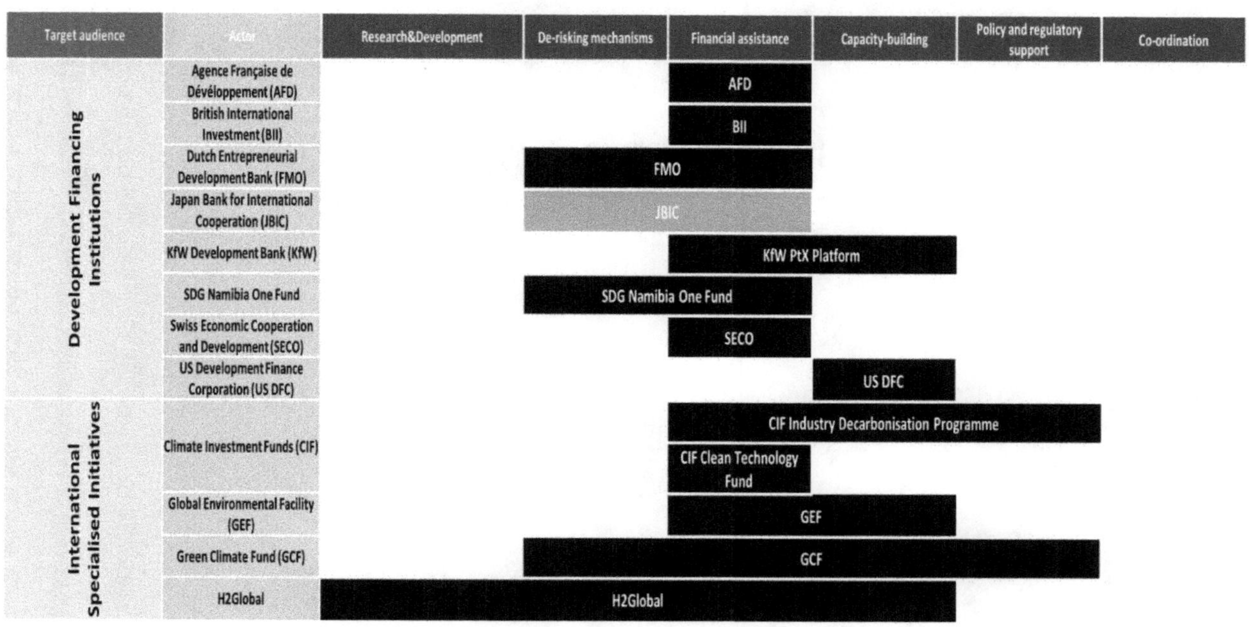

Note: The initiatives are coloured based on the step of the value chain they cover. Grey: Cross-cutting, dark blue: upstream phase, blue: midstream phase, light blue: downstream phase, black: non-specified.
Source: Authors

Figure A B.3. Mapping exercise of international initiatives for clean hydrogen in EMDEs [Panel 3]

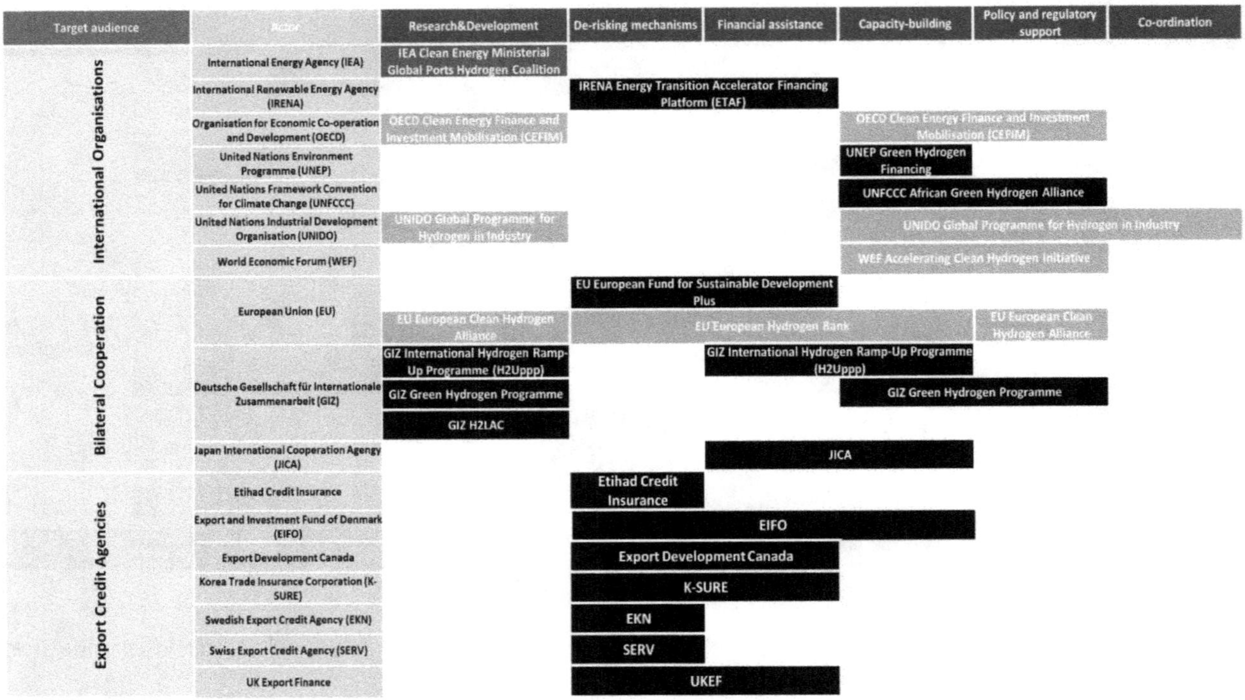

Note: The initiatives are coloured based on the step of the value chain they cover. Grey: Cross-cutting, dark blue: upstream phase, blue: midstream phase, light blue: downstream phase, black: non-specified.
Source: Authors

Annex C. List of OECD hydrogen case studies developed in 2022 and 2023

Table A C.1. List of OECD hydrogen case studies developed in 2022 and 2023

Type	Company	Description	Country
Project	ACWA	Ammonia	Uzbekistan
Project	Ad Astra	Trucks and buses	Costa Rica
Project	Chariot & Total Eren	Hydrogen, Ammonia	Mauritania
Project	CWP	Ammonia & Direct Reduced Iron (DRI)	Mauritania
Project	ENGIE/Yara	Ammonia	Australia
Project	Stegra (previously H2 Green Steel)	Steel	Sweden
Project	HIF Global	E-fuels	Chile
Project	HDF Energy	Dispatchable power	French Guiana / Indonesia
Project	Hychico	Power	Argentina
Project	Hyphen Hydrogen Energy	Ammonia	Namibia
Project	NEL	Electrolyser (Equipment)	Norway
Project	NEOM	Ammonia	Saudi Arabia
Project	Port of SOHAR	Hydrogen, Ammonia, Steel	Oman
Project	The Green Solutions	Ammonia	Viet Nam
Instrument (Financing)	Hintco / H2Global	Auctions and Contract for Difference (CfD) for hydrogen, ammonia, methanol and sustainable aviation fuels (SAF)	Global
Instrument (Financing)	Inter-American Development Bank (IDB)	Result based loans for hydrogen development	Chile

Note: e-fuels (also called synthetic fuels or electrofuels) are liquid fuels manufactured by combining captured CO_2 and renewable hydrogen
Sources: (Cordonnier and Saygin, 2022[1]), (Cordonnier and Saygin, 2023[2]), (Lee and Saygin, 2023[3]).

References

Cordonnier, J. and D. Saygin (2023), "Financing solutions to foster industrial decarbonisation in emerging and developing economies", *OECD Environment Working Papers*, No. 226, OECD Publishing, Paris, https://doi.org/10.1787/24a155ab-en. [2]

Cordonnier, J. and D. Saygin (2022), "Green hydrogen opportunities for emerging and developing economies: Identifying success factors for market development and building enabling conditions", *OECD Environment Working Papers*, No. 205, OECD Publishing, Paris, https://doi.org/10.1787/53ad9f22-en. [1]

Lee, M. and D. Saygin (2023), "Financing cost impacts on cost competitiveness of green hydrogen in emerging and developing economies", *OECD Environment Working Papers*, No. 227, OECD Publishing, Paris, https://doi.org/10.1787/15b16fc3-en. [3]

Annex D. Case studies developed in 2024

Case study 1 - Ceará Green Hydrogen Hub / Industrial and Port Complex of Pecém (CIPP)

Figure A D.1. Overview of Pecém complex

Source: Case study documentation

Table A D.1. Key indicators of the Ceará Green Hydrogen Hub

Indicator	Company / Project
Value Chain step / Application	Production / Clean hydrogen and ammonia
Country	Brazil
Status	Development: feasibility, pre-FID
Production route & type of renewable	Solar PV, onshore wind, from 2035 offshore wind expected (dedicated green field infrastructures) + grid electricity; electrolysis
Key project metrics (RE capacity / Electrolyser capacity / Ammonia Production / etc.)	Renewable power capacity: 6 GW Electrolyser capacity: 2 GW with potential to increase up to 3 GW Ammonia production volume: 2 million tonnes per year by 2030
Hydrogen production (kt/y)	Phase 1: 400 kt/y (500 MW electrolyser) Phase 2: 1 600 kt/y (2 GW electrolyser)
Start-up date	Phase 1: 2025 for the first project phase; Phase 2: 2027 (expected start of construction); 2030 (expected start of operations)
Amount	USD 7 billion

Source: Authors based on case study documentation

Basic description

The Ceará Green Hydrogen Hub (Complexo do Pecem, 2022[1]), located at the premises of the Pecém Industrial and Port Complex (CIPP) in Ceará, Brazil, aims to produce clean ammonia for export, targeting mainly the European market. CIPP is a joint venture formed by the State of Ceará (Brazil) and the Port of Rotterdam (Netherlands) conceived and designed to be an industrial and port space. Currently in its development phase, the Ceará Green Hydrogen project secured almost 40 Memoranda of Understanding (MoUs) with national and international companies. Some initial steps towards project implementation have been taken, including access to land reservation and grid connection.

The project focuses on the production of clean ammonia from clean hydrogen via electrolysis, using a mix of renewable energy sources such as onshore wind and solar power and grid electricity. The project focuses on clean ammonia production for export targeting mainly European countries via the port of Rotterdam.

Total investment is estimated at USD 7 billion. The total investment includes contributions from various parties, including USD 135 million infrastructure investment from the World Bank; USD 2 billion investment from Fortescue and Casa dos Ventos together with Total Energies; expected investment of USD 150-200 million from CIPP; expected investment of USD 200 million from local storage operator; expected investment of USD 50-100 million from local partners to be deployed before final investment decision (FID). A potential investor and operator for the ammonia pipeline, tank terminal and ship operations is pre-identified. The remaining amount is expected to be financed by private and public investors as well as senior debt providers.

The project will unfold in two phases with a total electrolysis production capacity of 2 GW, which may be further increased up to 3 GW. The first phase will involve the installation of 500 MW of electrolysers, aimed at producing 400 000 tons of ammonia annually, with an investment of USD 1.3 billion (BRL 7 billion). The second phase will expand the capacity by adding 1.5 GW of electrolysers, increasing production by 1.2 million tons to a total of 1.6 million tons per year. This second phase will require an additional USD 3.7 billion (BRL 20 billion) investment.

Project Rationale

The project is driven by the increasing global demand for clean hydrogen to achieve carbon reduction goals and the transition to a sustainable energy future. Ceará's strong commitment to sustainability since 2021, combined with its important potential for wind and solar energy generation, makes it an attractive location for clean hydrogen production. The site's strategic geographical location as the closest point in Brazil to Europe enhances trade opportunities. Additionally, Ceará benefits from extensive connectivity with Europe through its partnership with the Port of Rotterdam, which has launched several projects to become Europe's important clean hydrogen centre. The project is further supported by shared infrastructures available within operational port premises: an available electricity grid allowing capacity factor optimisation and water networks for electrolysis, shared tanking facilities for liquid ammonia, and over 1 700 hectares available for clean hydrogen production, for which the environmental permitting is pre-approved. There are six producer customers who pre-signed contracts with CIPP and paid a reservation fee for the land.

The project is expected to create significant employment opportunities during both the construction and operational phases, contributing to local economic development. Approximately 1 500 jobs are anticipated during construction and around 200 permanent jobs once operational.

By producing clean hydrogen, Brazil aims to establish itself as a key player in the international clean hydrogen market, with significant export opportunities to regions such as Europe and Asia, where demand for clean hydrogen is high. Relying on EU import projections, the project alone aims to supply around 15% of European import 2030 target and around 25% of Port of Rotterdam import volume target.

Governance

The Ceará state government plays a crucial role in facilitating the project by providing regulatory support and enabling infrastructure development, forming a public-private-academia partnership essential for the project's success. Additionally, under the guidance of the Ceará state government, main local universities and institutes joined forces to accelerate R&D on green fuels, under an initiative called Rede Verdes.

Business Model

The project aims to achieve competitive LCOH through the utilisation of abundant and low-cost renewable energy resources in Brazil. Clean hydrogen production is currently more expensive than conventional hydrogen production methods such as steam methane reforming. However, the competitive cost of renewable energy, advancements in electrolyser technology, scale effects, and tax break schemes for export processing zones (ZPE) are expected to enhance economic viability of the project.

The Ceará Green Hydrogen Hub encounters several viability barriers. Uncertainties in the clean ammonia offtake market could impact demand and price stability. Additionally, the cost gap between conventional and clean ammonia presents a challenge for competitiveness. Technological issues, particularly in scaling up production, pose further obstacles. The project also requires extensive infrastructure for hydrogen and ammonia storage, transportation, and distribution, which adds complexity. Moreover, both local and global regulatory and policy uncertainties could affect the project's long-term viability and attractiveness to investors. Addressing these barriers is essential for the project's successful execution.

Enabling Market Conditions

Several measures are being considered to enhance the economic feasibility of the CIPP hydrogen project. Although specific measures are not detailed, tax reliefs are expected to play a significant role, potentially including incentives linked to special export processing zones (ZPE) regulations. A dedicated tax break scheme has been approved. Additionally, offtake agreements with industrial consumers and energy companies are planned to secure long-term demand and stable revenue streams for the project.

Financing

The project primarily relies on private financing, with significant investments from international and local stakeholders. While specific details are not provided, development finance institutions, such as the World Bank, the European Union (EU), the Brazilian Development Bank (BNDES), and Banco do Nordeste, may participate to de-risk the project and attract further private investment. Exact equity/debt ratios are not disclosed, but a mix of equity and debt financing is typical for such large-scale infrastructure projects to manage risk and ensure financial viability. The project may involve senior and subordinated debt structures to distribute risk among investors and lenders. Public sector involvement likely provides additional risk mitigation.

Lessons Learnt

Robust infrastructure development is critical for the success of the CIPP hydrogen project. This includes large-scale production and conversion assets, as well as pipelines and storage facilities for the efficient distribution and export of clean hydrogen and ammonia. The project benefits from shared infrastructure within the operational port premises, which helps mitigate certain risks, reduces CAPEX concentration, and improves the likelihood of achieving a final investment decision (FID). Additionally, policy stability is crucial for attracting and maintaining investment, clear regulatory frameworks and incentives are necessary to enhance project feasibility. Furthermore, public-private partnerships (PPP) play a key role in ensuring industrial excellence, operational efficiency, and securing financing at the required scale.

Case study 2 – Egypt Green Hydrogen / Scatec

Table A D.2. Key indicators of Scatec's Egypt Green Hydrogen

Indicator	Company / Project
Value Chain step / Application	Production / Clean hydrogen and ammonia
Country	Egypt
Status	Under development
Production route & type of renewable	Solar PV, onshore wind, grid electricity, electrolysis
Key project metrics (RE capacity / Electrolyser capacity / Ammonia Production / etc.)	Renewable power capacity: 203 MW Electrolyser capacity: 70 MW Ammonia production volume: 70 000 t/y
Hydrogen production (kt/y)	13 kt/y (feedstock to ammonia production)
Start-up date	Phase 1: 2024 project development Phase 2: 2025 (expected start of construction); 2027 (expected start of operations)
Amount	USD 520 million

Source: Authors based on case study documentation

Basic description

The Egypt Green Hydrogen (Scatec, n.d.[2]) project aims to produce green ammonia and export it to European end-users. It is located in Ain Sokhna, in the Suez Canal Economic Zone, a green hydrogen production complex with a strategic location and unique features that incentivise green hydrogen development, including proximity to industrial zone, sea water desalination plants, and easy access to the Ain Sokhna Port.

Recently, the project secured an offtake agreement with Hintco GmbH, a subsidiary of the H2Global Foundation, through the first H2Global pilot auction for green ammonia. The auction, funded by the German Federal Ministry for Economic Affairs and Climate Action (BMWK), will provide a total of USD 440 million (EUR 397 million), with the aim to deliver around 397 kilotonnes (kt) of green ammonia cumulatively by 2033.

The project, led by a Norwegian company specialised in renewable energy, Scatec, comprises a 100 MW electrolyser facility (including renewable power assets and water sourcing) and an existing ammonia production plant using the Haber Bosch process. Electricity will be generated in an onshore windfarm of 203 MW located in Ras Ghareb (close to the Red Sea) and a newbuild solar PV plant of 70 MW capacity in Benban (south of Egypt). Egypt's national power grid will be used for electricity transmission to the production facility. Ammonia will be transported via a 7 km pipeline to Ein El Sukhna Port, and delivered to the Port of Rotterdam by Fertiglobe International Trading. Then, it will be sold by Hintco in batches of 500 tonnes as standardised quantities in annual auctions.

Figure A D.2. Description Scatec Green Hydrogen project

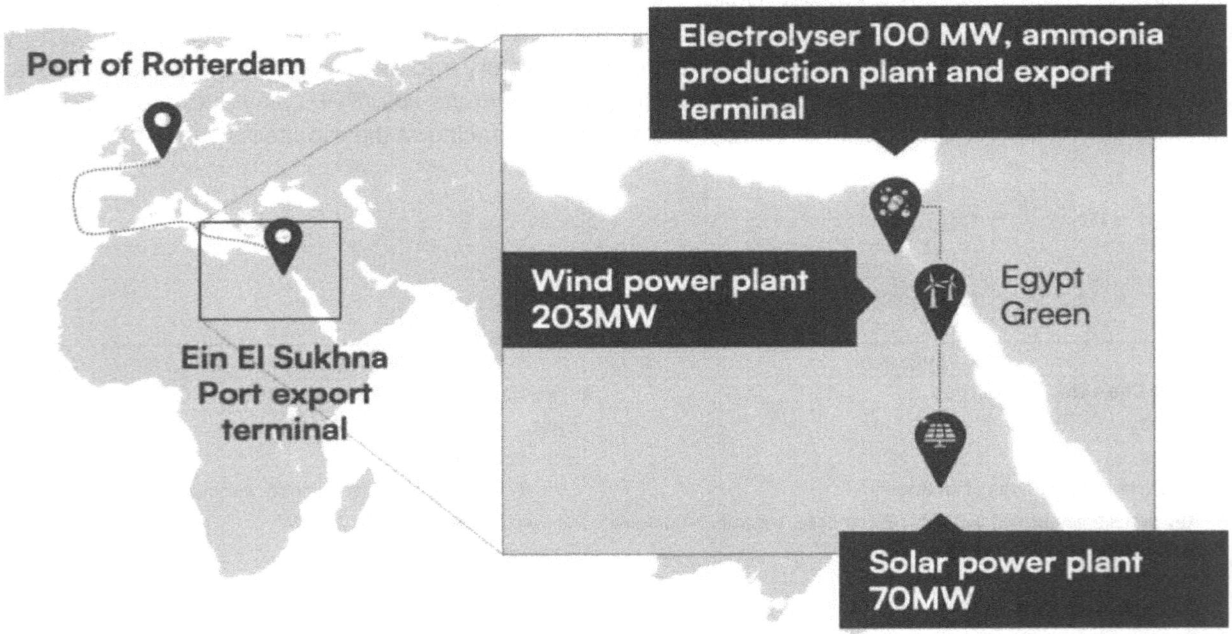

Source: (Hintco, 2024[3])

The total project value amounts to approximately USD 520 million. The construction and installation of the electrolysers will take place until 2027. Then, green ammonia will be produced, starting with 19 500 t in 2027, and 40 000 t/y from 2028 onwards.

Project Rationale

The project is part of Egypt's strategy to increase its domestic green hydrogen capacity, driven by its abundant renewable energy resources and strategic geographical location to export to Mediterranean countries through the Suez Canal. It is also well-suited to Europe's plans to import 10 million tons of green hydrogen by 2030. In 2023, Scatec reached a total annual production of 4 728 MW capacity in projects in operation, under construction or reaching FID, including projects for solar, hydro and wind power generation. The Norwegian company is currently targeting USD 50–70 million (NOK 500-750 million) of annual equity investments in renewable energy.

The project is expected to create significant employment opportunities during both the construction and operational phases, contributing to local economic development. Approximately 1 250 jobs are anticipated during construction and up to 80 jobs during the operation and maintenance phase.

By producing green ammonia, the project aims to strengthen Europe's energy security while reducing emissions. The mitigated CO_2 emissions via green ammonia imports would be equivalent to the annual emissions of 62 000 cars. The project marks a significant ramp-up in the European green ammonia market. Based on EU's Hydrogen Strategy, the Egypt Green Hydrogen project is expected to contribute to its 2030 import target of 10 million tons of green hydrogen, as well as to Germany's green ammonia supply, providing 10% of annual German ammonia production.

Governance

The project is led by Egypt Green Hydrogen S.A.E, a consortium formed by Scatec ASA, Fertiglobe, Orascom Construction, the Sovereign Fund of Egypt, and the Egyptian Electricity Transmission Company.

- Scatec is a Norwegian company specialised in renewable energy generation. It is the lead developer and majority sponsor of Egypt Green Hydrogen. The company will provide Engineering, Procurement and Construction (EPC) services in partnership with Orascom Construction, and will offer Operations & Management and Asset Management services for the project, working alongside key technology providers and project partners.
- Fertiglobe is the largest producer of nitrogen fertilisers in the Middle East and North Africa region, and a pioneer in sustainable ammonia. It operates in Egypt under its subsidiary, Egyptian Fertilizer Company, that will lead the production and trade of green ammonia through Fertiglobe International Trading.
- Orascom Construction: is a global engineering and construction contractor primarily focused on infrastructure, industrial and high-end commercial projects in the Middle East, Africa, and the United States. Orascom Construction is expected to execute the local works for the ammonia production facility, using state-of-the-art project technology and Egyptian engineers.
- The Sovereign Fund of Egypt provides investment in clean energy projects to support Egypt's roadmap towards zero emission targets. The Fund will provide financial support to the Egypt Green Hydrogen project throughout the construction and operations phases.
- Egyptian Electricity Transmission Company is a state-owned company for electrical power generation, transmission and distribution in Egypt. The company will be used for the transmission of electricity to the production site through Egypt's national power grid.

Business Model

The project has set a net product price of EUR 811 per tonne of ammonia and a total price of EUR 1000 per tonne of ammonia (including in addition transport and trading costs). The Contract-for-Difference approach provides an opportunity for Scatec to sell green ammonia at a lower price of supply and highest price of demand. Hintco will compensate the difference between supply and demand prices. Therefore, this mechanism will help to reduce the price, create investment certainty as well as the risks hindering the early-stage green hydrogen market. The 7-year auction will be timely until the market develops sufficiently and trading in hydrogen and hydrogen derivatives can take place via conventional market participants and platforms.

Egypt's green hydrogen production to replace grey hydrogen production is currently not economically viable. Yet, mechanisms that support low-carbon product development, such as EU's carbon border adjustment mechanism, can incentivise investors' appetite for renewable products and provide opportunities for Egypt to continue to develop and expand its hydrogen trade with the EU. The H2Global auction provides the financial support needed for Egypt to produce and trade green hydrogen/ammonia to international markets at competitive costs, and become a regional green hydrogen hub.

Currently, the project has secured offtake and is very likely to reach financial close in 2025, yet construction start still requires final governmental approval processes and completion of project finance processes.

Enabling Market Conditions

Egypt is well-positioned as a producer and exporter of green hydrogen and ammonia. Egypt has been experiencing a rapid increase of energy demand and expansion of renewable energy capacity, with a shared of renewables of 12% in total power generation in 2020/2021. The expansion of renewables accompanies the development of initiatives for green hydrogen development. Egypt holds great potential to develop a hydrogen economy, based on great capacity of renewable energy generation, access to water, and strategic locations with geographical proximity to Europe to trade the final product.

Public and governmental support plays a key role in the development of the hydrogen industry. The Egyptian Government has established a regulatory and institutional framework for green hydrogen deployment, including (Cabinet Decrees No. 981 of 2022, and No. 104 of 2022) and a law (Law No. 2 of 2024), along with different incentive policies and measures. The Green Hydrogen Incentives Law, for instance, provides significant tax incentives for new green hydrogen and derivatives projects in Egypt, including tax credits of 33-55% and tax exemptions. Recently, the Government of Egypt has published the National Low Carbon Hydrogen Strategy, which sets the target to produce 9.2 Mt of green hydrogen per year by 2040 (3.6Mt for domestic consumption and 5.6 Mt for export), devoting USD 60 billion of investment.

Additionally, the project has received technical assistance and financial support, which has helped to partially mitigate offtake risks and ensure project bankability. These includes the long-term offtake agreement with H2Global, as well as the feasibility study and guarantee provided by the European Bank for Reconstruction and Development (EBRD).

Financing

The project primarily relies on public and private financing, with significant investments from European stakeholders. While specific details are not provided, the consortium's partners cover a significant part of the project's investment requirements. Additionally, international development institutions and multilateral banks, have committed to provide financing for the project, including the European Bank for Reconstruction and Development (EBRD), with a USD 80 million equity investment, and the United States International Development Finance Corporation (DFC), that will invest USD 5 million in the project. Other investors include KfW, the European Investment Bank (EIB) and British International Investment (BII). The H2Global auction, with an additional USD 443 million into the initiative, is expected to play a key role in lowering the production costs and attracting further international investments. The project is likely to reach financial close by half of 2025.

Lessons Learnt

Long-term financial support: Facilitating access to financing mechanisms that support project's development in the long run is key to accelerate its implementation and mitigate risks. The H2Global auction secures long-term (7 years in the case of Scatec) purchase contracts on the supply side and short-term (1 year) sales contracts on the demand side, thereby ensuring stable prices and mitigating offtake risks.

Infrastructure and logistics: taking advantage of Egypt's existing infrastructure, including the Port of Ein El Sukhna and Egypt's national power grid for electricity transmission is crucial to make the project operable.

Strong commitment: The Government of Egypt's regulatory and financial support of green hydrogen economy, combined with the strong interest and commitment from the consortium's partners, will be critical for the successful implementation of the Egypt Green Hydrogen project.

Case study 3 – HyDuqm / Engie, POSCO Holdings

Figure A D.3. Signing ceremony for the green hydrogen project in Oman on June 21, 2023

Source: Case study documentation

Table A D.3. Key indicators of HyDuqm

Indicator	Company / Project
Value Chain step / Application	Clean hydrogen and ammonia production for decarbonisation of power and steel industries
Country	Oman
Status	Feasibility study, currently under industrial design
Production route & type of renewable	Dedicated renewables (onshore wind, solar PV), electrolysis, battery storage, ammonia conversion facility, hydrogen and ammonia storage facilities
Key project metrics (RE capacity / Electrolyser capacity / Ammonia Production / etc.)	Renewable power capacity: 5.25 GW Electrolyser capacity: 2.5 GW Ammonia production volume: 1.2 Mt/year by 2030
Hydrogen production (kt/y)	200 kt (for ammonia production)
Start-up date	Construction starts by 2027 First production and exports by 2030
Amount	USD 7 billion

Source: Authors based on case study documentation

Basic description

HyDuqm hydrogen project (Engoie, 2023[4]), carried out by a consortium led by POSCO Holdings and ENGIE, is planned in Duqm, a port town in east-central Oman. The project aims to develop 5.25 GW of solar and wind capacity, integrated with battery energy storage systems (BESS), and will produce approximately 200 kilotonnes (kt) per year of clean hydrogen (see Figure 1). This hydrogen will feed into a clean ammonia production facility with a capacity of 1.2 million tonnes per annum (Mt/year) by 2030, targeting exports to South Korea, for the purpose of decarbonising power assets in Korea, while local industrial use of hydrogen in Oman in the steel sector is envisioned as an additional business case. The total investment is estimated at USD 7 billion, with construction starting in 2027 and the first exports expected in 2030. The project is currently under industrial design process, with the feasibility studies ongoing.

Figure A D.4. HyDuqm project description

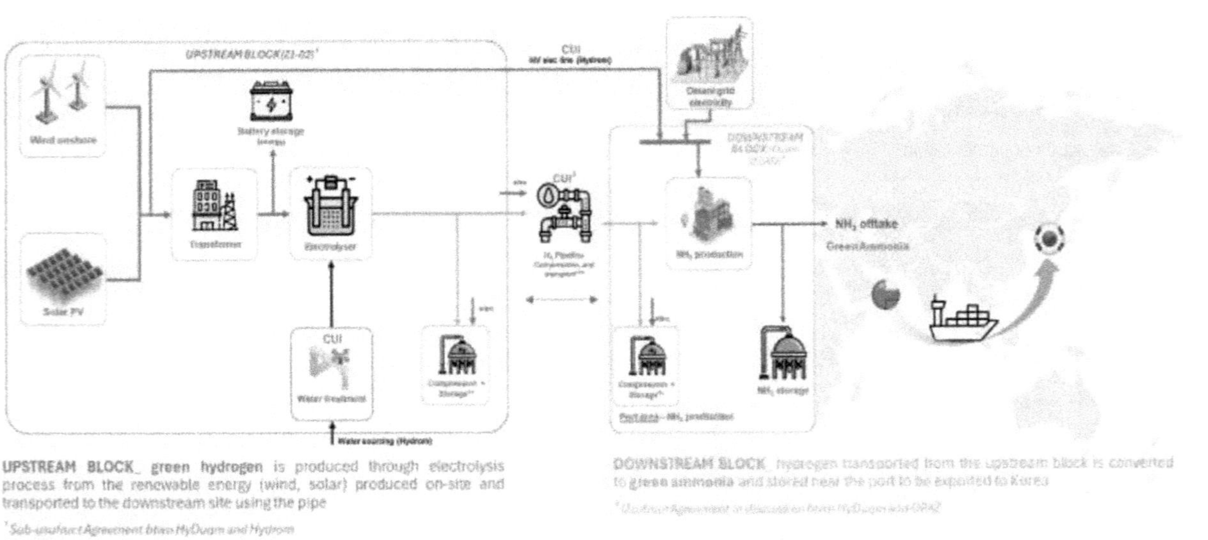

Source: Case study documentation

Project Rationale

This project supports multiple objectives, representing the carbon neutrality ambition of the project sponsors and their respective countries, i.e. South Korea, France and Thailand. In addition, it aligns with Oman's goal to become a leading hydrogen exporter and achieve net-zero carbon emissions by 2050, contributing to energy diversification and economic development.

For South Korea, the project facilitates its decarbonisation targets, including a 40% carbon reduction by 2030. The venture is also set to create substantial trade opportunities, focusing on clean ammonia exports, which are key to decarbonising industries such as generation of carbon neutral electricity and steel manufacturing. Notably, POSCO Holdings[1] plans to achieve net zero by 2050, according to its 2050 Carbon Neutrality Roadmap. To do that, POSCO aims to complete the development of commercial HyREX technology by 2030, and ultimately to ensure its steelmaking process does not generate GHG emissions. The generation assets owned by Korea Electric Power Corporation subsidiaries such as Korea East-West Power Company and Korea Southern Power Company are subject to decarbonisation through co-firing.

France is propelling an important part of the European Union's decarbonisation plan. ENGIE Group[2], with 115 GW power generation capacity, targets to achieve net zero carbon by 2045, with the interim goal of achieving 66% reduction in its scope 1 production and energy consumption to reach 110 grammes of CO_2 per kWh by 2030 compared to 2017. The group continues to commit to its "well below 2° SBTi certified target. Hydrogen is envisioned to take a critical role in the transformation, with 4 GW electrolyser capacity targeted by 2030.

Thailand pledged carbon neutrality by 2050 and net zero GHG emissions by 2065. In preparation for energy transition, Thai's PTT Exploration and Production Public Company Ltd[3] (PTTEP) has diversified into new businesses involving new forms of energy, advanced technology and decarbonization while emphasising on carbon emissions reduction. PTTEP aims to reach Net Zero Greenhouse Gas Emissions by 2050, through its EP Net Zero 2050 pathway (PTTEP, n.d.[5]).

Governance

The governance structure of the HyDuqm project is built on an usufruct grant model, where Oman's government, via Hydrom (Hydrom, n.d.[6])[4], the orchestrator of Omans Green Hydrogen Strategy execution, and administrator of renewable hydrogen projects in Oman, acts as the grantor of the land rights, granting usufruct and development rights to developers; in line with Royal Decree 10/2023, with the Ministry of Energy and Minerals serving as the regulator and policy maker; yet Hydrom does not hold equity in the project's Special Purpose Vehicle (SPV). The SPV is incorporated by POSCO Holdings and ENGIE as co-lead developers of the project. Samsung E&A[5], FutureTech Energy Ventures (PTTEP subsidiary), Korea East-West Power Co. (EWP), and Korea Southern Power co. (KOSPO) participate as direct and indirect project sponsors. As majority offtake is to be ensured by the Korean sponsors in the partnership, majority shareholding is also owned amongst the Korean sponsors. Each project sponsor leveraging its capabilities associated with hydrogen, contributes to respective roles and responsibilities of the various development activities. The consortium will develop the project for the first seven years and then operate the plants for the following 40 years.

Business Model

The project's business model leverages competitive renewable energy sources (solar and wind) to produce clean hydrogen, which is converted into ammonia. Clean ammonia has a high export value and is deemed to be a more commercially viable transportable form of hydrogen as of today's technology. The Levelised Cost of Hydrogen (LCOH) will depend heavily on achieving economies of scale, but challenges remain, such as the high initial capital costs and competition from the cheaper, fossil-based hydrogen production methods.

Enabling Market Conditions

Building on its LNG export expertise, Oman is actively developing hydrogen export capabilities. In 2021, the Ministry of Energy and Minerals launched the National Hydrogen Alliance (Hy-Fly), which unites 15 public and private entities to advance hydrogen production, transport, and utilisation. Oman's green hydrogen strategy, unveiled in October 2022, targets 1 to 1.5 Mt of production by 2030, rising to 7.5 to 8.5 Mt by 2050. This plan requires a cumulative investment of approximately USD 140 billion by 2050.

The government has designated Duqm, Dhofar, and Al-Jazir as hydrogen project hubs, with approximately 50 000 km² of land set aside. This area could produce 25 Mt of hydrogen annually for export to Europe and Asia. Hydrogen Oman (Hydrom) was established to manage large-scale projects, land auctions, and shared infrastructure coordination. In November 2022, Oman launched Phase A auction, awarding eight projects worth USD 49 billion, and supporting 34.8 GW of Renewables' capacity in both Al Wusta and Dhofar governorates. These projects will operate for 47 years, including 7 years of development. Oman is on course to become a major hydrogen exporter, potentially accounting for 61% of the Middle East's exports by 2030, primarily as ammonia due to its suitability for export via sea, currently as per IEA report.

The HyDuqm project is aiming for long term offtake agreements. Among the consortium members, POSCO Holdings, Samsung E&A, KOSPO, and EWP are considering offtake in line with their respective carbon neutrality plans. HyDuqm is also looking at the local industry in Oman, the EU, and Japan as alternative markets. Tax incentives and trade agreements between Oman and South Korea further support the project.

Financing

The project financing of USD 7 billion involves a mix of equity from the project sponsors and non-recourse debt financing. While specific details on the equity-debt ratio or the participation of development finance institutions are not yet fully disclosed, such large-scale infrastructure projects often include a combination of private and public funding. The key to achieving the financial closure of the project will depend on successful de-risking of the project and balanced risk allocation approach amongst the stakeholders.

Lessons Learnt

One key takeaway from this project is the importance of aligning energy projects with both national and international sustainability goals. The collaborative approach between Oman, South Korea, and EU member states, leveraging expertise from multiple countries, can serve as a model for other nations looking to develop large-scale hydrogen infrastructure. The project also highlights the necessity of securing government support for large-scale direct investment, investment in common infrastructure in line with project's schedule and long-term offtake agreements to ensure economic viability.

Case study 4 – Karnataka project / JSW Group

Table A D.4. Key indicators of JSW Group's Karnataka project

Indicator	Company / Project
Value Chain step / Application	Production / Renewable hydrogen and oxygen for steelmaking
Country	India
Status	Under construction: engineering and construction activities in progress
Production route & type of renewable	Solar PV, onshore wind + alkaline electrolysis
Key project metrics (RE capacity / Electrolyser capacity / Ammonia Production / etc.)	Renewable power capacity: 27 MW of RE power dedicated to clean hydrogen project out of total 965 MW RE capacity dedicated to green steel project (695 MW wind + 270 MW solar power) Electrolyser capacity: 25 MW
Hydrogen production (kt/y)	3.8 kt/y
Start-up date	2025
Amount	USD 24 million (excluding RE)

Source: Authors based on case study documentation

Basic description

JSW Energy's Clean Hydrogen project aims to produce renewable hydrogen for steelmaking (JSW, n.d.[7]). The company has partnered with JSW Steel for an offtake commitment, and the plant will be developed within its Vijayanagar energy complex, in Karnataka state. The project is expected to be commissioned by the fourth quarter of fiscal year 2024 – 2025 (March 2025).

The project focuses on producing renewable hydrogen via electrolysis, using a mix of renewable energy sources from JSW's existing renewable energy assets in Karnataka, which include 695 MW of wind power and 270 MW solar power. Clean hydrogen will be produced within the JSW energy complex and delivered via pipelines to both the direct iron reduction (DRI) plant and the blast furnace at JSW Steel's Vijayanagar facility. It will be blended with COREX gas and used in the DRI process, replacing fossil fuels such as coal and natural gas. In the long term, the company plans to expand its renewable hydrogen sales to other industries, including refining, fertilisers, and transportation.

The JSW Energy Clean Hydrogen project will support steel production at the Vijayanagar plant, with a DRI capacity of 1.2 million tonnes per annum. The use of renewable hydrogen is projected to result in the production of 50-60 thousand tonnes per annum of green steel. The project will generate 3.8 kilotonnes of renewable hydrogen annually, using approximately 27 MW of round-the-clock renewable energy (RTC-RE) and 25 MW alkaline electrolyser. To further expand hydrogen supply, JSW Energy has signed a Memorandum of Understanding (MoU) with JSW Steel to provide an additional 90 kilotonnes per year by 2030, contributing to reducing the carbon footprint of the steelmaking process.

Project Rationale

Key market drivers for JSW Energy's Clean Hydrogen project include the growing demand for green steel, driven by global decarbonisation efforts and the shift towards sustainable industrial practices. Potential customers are likely to come from industries with high carbon reduction targets, particularly in Europe, where green steel commands a premium due to stringent regulations and corporate sustainability goals. The project, as a pilot initiative, aims to strategically position JSW in the emerging green steel market, allowing the company to develop expertise in renewable hydrogen utilisation across various steelmaking processes. This long-term vision not only targets domestic demand but also opens potential revenue streams in international markets where green steel can attract a higher price premium.

Governance

The JSW Energy is a leading power company in India at the forefront of the energy transition by investing in renewable hydrogen initiatives. The company is part of JSW Group, a diversified conglomerate focused on steel, energy, infrastructure, cement, among other industries. In line with India's ambitious goal to achieve net-zero emissions by 2070, JSW Energy has made significant strides in renewable energy, particularly in the State of Karnataka.

JSW Steel, another listed company of the JSW Group, focuses on steel production, with an annual capacity of 28 million tonnes per annum. Vijayanagar is India's largest steel plant, with a total production capacity of 12 million tonnes per annum.

Business Model

The project targets a competitive Levelised Cost of Hydrogen (LCOH) by leveraging abundant and low-cost renewable energy resources. The anticipated LCOH for renewable hydrogen is approximately USD 3.5 to 4.0 per kilogramme, supported by electricity costs in the range of USD 4 to 4.25 cents per kWh. These cost efficiencies are key to making the project economically viable while contributing to the overall reduction in carbon emissions in the steelmaking process.

The strategic location of the JSW Clean Hydrogen project in Karnataka, a state with abundant solar and wind resources, enhances its economic viability. The region's falling renewable energy costs make renewable hydrogen production more competitive compared to conventional methods. By utilising local renewable energy capacity and existing infrastructure and storage at the Karnataka plant, the project is positioned to optimise costs and improve overall competitiveness in hydrogen production.

Despite the significant potential of JSW Energy's Clean Hydrogen project, several viability barriers exist. One major challenge is the high cost of round-the-clock renewable energy (RTC), which directly impacts hydrogen production costs. Additionally, starting production on a small scale limits the project's financial viability, as it misses out on economies of scale that could reduce unit costs. Another key barrier is the steelmaking process itself, which has a turndown constraint of approximately 50%. This requires incremental infrastructure development to ensure sufficient renewable hydrogen supply to meet the minimum process requirements. Scaling up production to meet industrial demands will further necessitate substantial investment in infrastructure.

Enabling Market Conditions

The Government of India is actively supporting the development of renewable hydrogen through policy support and subsidies. As part of this strategy, the Government launched in 2023 its National Green Hydrogen Mission to drive the production and use of clean hydrogen, supported by an USD 2.4 billion (INR 19 744 crore) budget. With a target of 5 Mt of clean hydrogen annual production by 2030, the Mission will support clean hydrogen demand creation, cost-effective production and use in various sectors, including steel.

As part of the Mission, India launched two auctions in 2023: (i) the first one offers subsidies for up to 1.5 GW of electrolyser manufacturing capacity, with a total envelope of USD 541 million (INR 4 440 crore); (ii) the second one supporting 450 kt per annum of clean hydrogen capacity for 3 years, offering up to USD 0.60/kg subsidy. In 2024, a second tranche of auctions was launched, offering similar subsidies for electrolyser manufacturing and clean hydrogen production, as well as further subsidies for clean hydrogen hubs. In early 2024, JSW Neo Energy, a subsidiary of JSW Energy, was among the auction winners, with the Production-Linked Incentive (PLI) corresponding to this project.

Financing

The JSW Energy Clean Hydrogen project is financed through a project financing structure, incorporating both debt and equity components. This approach allows the project to leverage external funding while managing financial risks associated with large-scale infrastructure investments. No concessional finance instruments have been reported as part of the financing structure, indicating that the project relies on conventional debt and equity sources.

Lessons Learnt

The JSW Energy Clean Hydrogen project provides several key lessons. First, government support is critical to its success, with incentives, subsidies, and regulatory backing under India's National Hydrogen Mission helping to reduce costs and improve financial viability. Additionally, as India seeks to expand its clean hydrogen applications, particularly with the decreasing cost of renewable energy, there is growing potential for hydrogen use in industries like transportation, steel, cement, fertilisers, chemicals, and refining. By positioning itself through this project, JSW Energy can become a major supplier of clean hydrogen to these sectors. Finally, as an early investor in renewable hydrogen, JSW Energy has the first-mover advantage, allowing it to establish partnerships, capture market share, and play a key role in shaping regulatory and operational standards in India's emerging hydrogen sector.

Case study 5 – Lyhfe Grand Canal du Havre / Lyhfe

Figure A D.5. Lhyfe Green Horizon project, artist view

Source: Case study documentation

Table A D.5. Key indicators of Lhyfe

Indicators	Company / Project
Value Chain step / Application	Production / Renewable hydrogen for industry and mobility
Country	France
Status	Development at pre-FID stage: public grant secured, land identified, construction and environmental permit submitted, electrical connection secured
Production route & type of renewable	Water electrolysis through renewable electricity via PPA and grid electricity
Key project metrics (RE capacity / Electrolyser capacity / Ammonia Production / etc.)	Renewable power consumption: 750 GWh/y Electrolyser capacity: 100 MW
Hydrogen production (kt/y)	12 kt/y
Start-up date	Phase 1: 2025 beginning of construction Phase 2: 2028 beginning of operations
Amount	estimated at EUR 250 million

Source: Authors based on case study documentation

Basic description

The Lhyfe Green Horizon project develops a clean hydrogen production facility in the industrial port area at Gonfreville-l'Orcher, near Le Havre, France (Lhyfe, n.d.[8]). Qualified as an Important Project of Common European Interest by EU and supported by a grant of up to EUR 149 million from the French government, approved by the EU, the project plans to produce 34 tonnes of hydrogen per day using a 100 MW electrolyser. The facility will occupy nearly 2.8 hectares in Havre's industrial port area, which counts on its premises multiple industrial actors including Yara and Total. The project is expected to be operational by 2028 and will contribute significantly to the decarbonisation of the area.

Project Development Stages:

- Development: currently in progress, involving detailed studies, consultations, and engineering plans; a significant public grant from the French government, approved by the EU, is secured; a land plot is identified; construction and environmental permit are submitted; electrical connection is secured.
- Construction: expected to start post-environmental authorisation in 2025, including site preparation, foundation work, and equipment installation.
- Operation: scheduled to start in 2028, with continuous monitoring and maintenance to ensure optimal performance.

Project Rationale

The project is driven by several factors. Firstly, it addresses the growing market demand for clean energy solutions to decarbonise various industries, including ammonia production. The construction, operation and maintenance of the Green Horizon production unit will create 15 direct jobs, 100% of which will be dedicated to the project, and will safeguard around 250 direct and indirect jobs (project development, equipment and electricity supply, studies, construction, operation and maintenance, etc.). Environmentally, it aims to reduce CO_2 emissions by over 90 000 tonnes annually by supplying locally produced clean hydrogen to nearby industries. Additionally, the project strengthens leading Lhyfe's position in clean hydrogen production in France.

Governance

Lhyfe leads the project, collaborating with public partners, including national and European authorities, as well as with private industrial partners. This public-private partnership is essential for the project's success, ensuring financial support and alignment with industry decarbonisation objectives.

Business Model

The business model for the Lhyfe Green Horizon project focuses on achieving a competitive Levelised Cost of Hydrogen (LCOH) through economies of scale and through using competitive renewable electricity secured via dedicated Power Purchase Agreements (PPA). Viability challenge linked to a high initial capital expenditure (CAPEX) is addressed by securing an important subsidy from the French government, approved by the EU. Economic viability is ensured by using renewable energy and advanced electrolysis technology to produce cost-effective clean hydrogen compared to fossil fuel-based alternatives.

Enabling Market Conditions

Supportive measures for the Lhyfe Green Horizon project include government grants of up to EUR 149 million from the French government, approved by the European Commission under the third wave of IPCEI (Important Projects of Common European Interest) for hydrogen. Offtake agreements are under discussion with potential industrial buyers, securing a stable market for the hydrogen produced and ensuring long-term revenue. Additionally, potential tax incentives and relief measures are being considered to improve the project's economic feasibility.

Financing

The financing structure is not disclosed, yet includes a mix of public and private funds. For the public financing, the project benefits from a substantial grant of up to EUR 149 million from the French government. As for private investment, additional funding is considered from private investors and industrial partners. While specific equity/debt ratios are not disclosed, the financing mix is designed to balance risk and return effectively as well as to reduce the project's weighted average cost of capital (WACC). Strategies for managing financial structure and mitigating risks are to be developed in order to ensure the project's financial stability.

Lessons Learnt

Key lessons from the Lhyfe Green Horizon project include the importance of robust public-private partnerships and state support as well as the integration of adapted technologies at scale with hydrogen production. Additionally, a thoughtful choice of location and proximity to consumers minimises transportation costs and enhances economic and environmental efficiency. This model can be replicated in other regions and countries to achieve scalable and sustainable energy solutions for local industries decarbonisation.

Case study 6 - Clean H_2 Infra Fund / Hy24

Table A D.6. Key indicators of the Clean H_2 Infra Fund

Indicator	Instrument
Type of instrument	Financing
Instrument	Private equity (equity and quasi equity investments)
Eligible step(s) of the value chain / technologies	Infrastructure over the whole low-carbon hydrogen value chain: from upstream projects like renewable and low-carbon hydrogen production, to downstream projects like captive fleet and refuelling stations
Eligible countries	Europe, North America, Asia Pacific, MENA
Status	Completed
Amount (USD)	Available: 2 billion Committed: ~0.7 billion
Date of implementation	Phase 1: 2021 (creation year) Phase 2: ~2035 (estimated end year for the closed end fund)

Source: Authors based on case study documentation

Instrument description – Theoretical Concept

Hy24 is a joint venture between Ardian, a leading private investment house, with EUR 164 billion under management, and FiveT Hydrogen, a clean hydrogen investment platform (Hy24, n.d.[9]). Hy24 has brought together an ecosystem of over 50 industrial and financial players - including the first supporters such as Air Liquide, VINCI Concessions, Total Energies, Plug, Schaeffler and Chart Industries - all committed to supporting the advent of the low-carbon hydrogen economy, tackling firstly the infrastructures challenge. The investment scope covers the whole low-carbon hydrogen value chain from upstream projects like renewable and low-carbon hydrogen production, to downstream projects like captive fleet and refuelling stations. The fund objective is to support the decarbonisation of hard-to-abate industries like chemicals and steel production, mobility and transport sectors including maritime and aviation via e-fuels (sustainable aviation fuels (SAF), e-methanol), while being aligned with the requirements of the article 9 of the Sustainable Finance Disclosure Regulation (SFDR) regulation and the EU taxonomy.

The platform primarily mobilises capital through its EUR 2 billion Clean H_2 Infra Fund, targeting large-scale hydrogen projects and infrastructures. The fund collected investments from industrial companies, institutional investors, pensions funds and sovereign funds, distributing the capital to hydrogen infrastructure projects that meet specific sustainability (according to the article 9 of the SFDR regulation) and criteria like the project geography, competitive access to renewable resources, team expertise and background and offtakers base. Hy24 aims to mobilise up to EUR 20 billion of investment capacity over the next six years using its financial power by leveraging on debt, subsidies and co-investments. Hy24 aims mainly for minority investments, with an average investment ticket of EUR 100 million, and a total portfolio of around 20 projects.

Governance/Organisation and Implementation

Hy24 operates as a general partner with a dedicated team of 45 collaborators. The implementation process includes:

- Project Selection: Rigorous evaluation of projects based on sustainability, feasibility, profitability and potential impact.
- Investment Committees: Decision-making bodies ensure investments align with strategic objectives and envisioned financial performance.

- Monitoring and Support: Ongoing oversight and technical support to ensure successful project execution, development and business expansion.

Key Challenges and Advantages

Challenges:

- Nascent market: The clean hydrogen market is still developing, embedding risks related to technological advancements, timely market adoption at scale and regulation uncertainties. Moreover, varying regulations and standards across countries can complicate project implementation and project replicability.
- Infrastructure availability: The timeline of infrastructure availability, notably the EU H2 backbone project, is needed to be clarified in the near future to make final investment decisions (FID) on large EU projects.

Advantages:

- Significant Capital Mobilisation: The EUR 2 billion fund provides substantial financial resources to support large-scale hydrogen projects.
- Finance-Industry Partnership: By involving both finance and industry actors, Hy24 leverages a broad base of industrial expertise and financial resources.
- Focus on Sustainability: The platform ensures that investments align with the standards of the article 9 of the SFDR regulation and the European taxonomy.

Supported Projects Description

Hy24's EUR 2 billion Clean H_2 Infra Fund is dedicated to deploying important low-carbon hydrogen infrastructures. From its inception in 2021 until summer 2024, Hy24 has committed around EUR 700 million through private equity (both equity and quasi equity) investments in 8 companies:

- HysetCo - France, hydrogen integrated offer of hydrogen infrastructures (hydrogen refuelling stations) and mobility solutions for professionals, mainly taxi operators, aiming to decarbonize the intensive urban mobility. Total investment round is of EUR 200 million led by Hy24 alongside RAISE Impact and Eiffel Investment Group, Hy24 became the main shareholder of the company.
- InterContinental Energy - Australia and Oman, renewable hydrogen and its derivatives production at scale. Joint equity investment of USD 115 million alongside GIC, a global long-term investor established in 1981 to manage Singapore's reserves.
- Elyse Energy - France and Spain, e-fuels production to support e-methanol and SAF projects in France and Spain aiming to decarbonize industrial, maritime and aviation sectors. Financing transaction (non-disclosed amount) signed with Hy24 and Mirova.
- Stegra (previously H2 Green Steel) - Sweden, building the most advanced large-scale, green steel plant in the world in Boden, Sweden, with Europe's largest electrolyser. Hy24 was lead investor in the EUR 1.5 billion private equity funding round closed in 2023 with the participation of other investors Altor, GIC and Just Climate.
- H2 MOBILITY - Germany, development of hydrogen refuelling stations network to decarbonize intensive and heavy mobility in urban areas. EUR 110 million investment round, led by Hy24 alongside significant investments from existing industrial shareholders. Next to the Hy24 fund, Air Liquide, Daimler Truck, Hyundai, Linde, OMV, Shell, and Total Energies contributed to the capital raise.

- Enagas Renovable - Spain, production of green hydrogen and biomethane. Hy24 signed an agreement with Enagás, the Spanish energy infrastructure company, to become a shareholder in Enagás Renovable (30%) to accelerate the development of its leading renewable-to-gas platform.
- Everfuel - Denmark, making green hydrogen for industry and heavy-duty mobility, and developing and operating large-scale hydrogen production projects to offer competitive hydrogen supply and fueling solutions. A Joint Venture (JV) between Everfuel (51%) and Hy24 (49%) brings EUR 200 million in equity. The JV's first investment was to acquire the HySynergy Phase 1 20 MW green hydrogen production plant in Fredericia, Denmark. The JV will further benefit from Everfuel's pipeline of hydrogen production projects as they are matured to final investment decision (FID) and transferred to the JV subject to predefined criteria.
- Hy2gen - France, Germany, Canada, Norway, and the United States, green hydrogen and e-fuels production to decarbonize maritime, ground transport, aviation and maritime applications. Hy24, Mirova, CDPQ and Technip Energies jointly made a EUR 200 million investment.

Total investment size including co-investors typically ranges from tens to hundreds of millions of euros, depending on the project's scale and scope, with a Hy24 average investment ticket size of around EUR 100 million.

Impact of the Solution on the Projects

Advantages vs. Conventional Financing:

- Dedicated Hydrogen Focus: Unlike conventional financing, Hy24 is specifically tailored for hydrogen projects, providing targeted industrial expertise and important financial resources.
- Venture to infrastructure approach: Hy24 supports globally the developers of hydrogen projects and equipment providers who are advanced in the value chain, and offer an important potential for industrialization.
- Risk Mitigation: Private investments in today's early market help alleviate the risk notably thanks to Hy24 bringing other investors to mutualize risk and making investments more attractive to private and institutional investors and debt providers.
- Long-term Commitment: The fund's substantial size, patient infra-like capital and strategic focus on hydrogen infrastructures ensure long-term support for project development at scale.

Impact on Business Model or Access to Finance:

- Enhanced Access to Capital: Projects gain easier access to significant funding, which might be challenging through traditional financing routes and get a possibility to find further support as their needs grow, either with the fund following-on on its initial investment or with Hy24 leveraging its capability to funnel external investments.
- Increased Credibility: Backing by a dedicated hydrogen fund enhances project credibility and attracts additional private investors and facilitates debt leverage.
- Innovative Financing Structures: Hy24 offers flexible financing solutions, including equity investments, quasi equity investments (such as convertible bonds), and hybrid instruments enabling fair risk and profit sharing for employees, founders and investors at different stages and maturity of a wide range of company types.

Improving Enabling Conditions:

- Policy Advocacy: Hy24 engages with policy makers via global hydrogen associations such Hydrogen Council and national hydrogen associations to facilitate favourable regulatory frameworks.

- Accelerating Hydrogen Market: Today's investment in hydrogen projects at scale accelerates global hydrogen market development.
- Stakeholder Collaboration: Facilitating partnerships and co-investments across the hydrogen value chain enhances project viability and scalability.

Lessons Learnt and Replicability

Hy24 has effectively mobilised a significant amount of private capital and engaged a diverse set of stakeholders, demonstrating the feasibility of large-scale hydrogen investment platforms today. The collaborative approach and robust governance model are crucial to its success. Additionally, having a team fully dedicated to clean hydrogen creates an alignment in the understanding of risk and long-term strategic value of projects.

While Hy24 has streamlined the investment process, the complex nature of hydrogen projects and evolving regulation implies that fund disbursement timelines can still be long. However, the platform's support has generally accelerated project timelines compared to conventional financing routes notably thanks to the support it brings in the execution and development of projects.

The involvement of industrial, private, institutional and public-backed funds has been instrumental in attracting private capital, reducing perceived risks, and enhancing investor confidence. Available country and region level public funding, often in the form of CAPEX and OPEX subsidies, serves as a catalyst for larger private investments with public funding being a direct attractor for any private funding including from the fund.

Hy24 employs adaptive equity and quasi equity investment approaches as well as co-investment strategies, to de-risk and ensure the efficient use and disbursement of funds. These instruments have successfully mitigated risks for co-investors and debt providers and facilitated project financing.

Conditions for replicability of the Hy24 model include establishing strong partnerships that ensure collaboration and strategic alignment between government, industrial, and private financial actors. Creating dedicated funding mechanisms is essential, with substantial, focused investment funds supported by industrial expertise and private equity mobilisation. Developing supportive regulatory frameworks is critical, involving long-term policies that address clean hydrogen production and usage, alongside comprehensive regulatory environments. Finally, leveraging specialised industry expertise in hydrogen technologies and project management is necessary to ensure the success and scalability of similar initiatives.

Case study 7 - Foreign Private Capital Mobilisation and Currency Hedging Programme / Inter-American Development Bank and Ministry of Finance of Brazil

Table A D.7. Key indicators of the Foreign Private Capital Mobilisation and Currency Hedging Programme

Indicator	Instrument
Type of instrument	Mixed (de-risking and financing)
Instrument	Loans and credit lines for blended finance, long term foreign exchange liquidity facility, foreign exchange derivatives
Eligible step(s) of the value chain / technologies	Projects aligned with the Ecological Transformation Plan, in the areas of Technological densification of the productive sector; Bioeconomy and agri-food systems, Energy transition, Circular economy, and Infrastructure and adaptation to climate change.
Eligible countries	Brazil
Status	Under implementation
Amount	Planned: USD 3.4 billion initial potential derivatives for hedging provided by IDB Planned: USD 2 billion from IDB + USD 1 billion from WB Disbursed: n/a
Date of implementation	Phase 1: 2023 conceptualisation year Phase 2: 2024 implementation year

Source: Authors based on case study documentation

Instrument description

Initiated in 2023 by the Brazilian Ministry of Finance and the Inter-American Development Bank (IDB),[6] the Foreign Private Capital Mobilisation and Currency Hedging Programme (also called Eco Invest Brazil) is a financial solution platform to reduce foreign exchange risk for investments aligned with socio-environmental principles and climate change adaptation and mitigation in Brazil (IDB, 2024[10]). Eco Invest Brazil, also known as The Brazilian Foreign Private Capital Mobilization and Currency Hedging Programme ("the Programme") under Brazil's National Climate Change Fund, is a sustainable financing platform designed to reduce the cost of capital and attract foreign investments into Brazil's green economy. It leverages blended finance, a long-term foreign exchange (FX) liquidity facility, foreign exchange derivatives, and project structuring to facilitate integrating Brazilian companies into the global financial system, ensuring sustainable and resilient economic growth.

Eco Invest Brazil objectives are to:

1. Foster and incentivise sustainable investments in projects that promote ecological transformation, particularly in the areas of technological advancement, bioeconomy, energy transition, circular economy, green infrastructure, and adaptation;
2. Attract foreign investments in sustainable projects to Brazil;
3. Enable transactions in capital markets to raise funds internationally for companies and investors based in Brazil to finance sustainable projects;
4. Support the development, liquidity, and efficiency of the long-term foreign currency hedging market in Brazil.

To attain those objectives, Eco Invest Brazil has put in place four different solutions, addressing both domestic and foreign companies and investors. The articulation between four solutions and addressed objectives is represented in Table A D.8. The Eco Invest Brazil program aims to create incentives to increase investment in the Brazilian Ecological Transition.

Table A D.8. Instruments of Eco Invest Brazil

Instruments	Description	Objectives addressed
Blended finance (in the form of long-term loans in BRL)	Aims to reduce the cost of capital through blended financing to facilitate integration of Brazilian companies into the global financial system, attract foreign investments, and foster a sustainable and resilient economy	1, 2, 3
Long term foreign exchange liquidity facility (in the form of contingent credit in BRL)	Aims to mitigate challenges faced by companies with foreign currency debt and revenues generated in Brazilian Real (BRL) in cases of material devaluation, allowing for effective cash management and credit enhancements	1, 2
Foreign exchange derivatives (in the form of credit lines in BRL)	Aims to mitigate challenges faced by companies with foreign currency debt and revenues generated in BRL in cases of material devaluation, allowing for effective cash management and credit enhancements	1, 2, 3, 4
Project structuring[1)] (in the form of long-term loans in BRL)	Aims to catalyse the development of large sustainable initiatives in Brazil, bridging the current gap in the nation's green project landscape	1, 2

Note: The project structuring is not an instrument as such yet an important assistance solution. This reimbursable financing is limited to the project preparation covering detailed plan and feasibility analysis stages.
Source: Authors based on case study documentation

Actors Involved:

- Ministry of Finance of Brazil is responsible for economic policy and public finance management, plays a crucial role in defining guidelines and allocating resources;
- Ministry of Environment and Climate Change provides the environmental vision, expertise, and technical depth necessary to align the Eco Invest Brazil program with sustainability and conservation goals;
- Inter-American Development Bank (IDB) 7 is the leading technical partner in the design and operationalisation of the derivatives pipeline and credit lines to be offered, as well as the primary provider of technical assistance for the design and implementation of governance, monitoring, and evaluation of the Eco Invest Brazil programme;
- Central Bank of Brazil, with its expertise in regulating and supervising the financial system, contributes to the financial structuring and economic stability of the transactions. It internalises the derivatives to be obtained by the IDB in the domestic market through accredited financial institutions;
- Financial institutions, commercial and investment banks, national and international, that complement the financing structure by offering various forms of credit and investment for projects, with impact in capital mobilisation.

Financial Flows: Initially, the Eco Invest Brazil platform has the potential to mobilise FX coverage of up to USD 3.4 billion. Financial flows for this FX derivatives pipeline are represented below in Figure A D.6. With the Central Bank, the IDB will support the development, liquidity, and efficiency of the long-term exchange-rate protection market in foreign currency. The IDB will offer Eco Invest Brazil an initial limit of USD 3.4 billion for exchange-rate coverage which may increase over time, the capacity to acquire derivatives for coverage under better conditions, facilitated by its AAA rating, and Treasury services.

Figure A D.6. Financial flows representation for FX derivatives pipeline of USD 3.4 billion

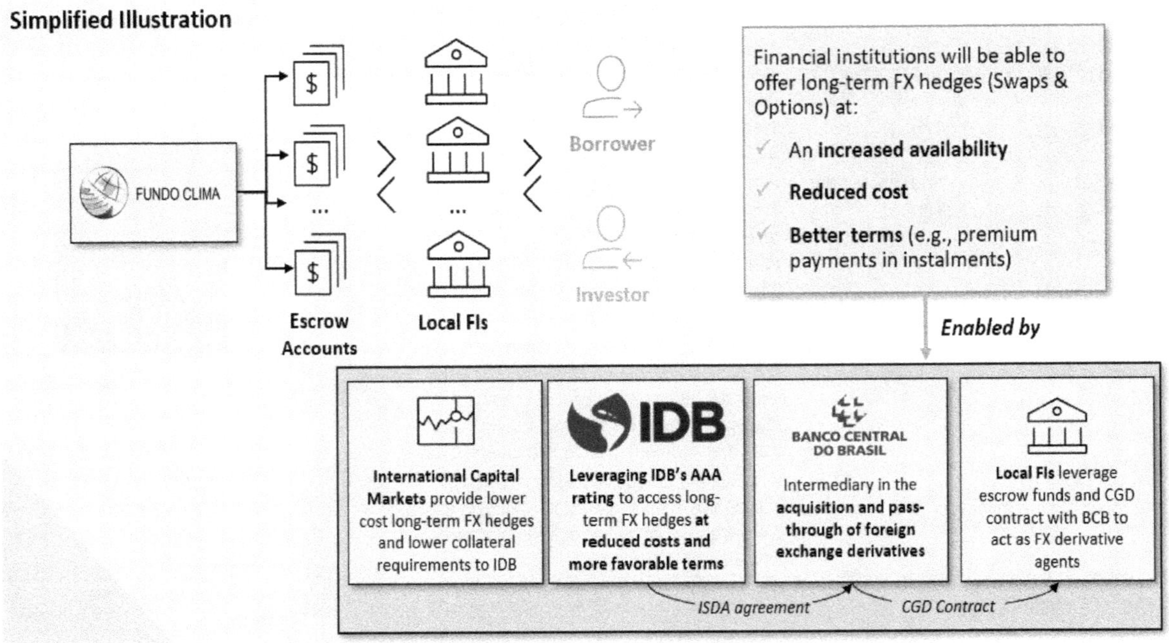

Source: Case study documentation

Moreover, the IDB might provide a USD 2 billion credit line and offer technical assistance to the Brazilian Ministry of Finance in implementing policy reforms associated with Eco Invest Brazil. The articulation of financial flows of this USD 2 billion credit line is represented in Figure A D.7 Figure A D.7. The mentioned amount will be provided through direct support and potentially leveraging additional sources through co-financing and donor mobilisation. The Programme promotes financial, fiscal, and environmental policy reforms on structural changes to the current regulatory framework, adopting new methodologies and institutional mechanisms, and the implementation of financial innovations under the Ecological Transformation Plan of Brazil (ETP).[8] Such reforms imply profound changes to the fiscal, financial, and environmental policies.

Figure A D.7. Financial flows representation for credit line of USD 2 billion

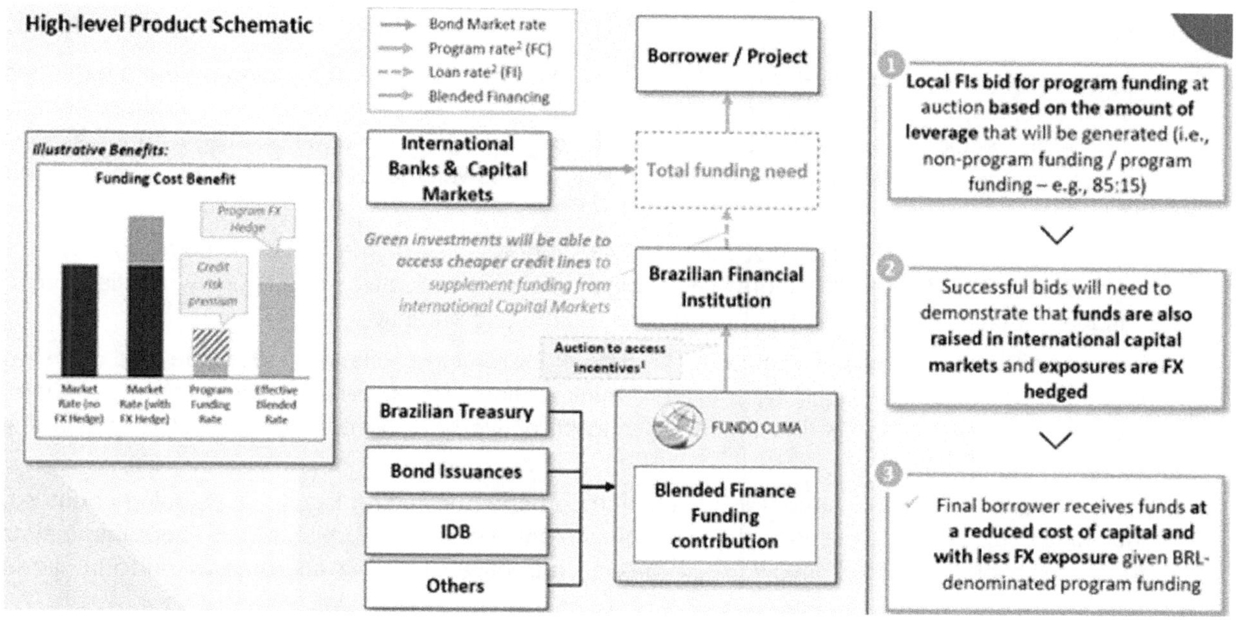

Source: Case study documentation

The World Bank contributes with the financial support of the International Bank for Reconstruction and Development (IBRD) with USD 1 billion. Related actions will be primarily directed towards developing projects dedicated to ecological transformation. This strategic partnership also seeks to mobilise significant financial resources and foster dialogue among various stakeholders, ensuring participants' autonomy in their operations and administration decisions.

Governance/Organisation and Implementation

The Eco Invest Brazil program will be overseen by the Ministry of Finance in collaboration with the Ministry of Environment and Climate Change. The Programme is supported by technical expertise from the IDB, internationally recognized consultants, and an independent verification company. The governance committee, composed of representatives from the Ministry of Finance and the Ministry of Environment and Climate Change, handles responsibilities such as defining the eligibility framework, accrediting implementation partners, and evaluating and approving transactions. Additionally, they will establish monitoring and evaluation indicators, including Key Performance Indicators (KPIs). They will oversee the approval and dissemination of allocation and impact reports.

The National Monetary Council regulates the financial conditions of the credit lines of Eco Invest, and the Ministry of Finance establishes the norms for participation in the Programme, encompassing the qualification and selection process for financial institutions, the allocation limits for resources, and the procedures for accountability and impact evaluation reports. The selection process for financial institutions will be conducted via public calls for proposals, with the National Treasury Secretariat reviewing submissions based on pre-defined criteria. The Executive Committee will homologate the results of the auctions. Transparency is ensured through the publication of selection results and periodic resource allocation reports on the Transparent Treasury website. Independent verification reports will also be regularly published, providing assessment and program improvement recommendations. This structured governance framework ensures accountability and makes the Programme a global model for climate change initiatives.

Challenges and key advantages to Implement the Instrument

Challenges:

- High costs of credit and long-term hedging: The costs associated with hedging for more extended time horizons are high and often prohibitive, making it financially challenging for investors to commit to long-term ecological projects. Blended finance and foreign exchange risk mitigation tools, such as the long-term liquidity facility and derivatives, can lower these costs, making hedging more affordable.
- High volatility of the Brazilian FX market: The high volatility of the Brazilian currency poses a significant risk for foreign investors. The Programme's FX derivatives and liquidity facilities aim to mitigate these risks, making investments more stable and attractive.
- Low liquidity for long-term FX hedges: The market for foreign exchange hedges beyond one year is characterised by low liquidity, with very minimal liquidity for periods longer than five years. Introducing a long-term FX liquidity facility and attractive hedging options can help address this issue.
- Low share of private investment in developing countries, including Brazil: Developing countries, including Brazil, face a low share of private investment in ecological projects. The Programme aims to increase private sector involvement through attractive financing instruments and structured support.
- Need to leverage investments for ecological transformation: Significant investment is required for ecological transformation, often beyond the capacity of public funding alone. The Programme's design to attract private capital is crucial for bridging this investment gap.
- Ensuring Robust Governance and Transparent Financial Flows: Maintaining robust governance and transparent financial flows is critical. The Programme's structured approach, involving independent verification and regular impact reports, addresses this challenge by ensuring accountability and transparency.

Advantages:

- Blended Finance: The Programme reduces the cost of capital through blended finance, making investments more attractive and financially viable. This can mitigate the high costs of long-term hedging by lowering the overall financial burden on investors.
- Long-Term FX Liquidity Facility: The creation of a long-term FX liquidity facility mitigates foreign exchange risks for companies with foreign currency debt and revenues in local currency, providing a cash management tool and credit enhancement for companies. This provides an alternative and a more cost-effective alternative to classical FX cross-currency swaps, directly addressing the challenge of high-cost for long-term FX hedges.
- Foreign Exchange Derivatives: The Programme will offer access to long-term FX hedging derivatives at favourable conditions through the IDB AAA status, attracting foreign direct investments. This advantage can counteract the low availability, and accessible conditions of long-term hedging and the deterrent effect of margin calls.
- Project Structuring: The Programme fosters the development of large sustainable projects by bridging Brazil's existing green project gap. Structured governance and technical support ensure that project structuring is effective and sustainable.
- Enhanced Climate Resilience: By mobilising foreign private capital for ecological projects, the Programme significantly contributes to climate resilience and sustainable development, aligning with global environmental goals.
- Structured Governance and Transparency: The involvement of the Ministry of Finance, the Ministry of Environment and Climate Change, the IDB, and independent verification ensures robust

governance, transparency, and accountability. This structured approach includes public calls for proposals, transparent publication of selection results, and regular impact reports. Such governance can manage the complexity of FX risk mitigation tools and ensure transparent financial flows.

Supported Projects Description

Eco Invest Brazil has the potential to mobilise coverage of up to USD 3.4 billion for green projects, focusing on infrastructure, renewable energy, and sustainable agriculture in Brazil. Projects span various sectors, including renewable energy, agribusiness, and infrastructure, with investments ranging from small to large scale. Examples of the projects include but are not limited to reforestation, storm-resilient infrastructure in cities, energy transition, green hydrogen, or low-carbon agriculture. The first auction for blended finance was published in July 2024 (Secretary of the National Treasury of Brazil, 2024[11]). The guidance on demand from financial institutions will be aggregated and revealed in a pre-allocation report in fall 2024.

Impact of the Solution on the Projects

Eco Invest Brazil offers several advantages over conventional financing mechanisms, particularly through its innovative financial structuring and risk management strategies. By utilising blended finance, the Programme significantly lowers the cost of capital for green projects, making sustainable investments more economically viable. Moreover, enhanced FX risk management capabilities further distinguish this Programme, providing robust hedging solutions that mitigate currency fluctuations and financial uncertainties. This comprehensive approach reduces financial risks, increasing the attractiveness of green investments and encouraging more foreign and domestic investors to participate in Brazil's ecological transformation initiatives. As a result, Eco Invest Brazil not only supports sustainable development but also promotes financial stability and investor confidence in the green economy.

The Programme significantly transforms the business model and financing landscape for Brazilian companies by enhancing access to international capital. By offering robust financial planning and risk management tools, particularly for businesses focused on green projects, the Programme reduces financial risks through innovative FX hedging and blended finance strategies. This support enables companies to secure essential funds more easily and at lower costs, fostering more predictable financial outcomes and stability. Consequently, this encourages broader participation in sustainable development, bolstering Brazil's green economy.

Strengthening policy frameworks and regulatory environments significantly boosts investment attractiveness by providing a stable and predictable context for investors. This stability is essential for attracting long-term capital. Additionally, offering technical assistance and capacity-building initiatives ensures effective implementation and long-term sustainability of projects. By creating a supportive environment, these improvements enhance the effectiveness of de-risking and financial solutions, making green investments more feasible and appealing, and driving sustainable development.

While it is not specific to a single sector, Eco Invest Brazil has significant implications for the clean hydrogen developments, particularly in addressing the financial and operational challenges associated with large-scale projects. Clean hydrogen initiatives typically involve high capital expenditures (CAPEX) and long development timelines, making long-term financial planning and risk management essential. The sector's challenges are addressed by the Programme as follows:

Currency Risk and FX Hedges: For green hydrogen projects, investments, operational costs, and sales can often occur in different currencies, leading to substantial foreign exchange (FX) risk. Long-term FX hedging solutions provided by the Eco Invest Brazil program addresses this risk, ensuring financial stability, and making the projects more attractive to foreign investors.

High CAPEX Intensity: Green hydrogen projects require significant upfront capital investment. Long-term hedging is essential to protect these large CAPEX investments from currency fluctuations over the project's lifecycle. The Programme's hedging solutions can lock in exchange rates, mitigating financial risks associated with currency volatility.

Natural Hedge Scenarios for export: In cases where green hydrogen is exported, there is a natural hedge as the revenues will be in foreign currency. The Programme can still support these projects through its blended finance line and project preparation line, enhancing financial viability and reducing the cost of capital.

Natural Hedge Scenarios for export for local consumption: For green hydrogen projects targeting local markets, the revenues will be in BRL. The FX Hedging solutions offered by the Eco Invest Brazil program will be beneficial in stabilising operational costs and revenues, ensuring that local currency earnings are protected from adverse exchange rate movements.

Lowering capital cost: The Programme's blended finance options and project preparation support are critical for the green hydrogen sector. They lower the overall cost of capital and provide necessary financial and technical backing, fostering the development and scaling of green hydrogen projects in Brazil.

Eco Invest Brazil addresses financial risks and supports the clean hydrogen sector through comprehensive FX risk management and long-term financial stability solutions. This alignment with Brazil's National Hydrogen Plan (Ministry of Minery and Energy, 2023[12]) is important for advancing the country's green hydrogen initiatives and promoting sustainable energy development.

Lessons Learnt and Replicability

Eco Invest Brazil is conceptualised, established by Provisional Measure (Secretaria Especial para Asuntos Jurídicos, 2024[13]), and with its governance established (Gabinet of the Ministry, 2024[14]). The blended finance credit line has already been regulated by the National Monetary Council (Central Bank of Brazil, 2024[15]), and the other three lines are currently under financial regulation. The first auction for the allocation of Eco Invest resources in the blended finance credit line has been published (Secretary of the National Treasury of Brazil, 2024[16]), with expected results in October 2024.

Mobilisation of capital for candidate projects will count from the day of publication of the blended finance auction process. In this sense it is not expected to increase the project preparation timeline. The blended finance model and risk mitigation strategies enhance the mobilisation of private local and international investments. The loans and credit lines under Eco Invest Brazil are not yet attributed, the first auction for blended finance being published in July 2024.

Replicating the Programme successfully requires strong institutional frameworks and effective public-private sector collaboration. Customising financing instruments to align with local market conditions is essential to address specific challenges. Continuous monitoring and adaptation to evolving economic and environmental factors are also crucial to ensure the Programme's long-term relevance and effectiveness. These elements combined create a foundation for replicating the Programme in various contexts, promoting sustainable investments on a global scale.

Case study 8 - Green Hydrogen Facility to support Green, Resilience, and Inclusive Economic Development Project for Chile / World Bank and CORFO

Table A D.9. Key indicators of the Green Hydrogen Facility

Indicator	Instrument
Type of instrument	Financing
Instrument	Concessional loans / Risk mitigation instruments
Eligible step(s) of the value chain / technologies	Electrolyser production / Electrolysis / Storage and transport infrastructure / End-Use / Cross-cutting / ...
Eligible countries	
Status	Planned
Amount (USD)	Planned: 260 million (private capital) Available: 150 million (IBRD) Disbursed: n/a
Date of implementation	Phase 1: July 2023 – June 2028

Source: Authors based on case study documentation

Financial instrument description

The Project supports the early deployment of green hydrogen production in Chile through the creation of a Green Hydrogen Facility (GHF) to be implemented by the Government of Chile (GoCl) through its Economic and Development Corporation (CORFO) and supported by Chile's public commercial bank, Banco de Estado (BE) (World Bank, n.d.[17]). Together with CORFO, the World Bank convened other multilateral partners, such as European Investment Bank (EIB), Interamerican Development Bank (IDB), German Development Bank (KfW) among other, to leverage a USD 1 billion GHF to support the development of the nascent green hydrogen industry.

The Project will establish a financing mechanism and capacity building to: (i) contribute to kick-start a new industry that will create local green jobs and value chains; (ii) decarbonize and increase the competitiveness of local industries (i.e. mining, agriculture, freight and heavy industry) and create new export opportunities through green hydrogen derivatives such as green ammonia and e-fuels; and (iii) help achieve Chile's vision of producing the world's cheapest green hydrogen by 2030.

The USD 150 million Investment Project Financing (IPF) loan aims at reducing the cost of producing a kilogramme of green hydrogen and help develop the enabling environment through the following components:

- Component 1: Green Hydrogen Investment Sub-loans and Risk-Mitigation Facility. Under this Component, the Project will provide investment sub-loans (by on-lending IBRD funds) on a preferential,9 but cost-covering basis to partially finance renewable green hydrogen production10 sub-projects in Chile and risk-mitigation reserve accounts.
- Component 2: Capacity Building and Project Management. This component will finance technical assistance, capacity-building activities, and overall Project management, including the establishment of an Implementation Support Unit (ISU) at Banco Estado, the public commrecial bank that will support CORFO.

Figure A D.8. Financial Mechanism for the World Bank Chile Green Hydrogen Facility Project

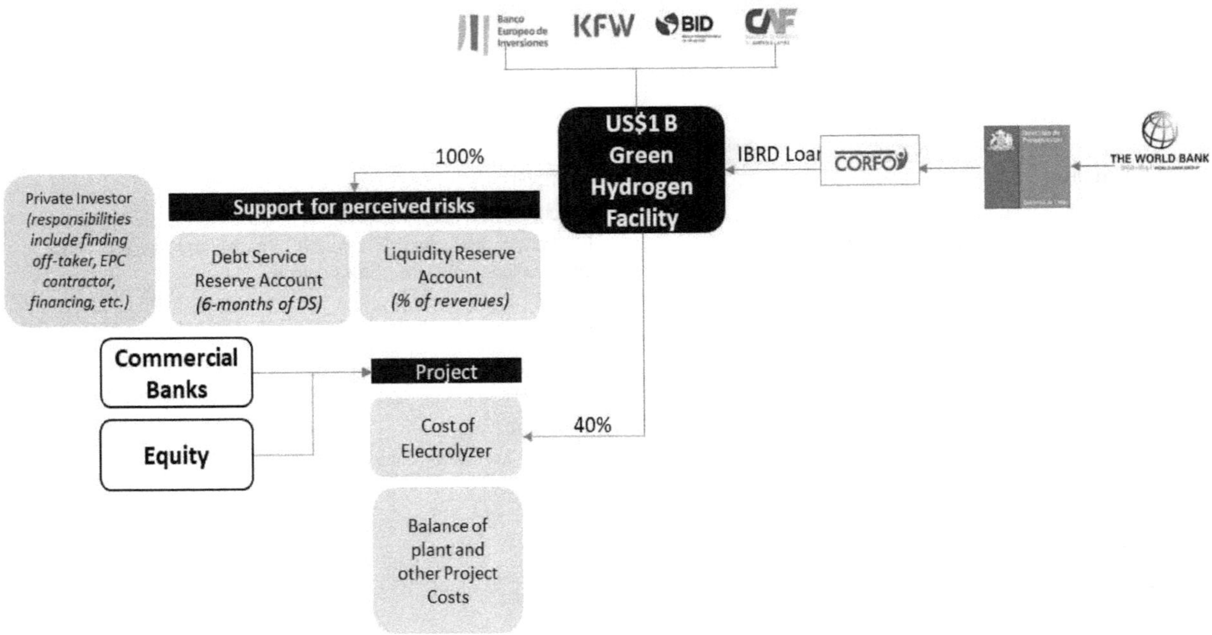

Source: Case study documentation

Supported project(s) description

Under the project, the GHF will provide:

- Green Hydrogen Investment Sub-loans to financial intermediaries and directly to green hydrogen sub-projects, for up to 40 percent of the investment costs (capital expenditures, CAPEX) for green hydrogen production. The IBRD loan resources will finance investment costs associated with the production of green hydrogen, including, *inter alia*, the capital cost of the electrolyser, compressor, storage, and dispenser equipment, as well as related installation, engineering, transport, and civil works—items that can represent between 60 and 80 percent of the total costs of a green hydrogen production plant.
- Risk-Mitigation Reserve Accounts, a typical instrument used in project finance, to mitigate the payment and operational risk associated to the green hydrogen production sub-projects. Specific characteristics of the reserve accounts are described below:
  - *Debt service reserve account (DSRA)*: The DSRA will mitigate risks related to debt repayment arising from the uncertainty of a continuous and stable cash flow due to the nascent nature of the technology. The DSRA will be available to cover 6 months,[11] of private sector debt instalment repayment of a GH project, thereby reducing the risks related to potential payment default by GH projects.
  - *Liquidity reserve account (LRA)*: The LRA will provide liquidity to a sub-project to cover unexpected short-term technical underperformance that impact the production level in the green hydrogen production plant. This risk-mitigation instrument is intended to reduce the cost of EPC performance guarantees and will strengthen confidence among EPC firms, financiers, or lenders in the operational performance of the green hydrogen sub-project. Given the limited track record of green hydrogen technology, the LRA would be available for the initial five years of a green hydrogen sub-project to mitigate its potential technical underperformance. The LRA will be created to provide additional liquidity and facilitate the sub-project's continued operation.

The LRA's triggering will be requested solely when sub-projects face non-structural technical challenges (especially early on) that could arise due to the early development stage of the green hydrogen industry.

It is expected the Chile GHF Project will support various sub-projects throughout Chile, to be evaluated and selected as part of the implementation phase. The potential sub-projects to be supported can be found in the Northern, central, and southern regions of Chile, in the country's main "hydrogen valleys." There is a robust pipeline of about 20 GH projects which are shown below.

Figure A D.9. Pipeline of green hydrogen projects in Chile

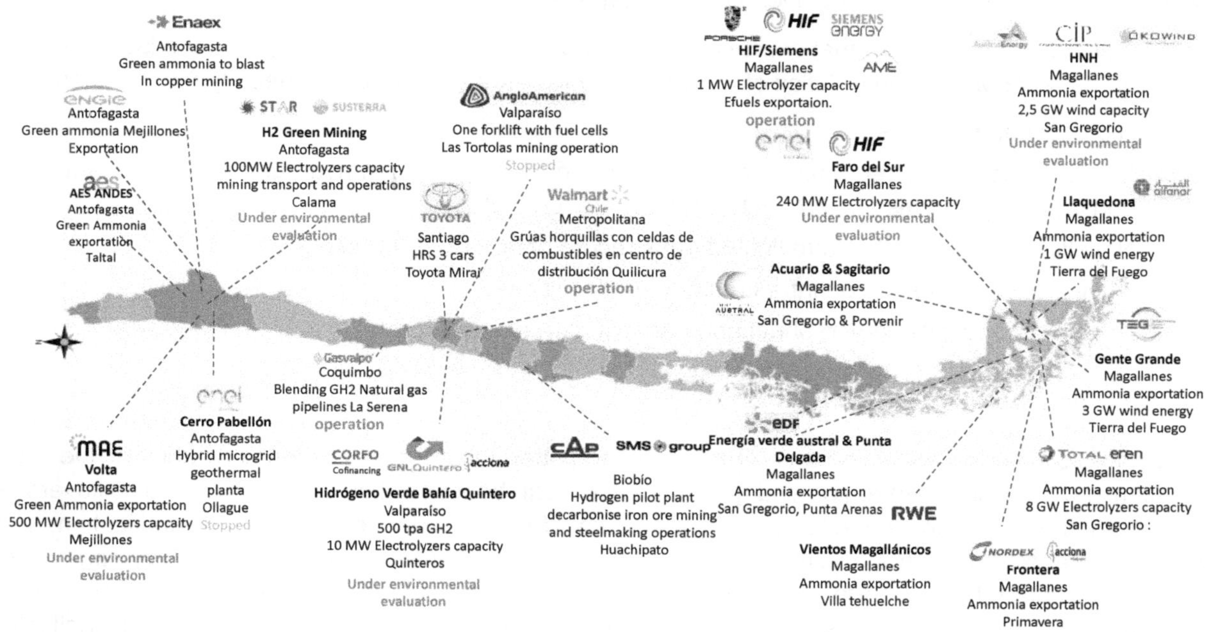

Note: Selected dynamic sample of projects.
Source: Case study documentation

Impact of the solution on the project

The hydrogen ecosystem is still at a nascent stage with the need to foster a market to develop the industry creating an investment environment that attracts not only equity but also debt investors as early as possible will be crucial for the development of Chile's Green Hydrogen industry. Typically, nascent industries are first developed by large and strategic equity investors, which use their own financial resources (R&D) to conduct prefeasibility and feasibility studies, as well as initial small testing pilot projects.

However, industrial development at scale can only be achieved with the participation of debt investors (e.g., commercial banks) that have the required financial resources to accelerate the transition from pilot projects to medium- and large-scale industrial projects. It is these large-scale projects that can have a meaningful impact on the development of a new industry and its market. When commercial banks are assessing whether to finance a GH project, risks related to the lack of a track record of the technology, large financing amounts involved, and the long tenors required are likely to result in high interest rates with standard grace periods and tenors, which are far from the soft financing terms that are critical to achieve competitiveness and industry development. It is thus essential for the creation of a green hydrogen market to pass on the cost of IBRD funding and using risk mitigation instruments to help lower the cost of producing green hydrogen, reducing the risk perceived by lenders on this nascent technology.

A robust market sounding undertaken by the World Bank identified key risks to developing green hydrogen projects in Chile as perceived by developers, financial institutions, and other stakeholders. The market sounding included engineers with experience in green hydrogen, equity investors pursuing pilot projects or with interest in future investments in the industry, and large international commercial banks with an extensive track record financing large energy-related projects (with and without a local presence in the country). The market sounding had two main objectives: (i) to identify key drivers of project and production costs that should be addressed to achieve market competitiveness and thus industry development as opposed to success of a single project; and (ii) to identify key issues that equity and debt investors consider as "industry-specific issues of concern/risk factors", which could have a defining role in their decision to invest or not in a green hydrogen production project. The second objective also included identifying the risk-mitigation instruments that could lead to an acceptable risk profile.

The market sounding identified that critical risks included the high cost of electrolysers, the lack of a track record for the technology, and a deficit of local capacity to assess and operate these types of projects:

- High cost of electrolysers
- Relative uncertainty regarding the technical performance of green hydrogen production and/or its derivatives due to the limited track record of the technology
- Novelty of the industry due to limited track record of large-scale projects
- High cost of transportation infrastructure and logistics
- Scarcity of specialised personnel and cost of international experts

Lessons learnt and replicability

The proposed Project can become a reference of a global public good to other countries in the Latin American and the Caribbean region and globally, since it can boost positive externalities and spillovers on decarbonizing hard-to-abate sectors, energy security, food security, productivity diversification, and innovative financing. In terms of climate change, (i) green hydrogen is a zero-carbon energy carrier, just like electricity, but it has an edge when it comes to decarbonizing sectors that are hard to electrify (e.g., heavy industry or long-haul transportation), and (ii) it can be stored for long periods, which facilitates greater integration of variable renewable energy and increases countries' energy security.

Key lessons learned that were included in the project design include:

- An adequate understanding of the local conditions and market is fundamental to design interventions that are fit for purpose.
- A coordinated set of institutional development and capacity-building tasks should be incorporated into projects to ensure that appropriate technical, financial, legal, and Environmental & Social assessments are conducted transparently.
- Risk-mitigation instruments can help support new clean-energy sources by enabling sub-projects to reach successful financial closure and by addressing market failures related to new technologies that remain relatively unknown to financiers.
- Implementing financial instruments together with parallel capacity-building activities helps increase their effectiveness and improves their design. This has been critical in other clean energy industries, such as renewable power generation.
- Committed partners and RFIs with strong environmental and social policies are critical for the success of sub-projects, for facilitating implementation, and to strengthen overall outcomes.
- Relying on third-party independent advisors or experienced financial institutions to assess new technologies and fill capacity gaps can be an effective approach to advance an incipient industry and share knowledge and expertise.

- Financial intermediaries must clearly define the eligibility criteria for sub-projects, and special attention should be paid to an adequate due diligence of the underlying risks.
- Enhanced dissemination of project objectives, components, and activities is recommended to ensure swift implementation. A valuable sub-project may be hampered by poor communication among the implementing agencies, sponsors, and other stakeholders.

The Chile GHF Project will establish a financing mechanism and capacity building to: (i) contribute to kick-start a new industry that will create local green jobs and value chains; (ii) decarbonize and increase the competitiveness of local industries (i.e. mining, agriculture, freight and heavy industry) and create new export opportunities through green hydrogen derivatives such as green ammonia and e-fuels; and (iii) help achieve Chile's vision of producing the world's cheapest green hydrogen by 2030. The investments supported by this operation are expected to generate local economic development, green jobs, and capacity building while decarbonizing local industries and reducing emissions.

The proposed GHF will act as a global public good by testing an innovative financing mechanism that proposes targeted public financing to leverage private investments and building local capacity to accelerate the deployment of green hydrogen sub-projects, providing a blueprint to other countries in the Latin America and Caribbean region and beyond. The GHF's innovative financing mechanism will mitigate the risks associated with this new technology, thus increasing investor confidence to spur the energy transition.

Case study 9 - Green Hydrogen Incentives Law – Government of Egypt

Table A D.10. Key indicators of Egypt's Green Hydrogen Incentives Law

Indicators	Instrument
Type of instrument	Tax credit and tax exempt
Eligible projects/technologies	Projects involving green hydrogen and its derivatives (such as green ammonia and green methanol), as well as upstream and midstream facilities where 95% of the output is dedicated to servicing green hydrogen. Projects focused exclusively on the transportation, storage, and distribution of green hydrogen and its derivatives in Egypt. The incentives also extend to projects that directly and exclusively manufacture production inputs and supplies for midstream and downstream facilities, provided a cabinet decree has been issued. Detailed executive regulation will be released by the end of 2024 (tbc) encompassing application procedures and how investors can benefit from both tax and non-tax incentives
Eligible countries	Egypt
Status	Under implementation
Date of implementation	27 January 2024

Source: Authors based on case study documentation

Context

The regulatory and institutional frameworks of Egypt to support green investment targeting low carbon technologies such as renewable energy or green hydrogen deployment have been rapidly evolving (see table 2). Egypt has established a regulatory and legislative framework in supporting the green hydrogen sector, including several decrees (Cabinet Decrees No. 20, 981, and 983) and a law (Law No. 2 of 2024), along with different incentive policies and measures. The approach of Egyptian government to have an integrated approach to developing renewable energy and hydrogen production capacity opens a new transition pathway for the country, as it provides more flexibility to utilise intermittent renewable energy capacities, particularly in a time of energy surplus and foreign exchange shortages.

Table A D.11. Key incentives law and decree announced in Egypt

Subject	Law	Ministerial Decree
Hydrogen	Gas Market Law No. 196 of 2017 Investment Law No. 72 of 2017[12] (Incentive law)	Ministerial Decree No. 239 for 2018 Cabinet Decrees No. 981 of 2022, and No. 104 of 2022 (incentive law)
Electricity	Electricity Law No. 87 of 2015	Ministerial Decree No. 230 of 2016
Renewable Energy	Renewable Energy Law No. 203/2014	
Environment	Environment Protection Law No. 4 for 1994	Ministerial Decree No. 228 for 1994
Suez Canal	Special Economic Zone Law No. 83 of 2002	Ministerial Decree No. 1625 of 2002 Ministerial Decree No. 2282 of 2015

Note: Law No. 2 of 2024, the Green Hydrogen Incentive Law, takes a stronger enforcement approach than other current laws or ministerial decrees, notwithstanding other laws and decrees.
Source: Authors based on case study documentation

For the production and usage of green hydrogen for both domestic use and export, the Egyptian Parliament has ratified a suite of incentives for green hydrogen producers, aiming to establish Egypt as a key player in the emerging export market. These incentives are designed to create an attractive investment climate through tax concessions and streamlined administrative processes. As a result of these plans and policy measures, Egypt anticipates over USD 60 billion in investments for green hydrogen and ammonia projects in the coming years, with a target to produce 5.6 million tonnes of green hydrogen and ammonia by 2040 for exporting according to the green scenario, in line with the country's green hydrogen strategy.

The provisions of this law apply to projects for the production of green hydrogen and its derivatives, provided the Project Agreements are concluded within five years from the law's effective date. The new law detailed the scope of the incentives, types of incentives, and the associated conditions and requirements.

Actors involved

Currently, four government authorities oversee Egypt's green hydrogen development: The New and Renewable Energy Authority (NREA), The General Authority of the Suez Canal Economic Zone (SCZone), the Egyptian Electricity Transmission Company (EETC), and The Sovereign Fund of Egypt (TSFE).

- NREA is responsible for granting land for renewable energy infrastructure development. It manages applications for green hydrogen project proposals and conducts pre-feasibility studies. NREA charges an annual land use fee of 2% of the renewable energy production revenue, aligning with existing BOO projects in operation.
- EETC provides transmission and distribution services, ensuring that green electricity reaches hydrogen production sites. It acts as the sole buyer of all electricity generated in Egypt and charges a 7% wheeling fee on electricity revenue for grid integration. This fee has raised concerns among developers about the increased costs of green hydrogen production, as electricity generation accounts for approximately 70% of total hydrogen production costs.
- The General Authority of SCZone manages and regulates green hydrogen facilities, most of which are located within the SCZone. It supports prospective investors by providing necessary administrative services and infrastructure support.
- The Sovereign Fund of Egypt (TSFE) coordinates all parties involved in green hydrogen projects. Established in 2018 with total assets of USD 2.42 billion, TSFE works closely with the Egyptian government to manage investment deals related to state-owned assets. It participates in green hydrogen projects as an equity partner and provides support for signing green hydrogen Memorandums of Understanding (MoUs).

Supported Scheme Description and Scope

Under the Green Hydrogen Incentives Law, Egypt outlines the targeted production of green hydrogen and its derivatives (the "Green Hydrogen Projects") as follows:

- Factories for the production of green hydrogen and its derivatives;
- Desalinated water production plants that allocate at least 95% of their production for use in the production of green hydrogen and its derivatives;
- Plants producing electrical energy from renewable energy sources, which shall allocate no less than 95% of their production to fuel the factories producing green hydrogen and its derivatives and desalinated water production plants;
- Projects whose activity is limited to the transport, storage or distribution of green hydrogen and its derivatives produced within the Arab Republic of Egypt;
- Projects whose activity is directly limited to the manufacture of production requirements or inputs necessary for the factories producing green hydrogen and its derivatives.

The Green Hydrogen Projects must meet the following criteria to benefit from the incentives of the law:

- The commercial operation date must be within five years from the date of the project agreements. Future expansions can benefit from the incentives if their project agreements are executed within seven years from the commercial operation date.
- Foreign currency financing must be sourced from offshore sources to cover no less than 70% of the investment cost.
- Local content, to the extent available in the local market, must be no less than 20% of the project components.
- Transfer and localization of technology into Egypt with the set-up and implementation of a training program to Egyptian labour.
- Corporate social responsibility activities for the areas in which the project is based.
- Once the project meets the criteria, the project developers can take advantage of taxation incentives and non-taxation incentives.

Table A D.12. Scope of Law No. 2 of 2024

Category	Law
Taxation Incentives	• A cash investment incentive known as the Green Hydrogen Incentive (State Information Service of Egypt, n.d.[18]), equivalent to 33% up to 55% of the tax paid upon declaring the income resulted from initiating activities in the project or its expansions. • VAT exemption on equipment, tools, machines, devices, raw materials, supplies, and necessary transportation means needed for initiating the project. VAT rate for exports of green hydrogen projects and their derivatives is 0%.
Non-taxation Incentives	• Regulatory Approval: Obtaining the single approval (i.e., Golden License) for the companies working in green hydrogen production project. • Import and Export Rights: Allowing the project company to import any necessities needed to establish the project or expand it or operate it from raw materials, production requirements, machines, spare parts, and the appropriate means of transportation to the activity's nature, without the need to register the project company in the importer's register. It is also entitled to export its own products without a license and without the need to register the project company in the exporter's register. • Employment of Foreign Worker The project company is entitled to use foreign employees within the limits of 30% of the total number of employees in the project during the first ten (10) years commencing from the date of signing the project agreements. • Special Customs Zones: Establishment of special customs ports for the project's exports and imports. • Special Customs Zones: A 30% deduction from the value and categories fees, for the use of seaports and sea transport and fee services provided to ships in the Egyptian seaports. • Land Use Fees Reduction A 25% deduction on the value of the usufruct right of industrial lands, which are allocated to establish a hydrogen production plant and its derivatives. In addition to, a 20% deduction on the right to use the storage warehouse lands at the ports. • Grace Period for Fees Granting a grace period for the payment of the usufruct right of the project's industrial and storage lands, where the payment starts from the project's commercial operational date, without imposing any interest and/or fines. Licenses Tenure Determining the terms of the licenses granted to green hydrogen production projects as the same term as the right of usufruct of the project's land.

Source: Law No. 2 of 2024 Regarding Investment Incentives for Green Hydrogen Production Projects and its Derivatives: Unofficial Translation, Deloitte

Challenges and key advantages

Egypt benefits from immediate access to the Mediterranean and, consequently, the European market. The newly enacted Green Hydrogen Incentives Law is positioning Egypt as a regional hub for green hydrogen and derivatives projects, driven primarily by renewable energy sources such as wind and solar. Beyond its environmental impact, the law is expected to generate positive spillover effects across various sectors. The attractive investment environment it creates for Project Companies is poised to bolster Egypt's economic standing by promoting sustainable development, increasing employment opportunities, reducing unemployment rates, and fostering competition among stakeholders. Furthermore, Egypt's commitment to advancing technological innovation and research in green hydrogen production solidifies its position as a leader in clean energy technology. However, many governments are now announcing lucrative incentive schemes, such as Oman's 47-year land concessions. The impact of these competing incentives on the global market remains to be seen.

To realise full intended impact of the incentive law, there remains a need for further clarification and refinement for law's enforcement scope and process. According to the law, certifications issued by the competent minister or an authorized representative, which grant incentives to Project Companies, are considered final and effective without the need for additional approvals from other related entities. As a result, investors are currently following two main approaches to benefit from the law: either by directly engaging with the EETC/NREA for preliminary approvals and signing MoUs, or by directly communicating with the Prime Minister, typically through embassies and foreign investment chambers in Egypt. It is important to note that meetings with the Prime Minister are generally reserved for concrete investment proposals. However, the types of project documents that qualify under the incentive law, as well as the processes and scope, have yet to be standardized. Currently Government is in the preparation of developing a detailed executive regulation for this law, which is currently under preparation and review. It is expected to be released by the end of 2024. This regulation will include all the necessary details regarding application procedures and how investors can benefit from both tax and non-tax incentives.

Case study 10 - HySure risk transfer / Munich Re

Table A D.13. Key indicators of HySure

Indicator	Instrument
Type of instrument	De-risking
Instrument	Warranty insurance for product, performance and availability warranties
Eligible step(s) of the value chain / technologies	Electrolyser systems and fuel cells
Eligible countries	Global
Status	Under implementation / Completed
Amount (USD)	n/a
Date of implementation	n/a

Source: Authors based on case study

Instrument description – Theoretical Concept

HySure is an innovative insurance solution developed by Munich Re, specifically designed to address the risks associated within the hydrogen industry. The product provides comprehensive risk coverage for electrolyser manufacturers or project developers, HySure covers three primary risk categories: (i) product warranty: protects against excessive maintenance costs due to product failures; (ii) performance warranty: insures against underperformance in terms of hydrogen production rate and efficiency metrics such as cell voltage; (iii) availability warranty: provides coverage for unforeseen downtime.

Munich Re's HySure product is designed to alleviate the financial burden on electrolyser manufacturers by covering excessive warranty costs associated with repairs or replacements (see Figure A D.10). The insurance structure includes three key elements: the deductible, co-payment, and limit. The deductible represents the amount of risk the manufacturer is willing to bear before the insurance coverage begins. Once the deductible is exceeded, Munich Re covers the majority of additional warranty costs, up to an agreed-upon limit. The manufacturer also shares a portion of the loss through a claims-proportional co-payment, allowing for a balanced risk-sharing approach that supports financial stability while managing insurance premiums.

Figure A D.10. HySure insurance structure

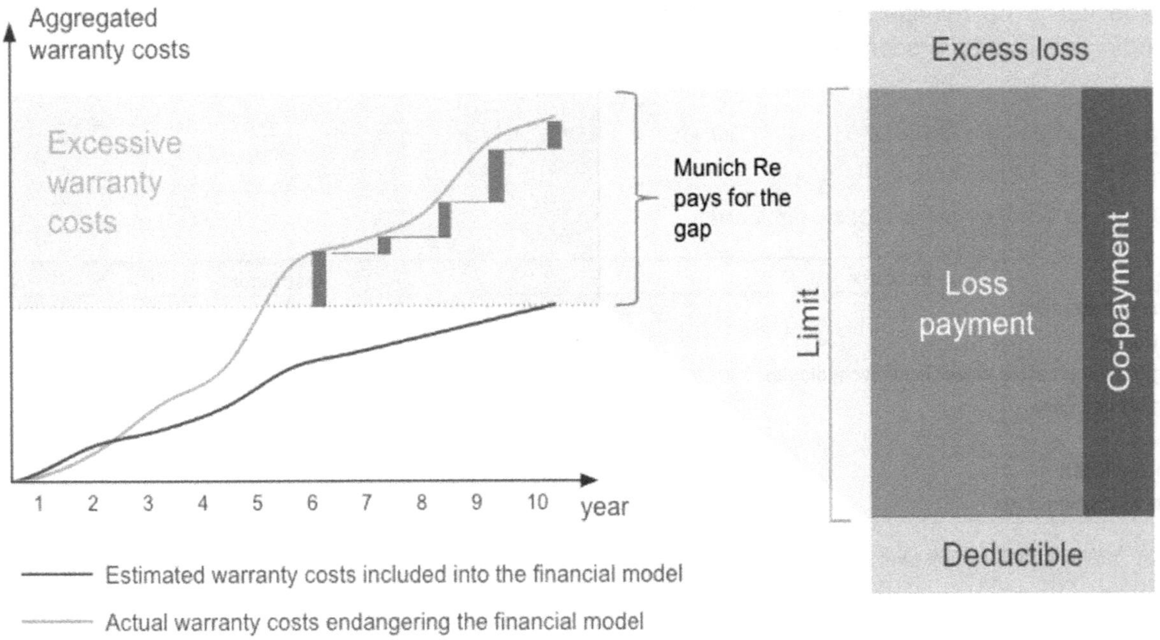

Source: Munich Re Green Tech Solutions - HySure documentation

The HySure solution ensures that manufacturers can offer long-term performance guarantees without overburdening their balance sheets, thus enhancing the overall bankability of clean hydrogen projects.

Key actors involved in HySure are:

- Munich Re[13]: as the insurer, Munich Re performs risk assessments, offers tailored insurance solutions, and underwrites the associated risks. Munich Re collects premiums from manufacturers and disburses payments in the event of a valid warranty claim.
- Electrolyser manufacturers: the primary users of the HySure insurance product. By leveraging this solution, manufacturers can offer enhanced warranties, which boost sales and enhance financial stability by mitigating the risks associated with excessive warranty claims.
- Project developers and owners: these entities benefit from the enhanced warranties provided by the manufacturers, reducing financial risks and improving the predictability of cash flows.
- Investors and banks: the financial stakeholders benefit from the reduced risk profile of projects insured under HySure. The enhanced warranties and performance guarantees make projects more attractive to financiers, leading to lower financing costs and increased investment security.

There are three main contracts/agreements in the HySure package: (i) insurance agreement: between Munich Re and the electrolyser manufacturers, defining the terms of coverage; (ii) warranty contracts: enhanced by the HySure insurance, these contracts are between the insured such as the manufacturer and their respective customers; (iii) financing agreements: between project developers and investors, improved by the risk mitigation provided by HySure.

Munich Re works closely with electrolyser manufacturers through a structured process that includes risk assessment, technical due diligence, and the development of a customised insurance solution. The process typically takes between 3 to 6 months, depending on data availability and project complexity.

HySure requires comprehensive technical due diligence and the customisation of insurance solutions to meet specific project needs. To achieve widespread market adoption, manufacturers and project developers will receive extensive education and targeted market development support to understand and embrace this new insurance solution. This is expected to enable especially smaller manufacturers or projects with constrained budgets to embrace the benefits of this innovative insurance solutions.

HySure offers several advantages for manufacturers and project developers. It improves liquidity by transferring a substantial portion of risk to Munich Re, enabling manufacturers to maintain stronger financial flexibility. The solution enhances the bankability of clean hydrogen projects by reducing perceived risks, making them more attractive to investors and financiers. Its scalability allows for adaptability, as manufacturers can tailor the insurance to suit their specific risk appetite and financial requirements. Additionally, HySure provides effective risk mitigation, shielding manufacturers from excessive warranty claims and allowing them to concentrate on growth and innovation.

Supported Projects Description

The exact number of projects supported by HySure is not publicly disclosed, but the solution is designed to support a wide range of clean hydrogen initiatives, from small pilot projects to large-scale industrial operations.

HySure is a global solution applicable to industry sub-sectors within the clean hydrogen space, particularly those involved in hydrogen production.

Impact of the Solution on the Projects

The capacity to provide extended and more comprehensive warranties enhances the appeal of clean hydrogen projects to developers and financiers, contributing to their overall attractiveness and potential for successful funding. HySure enables manufacturers to provide such warranties and acts as an enabler for improved bankability.

HySure aims to have a direct impact on business models and access to finance. It provides increased financial flexibility by transferring risk to Munich Re, allowing manufacturers to allocate capital more efficiently and support operational scaling. The insurance solution also improves market position, as it offers a form of validation that can enhance customer trust and potentially increase market share for manufacturers.

The involvement of a reputable reinsurer like Munich Re helps build confidence among investors and project developers, facilitating smoother project development and execution. This, in turn, supports the broader growth of the clean hydrogen industry by enabling the scaling of projects.

Lessons Learnt and Replicability

The structured co-creational process ensures that the insurance solutions are effectively tailored to the specific needs of each project, thereby improving their financial viability and attractiveness. While the detailed due diligence process might slightly extend the project preparation timeline, this is counterbalanced by the significant benefits in terms of reduced risk and improved financing conditions. The implementation of HySure has the potential to facilitate mobilisation of significant private capital by de-risking investments in clean hydrogen projects, thus attracting a broader range of investors.

The conditions for replicability of HySure include its scalability across various regions and project sizes, as long as adequate underwriting and risk assessment capabilities are in place. Market acceptance is also crucial, successful replication relies on manufacturers and project developers adopting insurance solutions as part of their standard financing and risk management strategies. Positive outcomes from early adopters can support wider market acceptance and adoption.

Case study 11 - Insurance facility / Marsh

Table A D.14. Key indicators of Marsh's Clean Hydrogen Insurance Facility

Indicator	Instrument
Type of instrument	De-risking
Instrument	Insurance solutions for construction and operational risk of clean hydrogen production and use projects
Eligible step(s) of the value chain / technologies	Electrolysis, fuel cell and CCS technologies, end-use sectors (incl. marine and cargo industries)
Eligible countries	Global
Status	Under implementation: implemented with use of facility ongoing
Amount (USD)	Planned: USD 400 million insurance capacity per project Available: USD 400 million insurance capacity per project Disbursed: disbursed value does not erode insurance capacity
Date of implementation	Launched in 2022

Source: Authors based on case study documentation

Instrument description – Theoretical Concept

The Marsh Clean Hydrogen Insurance Facility is an insurance platform designed to support and facilitate the insurance of clean hydrogen production and end-use projects (Marsh, n.d.[19]). It offers risk transfer solutions across all phases of hydrogen projects including both construction and operational stages.

The facility provides a tailored project risk management framework, with risks thoroughly reviewed and evaluated by a dedicated risk engineering team. Appropriate risk mitigation strategies and insurance products are proposed based on specific project factors such as location, technology, contractors, and project duration. To ensure effective risk transfer to the commercial insurance market, Marsh manages a competitive tender process involving A-rated global insurance carriers, selecting the most competitive and comprehensive coverage available. Core insurances include coverage for construction and operational property damage, delay in start-up, business interruption, third-party liability, and marine cargo, as well as associated financial risk insurance (see Figure A D.11). Launched in 2022, the facility provides up to USD 400 million in insurance capacity per project, supporting clean hydrogen projects with capital expenditures of up to USD 600 million and enhancing bankability through pre-approved financier-focused insurance programmes.

Figure A D.11. Marsh Clean Hydrogen Insurance Facility insurances

Construction phase	Operational phase	Additional coverage for construction and operational phases
• Construction all risks	• Operational all risks	• Reservoir leakage and emissions trading coverage
• Delay in start-up (DSU)	• Business interruption	• Sabotage and terrorism
• Third party liability	• Third party liability	• Environmental impairment liability
• Marine cargo	• Marine cargo	• Professional indemnity
		• Contractor's plant and equipment
		• Cyber

Source: Marsh Clean Hydrogen Insurance Facility documentation

The key actors involved in the Marsh Clean Hydrogen Insurance Facility are:

- Marsh: the risk and insurance advisor managing the facility. Marsh, part of Marsh McLennan, a New York, USA, headquartered and stock exchange listed company in the S&P 500, is an insurance broker and risk advisor, offering data-driven risk solutions and advisory services to commercial and individual clients in over 130 countries. As a business Marsh McLennan supports clients through comprehensive risk management, strategy, and people advisory.
- Project developers, EPC contractors, operators, owners and any parties with contractual risk of loss for the project: clients developing clean hydrogen projects and requiring appropriate risk advisory and insurance transfer products.
- Investors and lenders: financial institutions seeking to reduce exposure to risk before committing capital to clean hydrogen projects.
- Global insurers: A-rated (re)insurers providing pre-agreed coverage for projects.

In the contractual flows of Marsh's Clean Hydrogen Insurance Facility, clean hydrogen project developers pay insurance premiums to cover various project risks. Marsh serves as an intermediary, negotiating insurance coverage with global insurers and transferring these risks from the project owners' balance sheets to the commercial insurance marketplace. Financial investors provide capital investment for the projects, with their risk exposure mitigated by tailored insurance coverage. In the event of insured incidents, such as property damage or business interruption, Marsh manages the claims process, ensuring developers are properly compensated and project disruptions are minimised.

Clean hydrogen projects face several challenges that benefit from Marsh's clean hydrogen insurance facility. One common issue, especially in large-scale infrastructure projects, is the complex ownership structures, often involving multiple stakeholders, which can complicate both risk management and insurance arrangements. Additionally, technological uncertainty, as hydrogen production is sometimes perceived as relying on emerging technologies, requires thorough risk assessments, which differs for prototype or scale-up projects. Furthermore, the high production costs of clean hydrogen, compared to carbon-based hydrogen, make early-stage projects more financially challenging, potentially limiting investment appeal and heightening the need for customised insurance solutions.

The Marsh Clean Hydrogen Insurance Facility provides several practical advantages for project developers and investors. It simplifies the process of securing core insurance needs by offering a single platform with pre-agreed terms and competitive pricing from a global panel of A-rated insurers. The facility offers comprehensive risk coverage across both construction and operational phases, addressing risks such as technology failure, political uncertainty, and sabotage. Its flexible structure allows developers to select construction phase, operational phase, or combined coverage extending into the first year of operations. Marsh also tailors insurance solutions to the specific risk characteristics of each project, taking into account location, technology, contractors, and supply chain. Additionally, the facility is designed to meet lender requirements, including a Brokers Letter of Undertaking and appropriate lender insurance clauses. These advantages help reduce project risk, enhance investor confidence and improve access to financing.

Supported Projects Description

The Marsh Clean Hydrogen Insurance Facility offers risk transfer solutions for a variety of clean hydrogen projects globally, including renewable hydrogen, hydrogen production based on natural gas with carbon capture, clean steel production, and hydrogen fuel cell applications, although specific projects are not publicly disclosed. It serves a range of clients, such as local governments, independent project developers, and large-scale conglomerates, to manage their project risks. The facility is active in both OECD and select emerging markets, supporting clean hydrogen production and use, as well as carbon capture projects. It is structured to handle large investments, covering projects with capital expenditure up to USD 600 million and providing insurance capacity of up to USD 400 million.

Impact of the Solution on the Projects

The Marsh Clean Hydrogen Insurance Facility offers several advantages over conventional financing methods. It de-risks complex hydrogen projects by providing a comprehensive insurance package, simplifying risk management and enhancing investor confidence. The facility reduces complexity by allowing project developers to secure the majority of core insurances under a single platform, streamlining the risk transfer process and lowering administrative burdens. Additionally, by mitigating risks related to construction, operations, and political uncertainties, the facility improves access to both institutional and private financing, potentially reducing borrowing costs for project developers.

The Marsh Clean Hydrogen Insurance Facility improves access to finance by making projects more attractive to institutional and private investors through effective risk mitigation. This risk reduction supports developers in securing long-term financing. The facility offers flexible, tailored insurance coverage that aligns with the specific risk profile of each project, enabling more precise financial planning. This customisation further strengthens the project's investment appeal and financial viability.

Improving enabling conditions can complement the de-risking solution offered by the Marsh Clean Hydrogen Insurance Facility. Government incentives, such as tax breaks and revenue support, make clean hydrogen projects more attractive to investors and work in tandem with the risk transfer solutions provided by the facility. Additionally, as hydrogen production technologies and infrastructure mature and scale, the facility further reduces perceived risks associated with early-stage projects, supporting their viability and improving investor confidence. These factors contribute to a more favourable environment for financing hydrogen projects.

Lessons Learnt and Replicability

The Marsh Clean Hydrogen Insurance Facility has been effectively implemented in multiple projects globally, providing a comprehensive risk management framework that enhances project viability and secures financing. While the facility requires an upfront risk assessment and project evaluation by in-house risk engineers, typically taking up to six weeks, this preparation time helps reduce long-term risks and ensures smoother project execution. By simplifying the process of securing insurance coverage and de-risking hydrogen projects, the facility also helps mobilise private capital, making these projects more attractive to institutional and private investors.

The replicability of the Marsh Clean Hydrogen Insurance Facility depends on several key conditions. Countries with mature clean hydrogen policy frameworks and regulatory clarity are more likely to adopt and benefit from the facility. Its flexible design allows for application across a wide range of clean hydrogen projects with varying risk profiles, making it adaptable to different markets and project types. Successful replication also requires strong engagement between project developers, insurers, and financial institutions, as collaboration among these stakeholders is crucial to effectively implementing the facility in other sectors and regions.

Case study 12 - IRA Hydrogen / Government of the United States

Table A D.15. Key indicators of the IRA

Indicator	Instrument
Type of instrument	Economic
Instrument	Tax credits
Eligible step(s) of the value chain	Fuel cell electric vehicles, hydrogen infrastructure, electrolysers, and a range of other products
Eligible countries	United States
Status	Completed
Amount	There are multiple credits and the planned credit amounts vary by technology and other factors: • aggregate maximum USD 10 billion for advanced energy projects, including manufacturing of certain hydrogen technologies, such as electrolysers and fuel cells; • maximum USD 40 000 for commercial fuel cell buses and trucks; • maximum USD 3/kg of qualified clean hydrogen production.
Date of implementation	IRA was enacted on August 16, 2022. Rulemakings associated with individual tax credits are ongoing.

Source: Authors based on case study documentation

Instrument – Theoretical Concept

The Inflation Reduction Act of 2022 (IRA) provides a comprehensive suite of economic instruments, including tax credits and incentives aimed at fostering the production and adoption of clean energies, including clean hydrogen (White House, 2023[20]). These measures are designed to support the transition to a low carbon economy by enhancing the economic viability of hydrogen projects through various tax credits. The main instrument is the Clean Hydrogen Production Tax Credit (45V), offering a tax credit based on the carbon intensity of hydrogen production. Other relevant credits include those for carbon capture (45Q), clean vehicles (30D, 45W), and energy projects (48C). Incentives for clean hydrogen under IRA are summarised in the table below:

Table A D.16. Zoom on hydrogen-related tax incentives

Incentive	Description	Funding / Duration	Additional information
Advanced Energy Project Credit (48C)	Extends 30% investment tax credit for qualifying advanced energy projects, including those for manufacturing of hydrogen technologies (e.g. electrolysers, fuel cells, etc.).	USD 10 billion, ongoing	Includes retrofitting for low-carbon industrial heat, carbon capture, storage, recycling and energy efficiency projects. Taxpayers must adhere to wage and apprenticeship standards to access full credit value.
Alternative Fuel Refuelling Property Credit (30C)	Extends and increases 30% credit for alternative fuel refuelling property, with a cap of up to USD 100 000 per dispenser or storage unit.	Through 2032	Credit is only for property installed in low-income or rural areas. For business installations, taxpayers must adhere to wage and apprenticeship standards to access full credit value.
Carbon Capture Tax Credit (45Q)	Enhances tax credit for carbon capture and direct air capture, extending the deadline for construction to 2033.	Through 2032	Cannot be combined with the 45V hydrogen credit. Taxpayers must adhere to wage and apprenticeship standards to access full credit value.
Clean Hydrogen Production Tax Credit (45V)	Production tax credit for clean hydrogen production with a variable rate based on carbon intensity (up to USD 3 per kg of H2 with carbon intensity lower than 0.45 kg of CO2 per kg of H2), for projects that began construction before 2033.	Ongoing, 10 years incentive plan	Taxpayers must adhere to wage and apprenticeship standards to access full credit value, cannot stack with 45Q.
Clean Vehicle Credit (30D)	Maintains USD 7 500 credit for FCEVs with new limits on price, battery components, and income eligibility. Eliminates the previous manufacturers quotas, which phased out the tax credit for manufacturers as they neared 200 000 clean vehicles sold.	Through 2032	Reduces credit if components are not sourced from the US/FTA countries[14] or if EV is not assembled in North America.
Elective Payment for Clean Energy Projects	Allows direct payments in place of tax liability reduction for certain clean energy credits, including the clean hydrogen production credit, the energy investment tax credit, the carbon capture and sequestration credit, alternative fuel vehicle refuelling, property credit, advanced energy project credit, and others.	Direct pay available through 2032	Elective payment is generally limited to tax-exempt and governmental entities but businesses can also access elective payment for 45V and 45Q credits for five years.
Energy Credit (Extends 48)	Extends 30% fuel cell investment tax credit, transitioning to a technology-neutral credit in 2025.	Through 2024	Offers bonuses for domestic sourcing, projects in energy communities and projects in low-income communities. Taxpayers must adhere to wage and apprenticeship standards to access full credit value.
Energy Storage Credit (New, 48 and 48E)	Adds energy storage, including hydrogen storage, to the energy investment tax credit.	Through at least 2032; the transition from 48 to 48E will occur in 2025	Offers bonuses for domestic content, projects in energy communities and projects in low-income communities. Taxpayers must adhere to wage and apprenticeship standards to access full credit value.
Qualified Commercial Clean Vehicles Credit (New, 45W)	Creates a 30% credit for commercial FCEVs, capped at USD 40 000.	Through 2032	Includes USD 7 500 for smaller vehicles, and up to USD 40 000 for larger ones.

Source: Authors based on case study documentation

Being an important measure in the overall clean hydrogen incentives package, the Clean Hydrogen Production Tax Credit (45V) provides a 10-year incentive for the production of clean hydrogen based on lifecycle greenhouse gas (CO_2 equivalent) emissions. The credit amount is determined by multiplying the kilogrammes of qualified hydrogen produced annually by a credit rate that depends on the carbon intensity of hydrogen production and on whether the project meets prevailing wage and apprenticeship requirements. There are four tiers of credit rates, with a maximum of USD 3 per kilogramme of hydrogen for a carbon intensity of less than 0.45 kilogramme of CO_2 equivalent per kilogramme of hydrogen, as shown in Table A D.17.

Table A D.17. IRA four-tier incentives

Carbon intensity (kg CO_2 equivalent per kg H_2)	Max Hydrogen Production Tax Credit (USD per kg H_2)
4 - 2.5	USD 0.60
2.5 - 1.5	USD 0.75
1.5 - 0.45	USD 1.00
<0.45	USD 3.00

Source: Authors based on case study documentation

To qualify for the credit, projects must be placed into service before January 1, 2033, and may not be combined with the 45Q Carbon Capture and Sequestration Tax Credit. Hydrogen production is evaluated using 45VH2-GREET[15] , which calculates emissions from the production process, excluding downstream emissions. Retrofits of existing facilities may also qualify, offering flexibility for expanding clean hydrogen production.

Actors involved and Financial Flows

Under the 45V Clean Hydrogen Production Tax Credit, the key actors include the Treasury Department and the Internal Revenue Service (IRS) for administering the tax credits, and the U.S. Department of Energy (DOE) for maintaining the 45VH2-GREET model and evaluating applications for pathways not yet in 45VH2-GREET through the Emissions Value Request Process (IRS, n.d.[21]; Department of Energy (DOE), n.d.[22]).

Private sector entities, such as hydrogen producers and technology developers, are eligible for the tax credit in the years that they produce clean hydrogen. The tax credit incentivizes investment in hydrogen projects by reducing the cost of clean hydrogen production. Other tax credits, such as 48C, 48, 30C, and 45W, incentivize investments in manufacturing technologies, infrastructure, and transportation end uses. Incentives within IRA include production tax credits (i.e. an incentive for every unit of a particular good that is produced, such as clean hydrogen), investment tax credits (i.e. a one-time incentive for deployment of a particular type of facility, such as an electrolyser facility), and grants (i.e. funds provided for direct use in a particular type of qualifying project, such as construction of an electrolyser manufacturing facility).

Governance/Organisation and Implementation

The governance involves Treasury and IRS, which develop regulations and guidance developed to implement the IRA provisions. The IRS issues guidelines, while the DOE maintains the 45VH2-GREET model and reviews applications for pathways not yet in 45VH2-GREET (through DOE"s Emissions Value Request Process).

Challenges and key advantages

One of the key challenges in utilising the Clean Hydrogen Production Tax Credit is accurately verifying the carbon intensity of hydrogen production, which may require sophisticated tools, particularly regarding electricity tracking. Procedures for taxpayers to obtain emissions analyses if their pathway is not in 45VH$_2$-GREET may also be lengthy, which can delay the initiation of projects. Additionally, the need for effective coordination with international regulations introduces complexity, particularly for taxpayers intended to export hydrogen.

The Clean Hydrogen Production Tax Credit provides several advantages, particularly in encouraging investment by lowering costs through tax incentives. It drives technological advancements and deployment of hydrogen production facilities, while also promoting job creation via prevailing wage and apprenticeship schemes. The significant financial benefits improve project feasibility, and the availability of the credit for up to 10 years supports sustained local investments. Additionally, the flexibility to combine the credit with others, such as renewable energy production tax or zero-emission nuclear credits, strengthens overall project financing and feasibility.

Supported Projects Description

Projects supported under the 45V Clean Hydrogen Production Tax Credit primarily focus on the development of hydrogen production facilities with significantly reduced carbon emissions. These include both the retrofitting of existing facilities to meet clean hydrogen criteria and the construction of new plants designed to produce hydrogen with minimal lifecycle greenhouse gas emissions. The tax credit encourages projects that integrate innovative technologies for clean hydrogen production, with the goal of achieving lower emissions thresholds, thus contributing to the broader decarbonisation of the energy and industry sectors.

Under the 2022 Budget Reconciliation bill, IRA will invest approximately USD 369 billion in Energy Security and Climate Change programs over ten years. The exact number of hydrogen projects supported is contingent on projects meeting eligibility criteria and project commencement before 2033.

The supported projects are developed in the United States. Projects in a wide array of industry subsectors can benefit from this incentives: fuel cell electric vehicles (FCEVs), hydrogen infrastructure, electrolysers, and a range of other products including retrofitting facilities for low-carbon industrial heat, carbon capture, transport, utilisation, and storage systems, and equipment for recycling, waste reduction, and energy efficiency.

Impact of the Solution of the Projects

The IRA's economic incentives significantly reduce the financial burden on hydrogen projects and enhance project feasibility, making them more viable and attractive to local and international investors. It helps accelerate the transition towards clean hydrogen energy and build up new clean infrastructures locally.

Advantages vs Conventional Financing: The IRA offers more favourable terms compared to conventional financing by providing direct tax credits and incentives, reducing upfront capital requirements, and enabling faster cost recovery.

Impact on Business Model or Access to Finance: The introduction of tax credits and incentives under the IRA improves access to finance for hydrogen projects, making them more bankable and attractive to private investors.

How Improving the Enabling Conditions Can Complement the De-risking and Financial Solution: Enhancing regulatory clarity, streamlining application processes, and improving coordination with regulations in other countries (e.g. RED II) can reduce project timelines and increasing private sector participation.

Lessons Learnt and Replicability

Key lessons learned include the necessity of clear eligibility criteria and streamlined administrative processes to ensure efficiency and fairness in resource allocation. Additionally, maintaining high workforce standards is crucial for sustaining public support and trust. Adhering to these standards helps ensure that quality and integrity are upheld, which in turn supports continued public confidence.

The solution is implemented effectively through clear regulatory guidance and collaboration between government agencies, ensuring that the economic incentives are accessible and operational in a timely manner to support the clean hydrogen market uptake locally. The solution has successfully mobilised investment and accelerated clean hydrogen projects. Key indicators of success from the Bipartisan Infrastructure Law and the IRA include the announcement of over USD 2.9 billion in investments for electrolyser and fuel cell manufacturing facilities since 2021. These investments represent over 15 new or expanded facilities with an annual manufacturing capacity of approximately 12 GW for electrolysers and 4 GW for fuel cells. As of May 2024, existing and planned electrolyser installations in the U.S. (including firm commitments and projects under construction) totalled around 4.5 GW.

The regulatory complexity may increase preparation timelines, but the financial benefits often outweigh these delays. Plus, the solution successfully mobilised private capital, as mentioned above, by reducing investment risks and accelerated the implementation timeline through substantial tax credits and incentives.

The funds have begun to be used, though challenges in disbursement may arise due to the complexity of compliance. The funds are utilised effectively, with clear disbursement criteria ensuring that projects meet environmental and economic objectives.

Successful replication of clean hydrogen projects under the 45V Clean Hydrogen Production Tax Credit framework hinges on robust regulatory support, well-defined eligibility criteria, and region-specific economic frameworks. While replication in advanced economies can thrive under these conditions, emerging markets and developing economies (EMDEs) may face substantial barriers. The high capital costs and complex regulatory requirements could make the scheme too costly and difficult to implement in these regions, especially where financial and institutional capacities are limited. Tailored solutions may be needed to enable broader participation in clean hydrogen initiatives.

Case study 13 - Japanese government subsidy scheme / Government of Japan

Table A D.18. Key indicators of the Japanese government subsidy scheme

Indicator	Instrument
Type of instrument	Economic
Instrument	Contract-for-Difference Subsidy
Eligible step(s) of the value chain	Hydrogen production and derivatives
Eligible countries	Japan
Status	The Hydrogen Society Promotion Act was put into force on 23 October 2024.
Amount	Planned: USD 19.2 billion Available: n/a Disbursed: n/a
Date of implementation	The Hydrogen Society Promotion Act was put into force on 23 October 2024.

Source: Authors based on case study documentation

Instrument – Theoretical Concept

Japan's low-carbon hydrogen subsidy is an economic instrument set by the Japanese Government and the Japan Organisation for Metals and Energy Security (JOGMEC) in 2024 (JOGMEC, n.d.[23]). It aims to stimulate investment in robust international supply chains for low-carbon hydrogen and its derivatives that meet the following requirements:

Table A D.19. Criteria for low-carbon hydrogen derivatives

	System boundary	Carbon intensity
Hydrogen	Well-to-gate	3.4 kg-CO_2-eq/kg-H2 (or less)
Ammonia	Well-to-gate	0.87 kg-CO_2-eq/kg-NH3 (or less)
e-Fuel	Whole supply chain	39.9 g-CO_2-eq/MJ (or less)
E-methane	Whole supply chain	49.3 g-CO_2-eq/MJ (or less)

Note: CO_2-eq stands for CO_2 equivalent.
Source: Ministry of Economy, Trade and Industry (METI)

The supply-side subsidy is structured as a Contract for Difference (CfD), providing financial support to cover the cost gap of low-carbon hydrogen production with fossil fuels. The CfD will be in place during the first 15 years of the relevant low-carbon hydrogen supply period, with an obligation for the hydrogen supplier to extend the supply for another 10 years. The subsidy will be paid in Japanese Yen (JPY) and will be granted after a competitive selection process to determine the eligibility of hydrogen producers.

The subsidy will cover the amount by which low-carbon hydrogen production costs (and imports and transportation costs, if applicable), also called 'Strike Price', exceeds the Reference Price to be set, depending on the actual use of low-carbon hydrogen and its derivatives. If the 'Reference Price' exceeds the 'Strike Price', the supplier will be required to pay the difference (see Figure 1).

The applicants will have to present the 'Strike Price' in the form of a calculation formula in accordance with the Government and the JOGMEC, reflecting the price at which the supplier is able to recover its cost of production, importation and supply of fuels and make a reasonable profit. The 'Reference Price' will be determined project-by-project by the Japanese Government, based on the following criteria:

- If the low-carbon hydrogen type is used in an industry where it has not been generally or commercially used, the 'Reference Price' will be equivalent to the cost of comparable "conventional" products landed in Japan.
- If the low-carbon hydrogen type has already been generally and commercially used in a relevant industry, the 'Reference Price' will be equivalent to the historic cost.

It is expected that low-carbon hydrogen and ammonia products for power generation will get the 'Reference Price' based on Liquefied Natural Gas (LNG) and coal prices.

Figure A D.12. Contract for Difference low-carbon hydrogen subsidy strategy

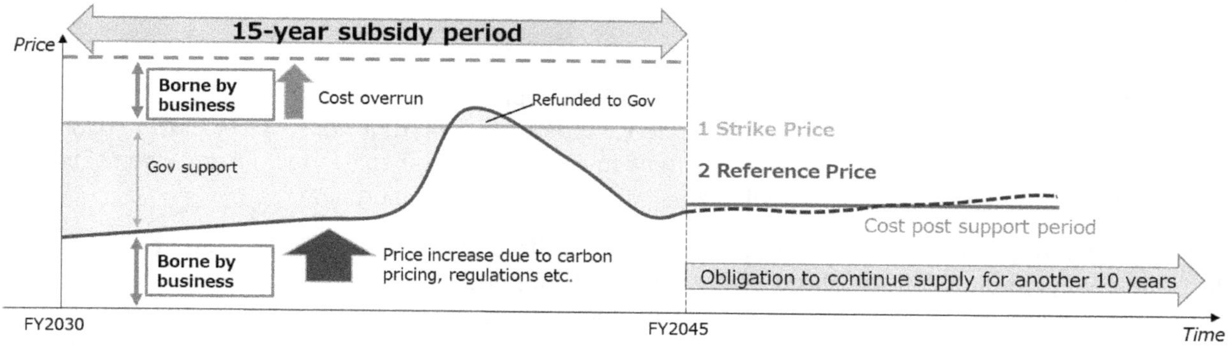

Source: Ministry of Economy, Trade and Industry (METI)

Actors involved and Financial Flows

- The Government of Japan is responsible for defining the criterion and requirements for the subsidy.
- The Ministry of Economy, Trade and Industry (METI) is mainly in charge of conducting the business plan evaluation and supervising the selection process.
- The Ministry of Land, Infrastructure, Transport and Tourism (MLIT) is in charge alongside with and provides support to METI if the candidate projects involve pipeline construction, roads or port sites.
- The Japan Organisation for Metals and Energy Security (JOGMEC) is responsible for supporting the selection process and paying the subsidy to the selected suppliers.

Governance/Organisation and Implementation

The Japanese Government is developing the subsidy pursuant to the Act on Promotion of Supply and Utilisation of Low-Carbon Hydrogen and its Derivatives for Smooth Transition to a Decarbonised, Growth-Oriented Economic Structure ("the Hydrogen Society Promotion Act"), which was passed on 17 May 2024. The Hydrogen Society Promotion Act establishes a basic policy, code of conduct and regulatory framework to promote the demand, supply and use of low-carbon hydrogen and its derivatives in Japan.

This act is part of the efforts to meet the Basic Hydrogen Strategy (2023), which aims to reach 12 million t/year of hydrogen use by 2040 (The Ministerial Council on Renewable Energy, Hydrogen and Related Issues, 2023[24]). It also aligns with the current sixth Strategic Energy Plan (2021), targeting 1% of hydrogen/ammonia in its power generation fuel mix by Fiscal Year 2030, with a goal of introducing and popularising 30% volume co-firing of hydrogen at gas-fired thermal power plants or mono-firing of hydrogen for power generation, and 20% co-firing of ammonia at coal-fired thermal power plants (Agency for Natural Resources and Energy, 2023[25]).

JOGMEC aims to ensure energy security by providing financial assistance to Japanese businesses to achieve carbon neutrality. It includes equity investments in hydrogen and fuel ammonia production and storage, as well as carbon dioxide capture and storage (CCS) projects.

Challenges and key advantages

Advantages:

- Promotes investment in Japan's clean hydrogen industry by covering the price gap.
- Ensures industrial competitiveness by covering hard-to-abate industry sectors.
- Offers long-term financial incentive (15-year) in forms of grant financing.

- Once commenced, quick implementation of the application process.

Supported Projects Description

To be considered for the subsidy, low-carbon hydrogen suppliers either produce in Japan or import into Japan low-carbon hydrogen products. Projects need to provide over 1000 tons of low-carbon hydrogen annually from 2030 onwards. The projects also need to contribute to Japan's industrial decarbonisation by supplying to hard-to-abate sectors, including steel, chemicals and transportation.

Low-carbon hydrogen supply projects proposed under the CfD subsidy scheme need to submit a business plan to the METI and MLIT (if involving pipeline installation, ports or roads). The business plan needs to include the duration and implementation structure and the source of funding for the development and operations of the project. Additionally, it needs to (1) be prepared jointly with the offtaker(s) or end-user(s), (2) include a capital investment plan, and (3) demonstrate that the supply of low-carbon hydrogen will start by the indicated time (i.e., Fiscal Year 2030[16]) and continue for at least 25 years, i.e. the 15-year subsidy period plus a further 10-year period.

In August 2024, the Government and JOGMEC circulated a set of draft basic principles and criterion for the country's new CfD subsidy scheme. This draft outlines the requirements for low-carbon hydrogen supply projects to be considered for the subsidy, in accordance with the Hydrogen Society Promotion Act, and was put into force on 23 October 2024.

The criterion to approve the business plan, currently under review, are the following:

- The business plan meets the criteria set out in the basic policy of the Hydrogen Society Promotion Act;
- The business plan is economically and commercially viable;
- The business plan will contribute to strengthening the industrial competitiveness.

The Japanese Government will invest approximately USD 19 billion (JPY 3 trillion) for the low-carbon hydrogen subsidy over fifteen years. The exact number of hydrogen projects supported is contingent on applications meeting eligibility criteria.

Country, Industry Subsector, Size of Investment:

- Country: Japan
  Industry Subsectors: Low-carbon hydrogen, ammonia, e-fuel and e-methane.
- Size of Investment: USD 19.2 billion (JPY 3 trillion).

Impact of the Solution of the Projects

Japan's CfD subsidy can allow producers to sell low-carbon hydrogen at the same price as fossil alternatives. Additionally, it helps accelerate the decarbonisation of the industry and the power sectors.

Advantages vs Conventional Financing: The CfD supply subsidy provides producers and importers a top-up payment above a pre-established reference price. By providing price protection, it can lower down the production costs and promote financial support from private investors. In the long term, the more the technology is deployed, the more the costs will decrease through economies of scale and learning curve effects, driving competitiveness against conventional technologies. Additionally, the CfD-based subsidy can help to achieve Japan's decarbonisation targets by allocating public money towards carbon neutrality goals.

Impact on Business Model or Access to Finance: The introduction of a government-led subsidy scheme improves access to finance for projects and attracts private investors seeking to enter the low-carbon hydrogen market, by providing a stable revenue profile for projects.

Enhancing regulatory clarity, streamlining application processes, and harmonising low-carbon hydrogen standards can benefit the subsidy scheme implementation, mitigating system complexities and reducing project timelines.

Lessons Learnt and Replicability

Key lessons learned include the importance of involving both supply and demand for the eligibility criteria and the necessity to implement a sound regulatory framework for the subsidy mechanism.

The regulatory complexity (i.e., setting basic criterion and requirements for the subsidy) may increase preparation timelines, with an expected delay of the application opening of two to five months. But once it is commenced, the selection process is likely to move quickly. It is expected to encourage private investments through public finance support.

Successful replication requires strong regulatory support, clear eligibility criteria, and robust co-ordination among public agencies involved in the implementation process.

Case Study 14 – National Hydrogen Mission / Government of India

Table A D.20. Key indicators of India's National Hydrogen Mission

Indicator	Instrument
Type of instrument	Economic
Instrument	Enabling policy framework under development, including consumption quotas for end use sectors and bidding auctions for clean hydrogen production; Financial incentives in the form of reimbursements for electrolyser manufacturing under PLI (Production Linked Incentives)
Eligible step(s) of the value chain	Electrolyser manufacturing / Electrolysis / Storage and transport infrastructure / End-Use Sectors
Eligible countries	India
Status	Under implementation
Amount	Planned: USD 2.4 billion (INR 19 744 crore) Available: n/a Disbursed: n/a
Date of implementation	Phase 1: 2023-26 partly addressing domestic demand of 5 Mt per year and increasing local electrolyser manufacturing capacity Phase 2: 2026-30 scaling up clean hydrogen production domestically up to 10 Mt per year and exploring export opportunities

Source: Authors based on case study documentation

Instrument – Theoretical Concept

Launched in August 2021 and formalised in January 2023, the India National Green Hydrogen Mission aims to establish the country as a global hub for the production, usage, and export of clean hydrogen by 2030. The mission's target is to build capabilities to produce 5 million metric tonnes (Mt) of clean hydrogen annually by 2030, with the potential to scale to 10 Mt as export markets grow. It focuses on replacing fossil fuels and fossil fuel-based feedstocks with renewable alternatives across various sectors, including ammonia production, petroleum refining, steel production, and in the mobility sector. The mission aims to decarbonise the economy, reduce dependency on fossil fuel imports and position India among leaders in the clean hydrogen sector by advancing the manufacturing of electrolysers locally and stimulating domestic clean hydrogen production (Ministry of New and Renewable Energy, 2023[26]).

Figure A D.13. National Green Hydrogen Mission components

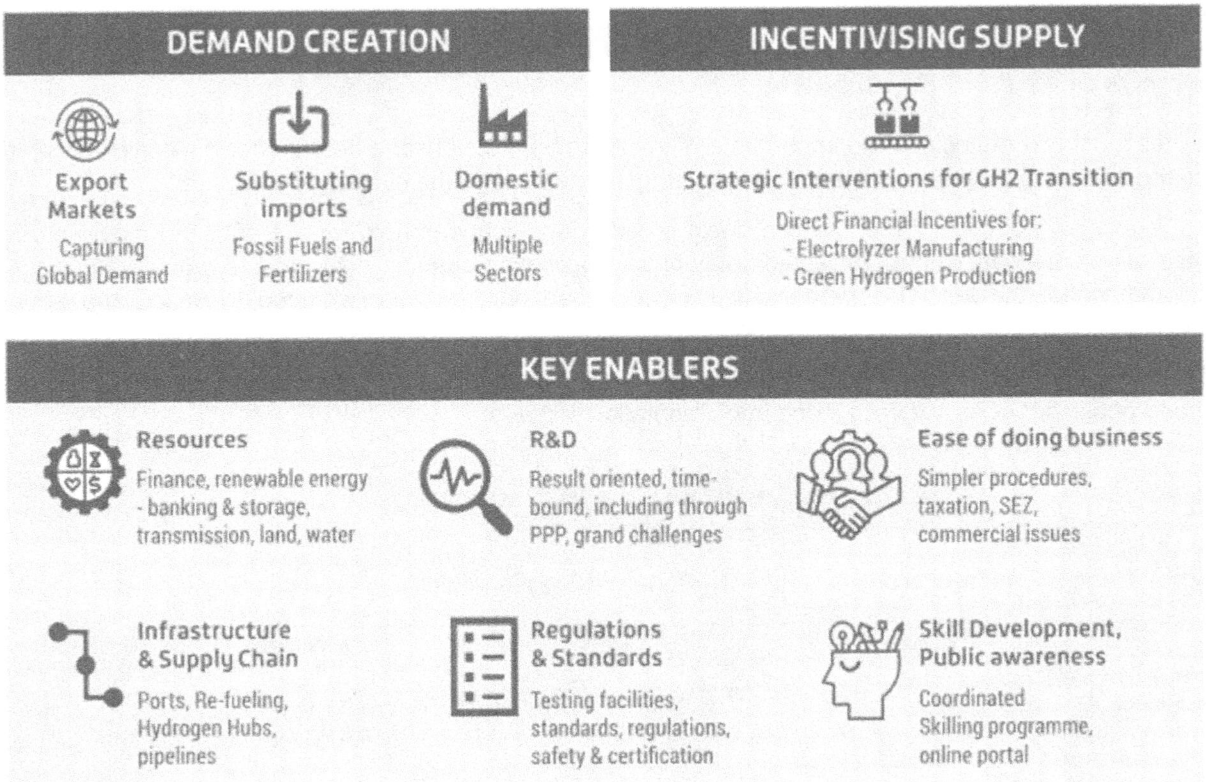

Source: Case study documentation

The National Green Hydrogen Mission will implement a wide incentive program to foster the growth of the clean hydrogen industry in India. The targeted sub-sectors include domestic and export-oriented clean hydrogen production, green ammonia for domestic fertilisers market, green steel, transport, shipping pilot project, and clean hydrogen hubs. The key enabling actions, on the top of elaborating enabling economic and policy frameworks, will be articulated around elaboration of regulations, costs and standards; support of research and development activities; set up of skill development programs for technology, operational and maintenance aspects; establishment of public awareness programs and stakeholder outreach; as well as establishing strategic international cooperation partnerships.

The mission's policy framework is expected to include financial and non-financial measures to support low-cost hydrogen production and domestic manufacturing of related technologies, including but not limited to consumption quotas for end use sectors and bidding auctions for clean hydrogen procurement. The Strategic Interventions for Green Hydrogen Transition (SIGHT) plan will include an incentive program designed to stimulate the growth of the clean hydrogen industry in India. Initially, the program will focus on providing financial incentives for electrolyser manufacturing and green hydrogen production. To ensure quality, eligibility criteria for procurement will require the use of government-approved equipment, with a list of approved models and manufacturers potentially updated over time. These interventions are expected to reduce production costs, support emerging sectors, and establish a domestic manufacturing base by mitigating risks for early adopters and innovators.

Some of measures were implemented by the Ministry of Power in February 2022, shortly before the formalisation of the National Green Hydrogen mission, and include for clean hydrogen and ammonia production projects. These include waiving of inter-state transmission charges for 25 years for projects commissioned before 2025; facilitating timelines and access to renewable energy; allotmenting land in renewable energy parks and manufacturing zones; streamlining the permitting process via a single governmental portal; and aggregating demand from different sectors through the Ministry of New and Renewable Energy (MNRE), with bid consolidation by designated agencies (Ministry of Power, 2022[27]).

Additionally, as part of the Atmanirbhar Bharat (Self-Reliant India) initiative, the Indian government launched in 2020 the Production Linked Incentive (PLI) scheme to strengthen domestic manufacturing competitiveness, including electrolysers manufacturing for clean hydrogen production (Cordonnier and Saygin, 2023[28]). With the total program amount of USD 26 billion (INR 1.97 lakh crore[17]), the PLI offers financial incentives in the form of reimbursement of between 1 and 10% of net sales over up to six years, fostering investment in advanced technologies, economies of scale, and export growth. While specific PLI programs target sectors like advanced chemistry cells and high-efficiency solar modules, electrolyser manufacturing is supported through the general scheme. This incentive promotes local production and advances India's clean hydrogen goals.

The National Green Hydrogen Mission will be implemented in phases, starting with Phase I, from 2022-23 to 2025-26, focusing on creating demand, enabling supply through domestic electrolyser manufacturing, and initiating pilot projects in hard-to-abate sectors. This phase includes pilot projects in refineries, fertilisers, and city gas sectors, alongside the development of R&D, regulations, and standards. Phase II, from 2026-27 to 2029-30, aims to make clean hydrogen cost-competitive in refineries and fertilisers, expand to sectors like steel and mobility, scaling up production and exploring commercial-scale projects.

Actors involved and Financial Flows

The National Green Hydrogen Mission in India involves a coordinated effort across multiple ministries and governmental bodies to achieve its ambitious goals. The Ministry of New and Renewable Energy (MNRE) leads the mission, responsible for overall coordination, financial incentives, and the development of the clean hydrogen ecosystem. Key line ministries, such as the Ministry of Power, Ministry of Petroleum and Natural Gas, or the Ministry of Chemicals and Fertilisers, play crucial roles in specific sectors like energy, transportation and industry. Scientific institutions, educational bodies, and international collaborations will further enhance the mission's success through research, innovation, and skill development.

State governments also contribute by establishing supportive subnational efforts and initiatives. Gujarat aims to produce 60% of India's clean hydrogen by 2030, targeting 3 million metric tonnes per year under its forthcoming Green Hydrogen Policy (Bioenergy Times, 2024[29]). Pilot projects are underway, such as hydrogen blending with Piped Natural Gas (PNG) in North Gujarat, led by Gujarat State Petroleum Corporation and Gujarat Power Corporation Ltd, supported by a 100 MW solar project. Further projects in Surat and Mehsana are also planned, with an estimated USD 240 million (INR 20 billion) investment by 2030 for 1 million metric tonnes annually clean hydrogen capacity.

Uttar Pradesh through its Green Hydrogen Policy 2024 promotes investments in clean hydrogen and clean ammonia production, aiming for 1 million metric tonnes annually by 2028 (Invest Up, n.d.[30]). Key incentives include a capital subsidy of up to 30%, with the first five projects receiving up to 40%. Land and power supply incentives are provided, such as discounted land prices, exemptions on electricity duties, and intra-state transmission costs. The policy also encourages ease of doing business through a single-window portal and environmental clearance under the White Category for clean hydrogen projects. The estimated maximum capital subsidy is USD 27 million (INR 225 crore).

Punjab, under its 2023 Green Hydrogen Policy, aims to achieve a production capacity of 100 kilo tonnes per annum of clean hydrogen by 2030. The policy leverages agricultural biomass, such as paddy straw and other residues, to produce hydrogen. The state has allocated a capital subsidy of up to USD 1.8 million (INR 15 crore) per project for biomass-based hydrogen production, targeting 10 projects. Additional incentives include land allocation, exemptions on electricity duties, and transmission cost reductions to promote clean hydrogen development and boost investment in renewable energy infrastructure (Punjab Energy Development Agency, n.d.[31]).

Governance/Organisation and Implementation

The National Green Hydrogen Mission is led by the Ministry of New and Renewable Energy (MNRE), with an empowered group chaired by the cabinet secretary, including officials from key ministries and industry experts. This group oversees policy, progress, and alignment with broader government initiatives. The MNRE's mission secretariat handles policy development, project management and risk assessment. Government agencies like the Solar Energy Corporation of India (SECI) are responsible for managing auctions and tenders for clean hydrogen projects, ensuring transparent procurement and competitive bidding to attract investments. An advisory group provides further technical and R&D support.

Challenges and key advantages

Challenges: The National Green Hydrogen Mission faces several challenges. First, establishing strong market demand for clean hydrogen, both domestically and internationally, remains difficult. High production costs due to expensive electrolysers and renewable energy inputs further hinder competitiveness. Currently, global electrolyser manufacturing capacity is limited to around 4 GW annually, posing a challenge to meeting the 200 GW target by 2030. Additionally, the absence of a fully established policy framework creates uncertainty, potentially delaying the mission's key milestones for 2026 and 2030, along with related investments.

Advantages: The National Green Hydrogen Mission offers several advantages. It contributes to decarbonisation by replacing fossil fuels across different sectors with clean hydrogen, aligning with India's Net Zero emissions goal by 2070. Financial incentives and R&D support help reduce production costs, making clean hydrogen more economically viable. Expanding domestic electrolyser manufacturing strengthens India's position as a leader in clean hydrogen technology and integrates it into global supply chains. Additionally, fostering domestic clean hydrogen production reduces dependence on imported fossil fuels, enhancing energy security and lowering energy import costs.

Supported Projects Description

The National Green Hydrogen Mission, with a budget of USD 2.4 billion (INR 19 744 crore), supports a range of clean hydrogen projects and R&D initiatives across various sectors. Initial focus includes driving demand in refining, fertilisers, and city gas, with pilot projects in steel, mobility, and shipping. Several auctions have been organised for electrolyser capacity and clean hydrogen production (see table below):

Table A D.21. Auctions of the National Green Hydrogen Mission

Date	Auction Title/Scope	Capacity	Financial Support	Winners (if available)
April 2023	Electrolyser manufacturing Tender under SIGHT scheme (1st Auction)	1.5 GW of manufacturing capacity	PLI incentives	RIL, Adani, L&T
July 2024	Electrolyser manufacturing Tender under SIGHT scheme (2nd Auction)	1.5 GW of manufacturing capacity	PLI incentives	Ongoing, proposals received
July 2023	Green Hydrogen Production Tender under SIGHT scheme	450 000 tonnes of clean hydrogen per year of production capacity	An average incentive for kg of clean hydrogen from USD 0.2 (INR 19) to USD 0.4 (INR 35)	Greenko, ACME, Reliance, Hygenco for capacities over 75 000 tonnes of clean hydrogen per year
September 2024	Green Hydrogen Hubs Tender under National Green Hydrogen Mission	N/A	N/A	Ongoing, N/A
June 2024	Green Ammonia Production Auction under SIGHT scheme	539 000 tonnes of clean ammonia per year of production capacity (5.39 lakh tonnes per year)	N/A	Ongoing, N/A

Source: Authors based on (Solar Energy Corporation of India, n.d.[32]; ManufacturingToday, 2024[33]; PV Magazine, 2024[34]; MERCOM, 2024[35]; Ministry of New and Renewable Energy, 2024[36])

The auction summary table above provides insights into India's growing clean hydrogen sector. Major auctions for electrolyser manufacturing and clean hydrogen production have seen significant interest from key players like Reliance, Adani, and L&T, signalling strong industry participation. The second electrolyser auction, with proposals exceeding 2.8 GW, reflects the rapid scaling of production capacity. Additionally, upcoming auctions for green ammonia further indicate the government's push to diversify hydrogen applications. These auctions aim to meet national hydrogen production targets and foster technological advancements through competitive bidding. Further auctions target clean hydrogen hubs and ammonia production, reflecting growing capacity and investment in the sector.

Impact of the Solution of the Projects

Advantages vs Conventional Financing: The mission addresses the entire clean hydrogen value chain. Leveraging on the public budget for the first domestic clean hydrogen projects it targets to promote use of clean hydrogen in different industrial sectors as well as increase local electrolysis production capacity for the needs of both domestic and export markets.

Impact on Business Model or Access to Finance: The mission's support framework, which is currently under development and formalisation, will enable the implementation of new business cases and industrial projects in the clean hydrogen sector and can facilitate future private investments.

To complement envisioned economic and financial support, the mission will include regulatory frameworks, standards, and international collaborations to create a conducive environment for clean hydrogen adoption at scale.

Lessons Learnt and Replicability

Key lessons learned include the importance of involving both supply and demand for the eligibility criteria and the necessity to implement a sound regulatory framework for the subsidy mechanism.

The National Green Hydrogen Mission covers the entire value chain, but its full impact remains to be assessed as it progresses through its phases. Early auctions, such as those for electrolyser manufacturing, have demonstrated effective mobilisation of industry stakeholders, showing initial success in the implementation.

The mission may extend project timelines due to the complexity of supporting mechanisms, such as bidding auctions, and condition the final investment decisions upon implementation timeline of dedicated policy frameworks.

The mission has successfully attracted private capital, as seen in the electrolyser auctions, where major players like Reliance, Adani, and L&T secured bids. Government incentives reduce risks and support the higher costs of early clean hydrogen projects, encouraging private sector participation and enabling first domestic clean hydrogen projects.

For replicability, a robust governance structure, clear policy support, and significant public investment are crucial. The mission's phased approach and comprehensive focus on the demand-supply ecosystem can serve as a model for other countries, especially given the success of early auctions in mobilising both private and public resources.

Case study 15 - SDG Namibia One Fund / Climate Fund Managers and Environmental Investment Fund of Namibia and Invest International

Table A D.22. Key indicators of SDG Namibia One Fund

Indicator	Instrument
Type of instrument	Financing
Instrument	Blended Finance: development loans and equity (junior, ordinary, and senior equity)
Eligible step(s) of the value chain / technologies	Green Hydrogen project, including but not limited to green hydrogen and ammonia production, hydrogen refuelling stations, green iron production
Eligible countries	Namibia
Status	Under implementation
Amount (USD)	Planned: 1.1 billion Available: 70 million Disbursed: 25 million
Date of implementation	Phase 1: 2023 (creation year) Phase 2: 2038 (estimated end year for closed end fund)

Source: Authors based on case study documentation

Instrument description – Theoretical Concept

SDG Namibia One is a USD 1.1 billion blended finance vehicle designed to mobilise investment in Namibia's green hydrogen sector (Environmental Investment Fund of Namibia, 2023[37]). It combines public and private funds to support clean hydrogen projects, leveraging grants and investment capital to reduce financial risk and attract further private sector financing. SDG Namibia One was created in 2023 through a partnership between Climate Fund Managers, the Environmental Investment Fund of Namibia and Invest International.

Climate Fund Managers (CFM) is a joint venture between Dutch Development Bank (FMO), a development finance institution, and Sanlam Infraworks, Africa's largest non-banking financial institution. CFM is a Dutch partner bringing expertise in climate finance. The Environmental Investment Fund of Namibia (EIF) is a fund established by the Government of Namibia, with a mandate to raise and provide funding for Namibia's economic and sustainable development. Invest International (II) is a joint venture between the Dutch Government and Dutch Development Bank (FMO), with a mandate to support Dutch-linked companies in financing impactful projects that contribute to the achievement of the SDGs.

SDG Namibia One articulates different types of instruments including development funding, junior equity, ordinary equity and senior equity (see Figure A D.14). The development funding is attributed at the pre-financial close state and addresses mainly project's development risk. The junior, ordinary and senior equity are generally attributed at the post financial close state prior to the project's construction phase and project's capital expenditure needs. The junior, ordinary, and senior equity within its priority order benefit the project's cash waterfall, being exposed to different risk levels.

Figure A D.14. Different types of instruments articulated by SDG Namibia One Fund

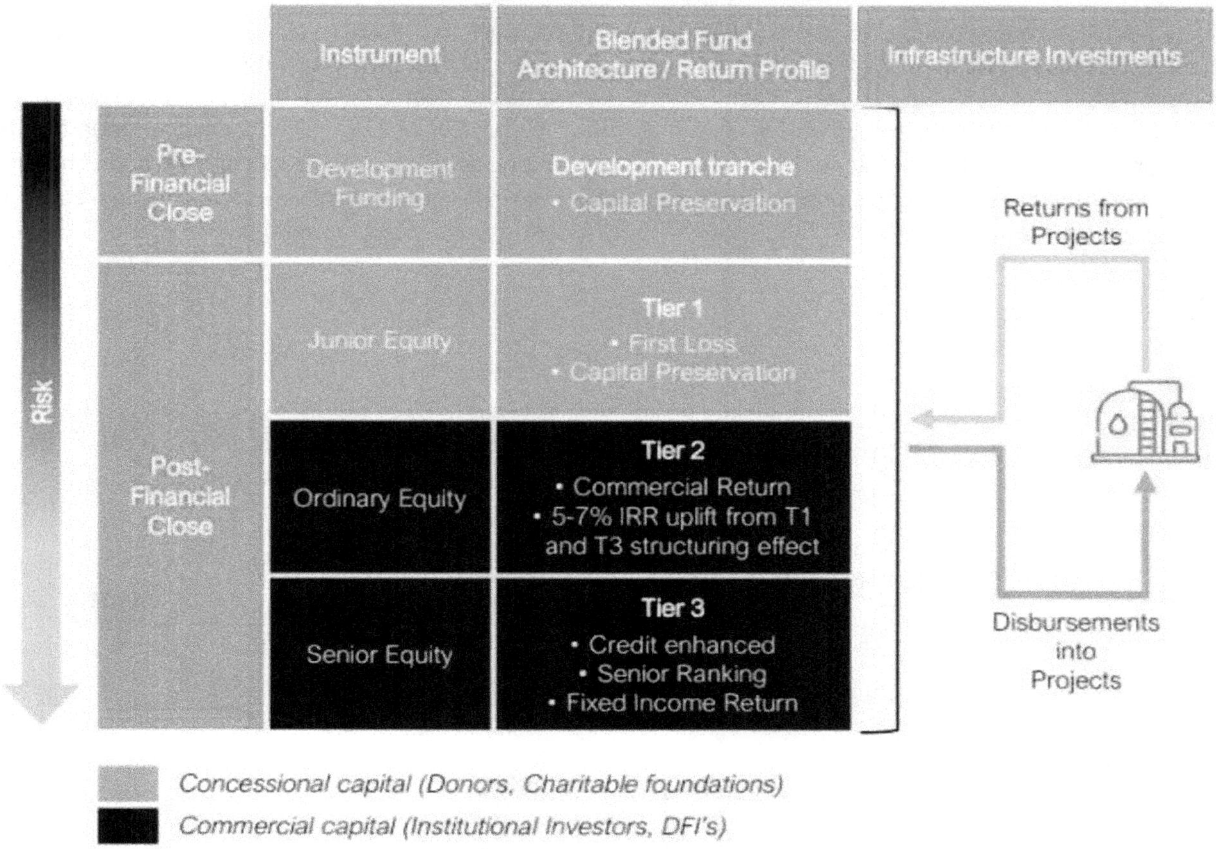

Source: SDG Namibia One Fund documentation

SDG Namibia One addresses the development risk through its development tranche of USD 100 million, as well as construction risk through its equity tranche of USD 1 billion (covering junior, ordinary and senior equity financing), while the long term debt is being externalised.

Financial/Contractual Flows

Financial flows involve an initial grant of EUR 40 million from Invest International. The European Commission gave approval, within its Global Gateway strategy, for EUR 25 million additional investment. EIF and CFM, as general partners (GP), will contribute 1% of the total fund size in the tier two, as per private equity (PE) market standard. The European Investment Bank and the Government of the Republic of Namibia concluded a letter of intent at COP27 for the raising of EUR 500 million, a portion of which is to be proposed to be designated for investment via SDG Namibia One. Further on, the vehicle will look to raise money from local institutional investors and investors from around the world, including development finance institutions and multilateral development banks as likely candidates, to develop Namibian green hydrogen projects and related infrastructures.

Governance/Organisation and Implementation

SDG Namibia One is managed by NH_2 Fund Managers, a partnership between EIF and CFM. The establishment involved Memorandum of Understandings (MOUs) and agreements with various stakeholders, aligning with Namibia's Harambee Prosperity Plan II[18] and the EU climate objectives.

SDG Namibia One governance boards structure is represented in Figure 2 and is as follows. NH_2 Fund Manager is 51% owned by CFM NL, which is a 75% – 25% joint venture between CFM and Invest International, and 49% by EIF. SDG Namibia One replicates typical GP - LP (general partner - limited partner) structure with a discretionary investment committee, which includes an independent member, an advisory board, which includes all investors from a certain level of investment, and general member meetings. Any investment decisions are to be approved by its investment committee, while certain strategic decisions need to be approved by the advisory board or general member meetings.

Figure A D.15. SDG Namibia One governance boards' structure

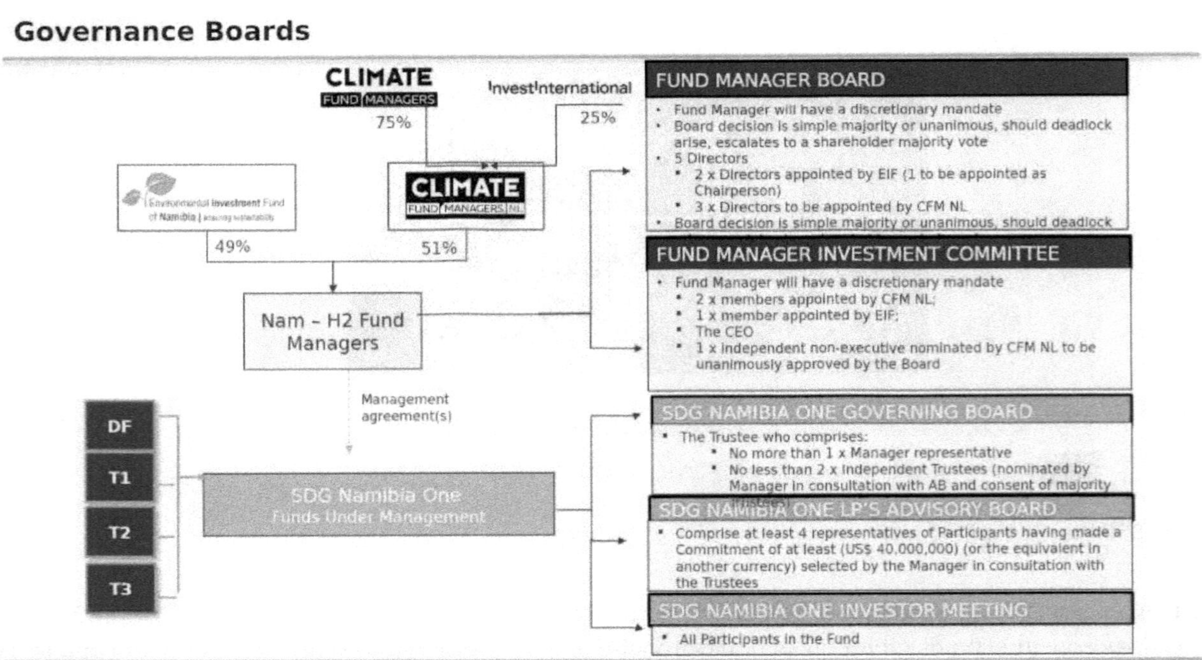

Source: Case study documentation

The investment process is best seen as a two-phased one, where the investment committee first approves the development work, after which it will look at approving the construction work only when development has successfully commenced. Decision making process at project level differs per project, as SDG Namibia One will not always be a majority investor, yet NH_2 Fund Manager endeavours to be an active investor, and ensure important financial and ESG related topics to remain reserved matters.

Key Advantages and Challenges to Implement the Instrument

Challenges:

- Co-ordination among multiple international and local stakeholders;
- Ensuring long-term financial sustainability and risk management within an evolving policy framework;
- Overcoming technological and infrastructural challenges in a developing market.

Advantages:

- Mobilises significant capital without burdening Namibia's fiscal budget;
- Attracts international investment and expertise;
- Supports the development of a nascent green hydrogen sector, fostering economic growth and energy independence;
- Ensure International Finance Corporation (IFC) Performance Standards on Environmental and Social Sustainability (PS)[19] compliance for all projects by bringing along donor or development financial institutions (DFI) investors.

Supported Projects Description

The platform aims to mobilise USD 1.1 billion for renewable hydrogen projects and targets to finance 207 kilotonnes (kt) of renewable hydrogen production per year. The fund solely focuses on investments in Namibia under the Southern Corridor Development Initiative (SCDI). The realisation of the SCDI aims to generate significant energy propelling Namibia to become energy self-sufficient, improve regional energy security by exporting 14 GW of clean power into the Southern Africa Power Pool and supply various international ports, including the Port of Rotterdam will clean molecules to decarbonise hard-to-abate sectors.

SDG Namibia One fund targets 15-25 investments, with an average ticket size varying between USD 25 million and USD 200 million. The investment scope covers the entire supply chain with a particular focus on production assets for green hydrogen and ammonia, including desalination, renewable energy, and electrolysis assets. Other sectors covered are transportation and transmission up until the port as well as downstream use, including green iron production. Projects with clear local benefits such as local offtake, job creation, energy generation etc. will be prioritised.

SDG Namibia One invested USD 25 million to support the development budget of Hyphen's renewable ammonia production project in Lüderitz, Namibia (OECD, 2022[38]). The commissioning of the first phase of the project is foreseen at the end of 2026, aiming for an annual output of 1 000 kt of green ammonia, produced from 175 kt of renewable hydrogen. The installed electrolysis capacity is 1.5 GW coupled with almost 2 GW of wind and 2 GW of solar generation installations. The total project cost is estimated at USD 7 billion, out of which USD 100 million of development cost. Targeted Levelised Cost of Green Ammonia (LCOA) is USD 400 per tonne by 2030, with weighted average cost of capital (WACC) seen as the key lever to drive down LCOA.

3. Impact of the Solution on the Projects

Blended finance offers significant advantages over conventional financing methods, particularly for large-scale, capital-intensive projects. By combining public and private investment, blended finance reduces risk, making projects more attractive to private investors and accelerating their implementation. This approach enables the undertaking of projects that might not be feasible with traditional financing alone due to their scale and capital requirements. Additionally, blended finance provides a mechanism for multilateral development banks and other public sector-oriented investors to participate in private sector finance, fostering greater collaboration and resource mobilisation. This structure also promotes country ownership, as evidenced by the involvement of the Environmental Investment Fund of Namibia in similar frameworks, ensuring that governments have a stake in the projects' success. Moreover, blended finance typically offers a lower cost of capital compared to conventional finance, which helps to lower the levelised cost of clean hydrogen, making it more competitive with conventional hydrogen. This financial model thus enhances the economic viability and attractiveness of green hydrogen projects.

Blended finance significantly enhances the business model and access to finance for clean hydrogen projects. For instance, it boosts Namibia's ability to attract international investment by demonstrating a lower-risk financial structure. This improved access to finance supports the growth of the clean hydrogen sector and stimulates the local economy growth.

Improving enabling conditions plays a crucial role in complementing financial solutions for clean hydrogen projects at scale. International partnerships and knowledge-sharing are instrumental in mitigating risks and accelerating technological advancements, making these projects more viable and attractive. These collaborations bring in expertise and innovative solutions that enhance project implementation and operational efficiency. Additionally, establishing a clearer hydrogen policy framework can significantly increase the region's attractiveness for private international investments. Well-defined policies provide investors with the confidence and stability needed to commit to long-term investments, thereby fostering a more supportive environment for the growth of the hydrogen sector.

Lessons Learnt and Replicability

Initial steps, including the signing of MOUs and the allocation of grant funding, suggest effective start of the implementation. The successful implementation will be achieved with further mobilisation of additional funds and project execution. Given the complexity and scale, project preparation timelines may be extended. However, the blended finance approach aims to streamline processes through clear frameworks and extensive partnerships.

The initial public grant funding from Invest International and the European Commission aims to de-risk the fund project and attract private investment. NamH_2, and CFM, are currently in active conversations with several private sector investors. The funds are allocated to address the development risk through development tranche and construction risk through a junior equity tranche.

Several conditions can be generalised for the replicability of successful clean hydrogen projects. First, there should be a strong alignment with national and international climate policies and objectives, ensuring that the project supports broader environmental goals and benefits from regulatory support. Second, effective public-private partnerships are crucial, combining the strengths of government entities and private companies to leverage resources, expertise, and risk-sharing mechanisms. Lastly, commitment from both local and international financial stakeholders is necessary to provide the funding and financial stability required for such capital-intensive projects. These conditions create a robust framework that can be adapted and replicated in different regions, fostering the global expansion of green hydrogen initiatives.

References

Agency for Natural Resources and Energy (2023), *Strategic Energy Plan*, https://www.enecho.meti.go.jp/category/others/basic_plan/pdf/strategic_energy_plan.pdf. [25]

Bioenergy Times (2024), *Gujarat plans to launch “Green Hydrogen Policy”*, https://bioenergytimes.com/gujarat-plans-to-launch-a-green-hydrogen-policy/. [29]

Central Bank of Brazil (2024), *Resolução CMN n° 5.130 de 25/4/2024*, https://www.bcb.gov.br/estabilidadefinanceira/exibenormativo?tipo=Resolu%C3%A7%C3%A3o%20CMN&numero=5130. [15]

Complexo do Pecem (2022), *Green Hydrogen*, https://www.complexodopecem.com.br/wp-content/uploads/2022/10/FAQ-Green-Hydrogen.pdf. [1]

Cordonnier, J. and D. Saygin (2023), “Financing solutions to foster industrial decarbonisation in emerging and developing economies”, *OECD Environment Working Papers*, No. 226, OECD Publishing, Paris, https://doi.org/10.1787/24a155ab-en. [28]

Department of Energy (DOE) (n.d.), *DOE official website*, https://www.energy.gov/. [22]

ENGIE (n.d.), *ENGIE official website*, https://www.engie.com. [40]

Engoie (2023), *ENGIE and POSCO Led Consortium to develop a Green Ammonia Project of up to a 1.2mtpa in Oman*, https://en.newsroom.engie.com/news/engie-and-posco-led-consortium-to-develop-a-green-ammonia-project-of-up-to-a-1-2mtpa-in-oman-8360-314df.html. [4]

Environmental Investment Fund of Namibia (2023), *SDG Namibia One Press Release 20 June 2023*, https://www.eif.org.na/post/sdg-namibia-one-press-release-20-june-2023. [37]

Gabinet of the Ministry (2024), *PORTARIA MF Nº 964, DE 11 DE JUNHO DE 2024*, https://www.in.gov.br/en/web/dou/-/portaria-mf-n-964-de-11-de-junho-de-2024-565122740. [14]

Hintco (2024), *H2Global Pilot Auction Results*, https://cdn.sanity.io/files/u4w9plcz/production/aa27b7842b9fa1015e9395e65ab1d9aa2a53147a.pdf. [3]

Hy24 (n.d.), *Hy24 official website*, https://www.hy24partners.com/. [9]

Hydrom (n.d.), *Hydrogen Oman official website*, https://www.hydrom.om/. [6]

IDB (2024), *IDB, Brazil’s Ministry of Finance, Ministry of Environment and Climate Change, and Central Bank Join Forces to Boost Green Investments*, https://www.iadb.org/en/news/idb-brazils-ministry-finance-ministry-environment-and-climate-change-and-central-bank-join. [10]

IDB (n.d.), *IDB official website*, https://www.iadb.org/en. [43]

Invest Up (n.d.), *Green Hydrogen Policy*, https://invest.up.gov.in/green-hydrogen-policy/. [30]

IRS (n.d.), *IRS official website*, https://www.irs.gov/. [21]

JOGMEC (n.d.), *JOGMEC official website*, https://www.jogmec.go.jp/english/news/release/news_10_00079.html. [23]

JSW (n.d.), *JSW Energy*, https://www.jsw.in/energy. [7]

Lhyfe (n.d.), *Lhye official website*, https://www.lhyfe.com/. [8]

ManufacturingToday (2024), *RIL, Adani, and L&T triumph in India's first electrolyser manufacturing tender*, https://www.manufacturingtodayindia.com/ril-adani-and-lt-triumph-in-indias-first-electrolyser-manufacturing-tender#:~:text=RIL%2C%20Adani%2C%20and%20L%26T%20triumph%20in%20India's%20first%20electrolyser%20manufacturing%20tender,-by%20Staff%20Writer&text. [33]

Marsh (n.d.), *Hydrogen*, https://www.marsh.com/en-gb/industries/energy-and-power/expertise/hydrogen.html. [19]

MERCOM (2024), *Greenko, ACME, Reliance among Winners of SECI's Green Hydrogen Manufacturing Auction*, https://www.mercomindia.com/greenko-acme-reliance-winners-secis-green-hydrogen-auction. [35]

Ministerio da Fazenda (2023), *Ecological Transformation Plan*, https://www.gov.br/fazenda/pt-br/acesso-a-informacao/acoes-e-programas/transformacao-ecologica/english-version/documents/pte-19-10-2023-ecological-transformation-plan.pdf. [44]

Ministry of Minery and Energy (2023), *Plano de Trabalho Trienal 2023-2025*, https://www.gov.br/mme/pt-br/programa-nacional-do-hidrogenio-1/planodetrabalhotrienalpnh2.pdf. [12]

Ministry of New and Renewable Energy (2024), *Solar Energy Corporation of India issues RfS for selection of Green Ammonia Producers under SIGHT Programme of the National Green Hydrogen Mission (NGHM)*, https://pib.gov.in/PressReleasePage.aspx?PRID=2023625. [36]

Ministry of New and Renewable Energy (2023), *National Green Hydrogen Mission*, https://cdnbbsr.s3waas.gov.in/s3716e1b8c6cd17b771da77391355749f3/uploads/2023/01/2023012338.pdf. [26]

Ministry of Power (2022), *Green Hydrogen Policy*, https://powermin.gov.in/sites/default/files/webform/notices/Green_Hydrogen_Policy.pdf. [27]

Munich Re (n.d.), *Munichg Re official website*, https://www.munichre.com/en/solutions/for-industry-clients/green-hydrogen.html. [45]

OECD (2022), *Hyphen Hydrogen Energy*, https://www.oecd.org/content/dam/oecd/en/about/programmes/cefim/green-hydrogen/hyphen-namibia-case-study.pdf/_jcr_content/renditions/original./hyphen-namibia-case-study.pdf. [38]

Office of the Energy Efficiency and Renewable Energy (n.d.), *GREET*, https://www.energy.gov/eere/greet. [47]

Office of the US Trade Representative (n.d.), *Free Trade Agreements*, https://ustr.gov/trade-agreements/free-trade-agreements. [46]

POSCO (n.d.), *POSCO Holdings*, https://www.posco-inc.com/. [39]

PTT Exploration and Production Public Company (n.d.), *PTTEP official website*, https://www.pttep.com/en/home. [41]

PTTEP (n.d.), *EP Net Zero 2050*, https://www.pttep.com/en/our-company/ep-net-zero-2050. [5]

Punjab Energy Development Agency (n.d.), *Punjab Green Hydrogen Policy*, https://www.peda.gov.in/assets/media/news/GH_Policy.pdf. [31]

PV Magazine (2024), *The Hydrogen Stream: India's second electrolyzer tender attracts proposals for more than 2.8 GW*, https://www.pv-magazine-india.com/2024/07/11/the-hydrogen-stream-indias-second-electrolyzer-tender-attracts-proposals-for-more-than-2-8-gw/. [34]

Samsung E&A (n.d.), *Samsung E&A official website*, https://www.samsungena.com/en/index. [42]

Scatec (n.d.), *Green Hydrogen Egypt*, https://scatec.com/locations/egypt/#green-hydrogen-egypt. [2]

Secretaria Especial para Asuntos Jurídicos (2024), *MEDIDA PROVISÓRIA Nº 1.213, DE 22 DE ABRIL DE 2024*, https://www.planalto.gov.br/ccivil_03/_Ato2023-2026/2024/Mpv/mpv1213.htm. [13]

Secretary of the National Treasury of Brazil (2024), *PORTARIA STN/MF Nº 1.135, DE 11 DE JULHO DE 2024*, https://www.in.gov.br/en/web/dou/-/portaria-stn/mf-n-1.135-de-11-de-julho-de-2024-571469142. [11]

Secretary of the National Treasury of Brazil (2024), *PORTARIA STN/MF Nº 1.135, DE 11 DE JULHO DE 2024*, https://www.in.gov.br/en/web/dou/-/portaria-stn/mf-n-1.135-de-11-de-julho-de-2024-571469142. [16]

Solar Energy Corporation of India (n.d.), *RfS for setting up Manufacturing Capacities for Electrolysers in India under SIGHT scheme (Tranche-II)*, https://www.seci.co.in/whats-new-detail/2651. [32]

State Information Service of Egypt (n.d.), *SIS official website*, https://sis.gov.eg/?lang=en-us. [18]

The Ministerial Council on Renewable Energy, Hydrogen and Related Issues (2023), *Basic Hydrogen Strategy*, https://www.meti.go.jp/shingikai/enecho/shoene_shinene/suiso_seisaku/pdf/20230606_5.pdf. [24]

White House (2023), *Inflation Reduction Act Guidebook*, https://www.whitehouse.gov/cleanenergy/inflation-reduction-act-guidebook/. [20]

World Bank (n.d.), *Chile Green Hydrogen Facility to Support a Green, Resilient and Inclusive Economic Development*, https://projects.worldbank.org/en/projects-operations/project-detail/P177533. [17]

Notes

[1] POSCO Holdings, headquartered in Seoul, South Korea, is Holding company of the POSCO Group, whose main business areas include steel, rechargeable battery materials, lithium/nickel, hydrogen, energy etc. (POSCO, n.d.[39])

[2] ENGIE is a French multinational utility company headquartered in La Defense, France, and operates in the fields of electricity generation and distribution, natural gas, nuclear, renewable energy, energy services and green hydrogen (ENGIE, n.d.[40]).

[3] PTT Exploration and Production Public Company Ltd, also known as PTTEP, is a national petroleum exploration and production company based in Thailand (PTT Exploration and Production Public Company, n.d.[41]).

[4] Hydrom is an Oman Government entity responsible for planning and overseeing green hydrogen projects in Oman.

[5] Samsung E&A, headquartered in Seoul, South Korea, is a global engineering, procurement and construction (EPC) company, focusing on energy and environmental sectors (Samsung E&A, n.d.[42]).

[6] The Inter-American Development Bank (IDB) is an international development finance institution headquartered in Washington, D.C., United States of America, and serving as the largest source of development financing for Latin America and the Caribbean. Established in 1959, the IDB supports Latin American and Caribbean economic development, social development and regional integration by lending to governments and government agencies, including State corporations.

[7] Established in 1959, IDB is a leading source of long-term financing for economic, social and institutional development in Latin America and the Caribbean (IDB, n.d.[43]).

[8] ETP is a comprehensive, inclusive, and sustainable development strategy to promote employment, productivity, environmental sustainability, and social justice. Such reforms imply profound changes to the fiscal, financial, and environmental policies (Ministerio da Fazenda, 2023[44]).

[9] Compared to commercial market rates.

[10] Green hydrogen production means renewable energy-powered electrolysis.

[11] The DSRA can go up to 12 months in certain specific cases.

[12] The Golden Licence is defined as a "single approval" issued by the Cabinet on establishing, operating and managing a project, which includes building licences and the approval on the allocation of the properties necessary for such project. It may be granted to companies upon a decree of the Council of Ministers. Under Article 5(1) of the Green Hydrogen Incentives Law, the Investment Law and the Cabinet Decrees, green hydrogen projects are entitled to obtain a Golden Licence.

[13] Munich Re, or Munich Reinsurance Company, is a German multinational insurance company, established in 1880 and headquartered in Munich, Germany. It's among the world's largest reinsurer. The company is offers an extensive range of insurance and reinsurance services, which cover a variety of sectors, including solutions like HySure for hydrogen projects. With operations worldwide, Munich Re aims to play a critical role in managing risk and supporting financial stability across industries, leveraging its deep technical expertise and strong financial position (Munich Re, n.d.[45]).

[14] FTE country is a Free Trade Agreement country. The US has free trade agreements in force with 21 countries, including 20 countries listed on the United States Trade Representative website (Office of the US Trade Representative, n.d.[46]), plus Japan.

[15] Office of Energy Efficiency and Renewable Energy (Office of the Energy Efficiency and Renewable Energy, n.d.[47]).

[16] In Japan, the government's financial year is from 1 April to 31 March.

[17] Crore and lakh are units commonly used in the Indian numbering system to represent large numbers. A crore amounts to 10 000 000 (ten million) in the international numbering system. A lakh amounts to 100 000 (a hundred thousand).

[18] Namibia's Harambee Prosperity Plan II (HPP II) is a comprehensive government initiative designed to drive economic recovery and inclusive growth from 2021 to 2025. The plan focuses on five key pillars: effective governance, economic advancement, social progression, infrastructure development, and international relations. It emphasises job creation, youth empowerment, digital transformation, and sustainable development to enhance the quality of life for all Namibians. A key aspect of the plan includes developing a green hydrogen industry, positioning Namibia as a leader in renewable energy and creating new economic opportunities. HPP II website for more information: https://hppii.gov.na/.

[19] IFC's Performance Standards on Environmental and Social Sustainability website for more information: https://www.ifc.org/en/insights-reports/2012/ifc-performance-standards.

www.ingramcontent.com/pod-product-compliance
Lightning Source LLC
Chambersburg PA
CBHW061217240926
51846CB00006B/1254
* 9 7 8 9 2 6 4 4 2 1 9 1 2 *